LORD WILLIAMS'S SCHOOL, THAME

A New History 1559 - 2020. Volume 1

Graham Thomas &
Derek Turner

SAGUS

I wil bequeath the rectories and parsonages of Brill, Okeley, Burstall and Eastneston to mine Executors for ever, to the intent that they, or the survivor or survivors of them, shall within the same erect a Free School in the town of Thame, and to find and sustain with the profits thereof, a schoolmaster and an usher, forever in such sort and time, as my said Executors shall think most convenient for the maintenance of the said School for ever.

John Williams. 18 March 1559.

Sic itur ad astra (thus the way to the stars)
A tous venaunts (for all comers)

CONTENTS

Pressures

Lord Williams, and a rendition of his coat of arms.

INTRODUCTION

WHY A BOOK and why a history?

The last book to cover the School's history was published as long ago as 1927 by John Howard Brown, a teacher at the School. *A Short History of Thame School* only covered the years from the School's founding to 1900. An update, in terms of extending the coverage to the 21st century was overdue not least because the School has since gone through some momentous changes and has become a significant player on the national stage.

Not that ours is a new idea. In 1997, the School Governors were anxious to produce an updated history but the difficulty in finding someone to undertake such a project proved insurmountable, and they dropped the idea. However Gerald Howat who had given a lecture in 1995 called *From Taunton to Butler: Lord Williams's School From 1866-1944* did expand this into a short history that we have consulted extensively.

Some years later, a valuable start was made, in connection with the 450th anniversary celebrations in 2009, with *A 20th Century Chronicle* compiled by one of the present authors. As its title implies, it comprises a year-by-year pithy account of happenings in the School, together with an introductory section summarising the School's history in the late 19th century. By its very nature, however, it could not tell the whole story. Something more was needed not least because the research that both of us have undertaken in recent years revealed that Howard Brown's history needed to be both revised and amplified as well as extended. His book deals with some topics in considerable detail; others rather less so. It is not without errors. At times he relied too uncritically on FG Lee's earlier history of Thame published in the late 19th century, and Lee's mistakes are repeated. For example, more recent historians - see Chapter 3 - have modified his benign view of Lord Williams.

Howard Brown consulted some primary sources in his research, but he did not use, or was not aware of, some key documentary evidence in the archives of New College. So as well as taking the School's history forward to the present day, the purpose of this work has been to expand, correct, and modify Howard Brown's book for the period before 1900.

Though the scale and breadth of the work have increased since we originally considered what it might contain, we have never aspired to write a comprehensive history. We have deliberately not repeated at length Howard Brown's history where we have found nothing new or different.

For the post-1900 period, our decisions about what to include are based on a variety of considerations. We wanted to include periods of high achievement, such as the final flowering decade of the grammar school - see Chapter 25; also periods of significant change or recovery during the headships of Shaw, Bye and Mullens– see Chapters 17, 18 and 22.

Important for a full understanding of the School's history are the proceedings that led to the main turning points; the refounding in 1879, comprehensive reorganisation in 1971 and, less immediately obvious but equally significant for the management of the School, the change from an independent to a state school. Chapters 15, 21 and 27 respectively cover these three crucial periods.

A truism amply illustrated in this book is the important role that the head teacher plays in the success or otherwise of a school. Consequently, choosing the right person to become head teacher is by far the most important decision that a school's governors have to take. We have therefore included a history of how the heads were appointed: who made the appointment, by what process, and the kind of person they chose? See Chapter 8.

We also wanted to provide a more permanent record of a series of themed exhibitions about the School's history. This started with the 2009 exhibition mounted in Thame Museum as part of the 450th anniversary celebrations and continued up to 2019 with annual Founder's Day exhibitions on various aspects of the life and work of the School and Old Tamensians (OTs).

These aspects included the achievements of the staff, pupils, and former pupils in a range of subjects and other activities such as drama, dance and music, sport and links with the wider world. As the period of these exhibitions included the centenary of the First World War, more than one exhibition commemorated the war service, bravery and self-sacrifice of the 200 OTs who served in that war. Because of length, these thematic chapters are all contained in Volume 2.

Exhibitions normally contain more images than text and this raised for us the issue of whether photographs should be included in our book. There is no lack of photographic evidence but most of it is already easily accessible in the Old Tamensians's Association's (OTA) vast collection on Flickr, compiled and maintained by one of the authors. In the end, we decided not to include any images.

Some of the topics included owe their place mainly to serendipity. Although our connections with the School are very different, a pleasure common to us both is to receive enquiries from, often far-flung, Old Tamensians or their descendants.

One such contact, for example, from the Australian granddaughter of the Headmaster, Arthur Dyer, linked quite coincidentally to a recently published memoir by one of his pupils, edited and presented to the School by his daughter, was the starting point for a re-appraisal of someone who was unpopular during his period as Headmaster – see Chapter 19.

Some of the topics may be regarded as niche interests. We appreciate that not every reader will want to learn how the School came to adopt an inaccurate crest but we hope that there will be some with an interest in heraldry, or historians who enjoy a good story of how historical errors can keep creeping in, who will be entertained by the chapter found in Volume 2, on choughs or moorcocks?

After some debate, we eventually decided to include a short chapter on one topic for which the School was in no way particularly significant nor untypical of schools in general, that is bullying. Over the two volumes we have attempted to provide a balanced history of the School's strengths and weaknesses, and in an age that rightly preaches the value of transparency even if it does not always practice it, we felt that it would be wrong to ignore the fact that, like all other schools, bullying took place at LWS. We have deliberately kept this chapter short and anecdotal. The history of bullying over the whole of the School's existence would be little different from that of hosts of other schools, ancient and modern - see Chapter 26.

Finally, on subject of providing entertainment rather than verifiable facts, we do not apologise for including a chapter on what is probably more legend than history, but either way an intriguing story involving royalty – see Chapter 5.

At this point we need to acknowledge that as joint authors we are wholly responsible for all the text as it stands, including any errors, ommissions and typographic mistakes. Any opinions expressed are of course our own as are any judgements about what to include or exclude. Inevitably, even with the greater flexibility of new technology, we were unable to include every milestone and achievement. Our choices have tried to capture the representative characteristics and essence of the School at that particular moment. Sometimes we do this at greater depth, sometimes just a sketch. There are also times when we have looked at one aspect of the School but only at a particular time whereas that aspect has been persistent for possibly decades. What we have attempted to avoid is to include anecdotes that create a false impression.

Of course we are open to receive comments and corrections. Contact details can be found at the rear of this volume.

One final point: this volume is updated from time to time as new, important information emerges. If the reader uses Kindle, the text will be automatically updated.

Graham Thomas & Derek Turner. 2020

BACKGROUND

ACKNOWLEDGEMENTS

We would like to extend our thanks to the many people who have helped us with our research, donated items or information to the archives over the years, or who provided information to many of the books listed in the bibliography.

Special mention must be made of Jennifer Thorpe archivist at New College, Suzanne Foster, archivist at Winchester College, the late Gerald Howat, historian, *The Tamensian* editor, and school archivist who did much to put order into the archives in the 1980s and '90s, and Michael Beech, former head of history at the School.

It should also be noted that the School has been blessed with possibly more books written about it than most. We have deliberately not attempted to re-cover the ground that they have done so well, although they have been consulted as sources. A list of these is contained within the bibliography.

STRUCTURE: Volume 1

As work progressed it grew longer than we had originally planned, and to justify a division into parts as well as chapters.

Part 1 covers the rise and decline of Thame School from its beginnings in the 1560s to its collapse in the 1870s.

Part 2 relates the initially stuttering growth and eventual high achievement of Lord Williams's Grammar School (LWGS) from its re-foundation in new premises in 1879 to its close as a boys' grammar school in 1971.

Part 3 recounts the first fifty years of Lord Williams's School (LWS) as a comprehensive.

NOMENCLATURE

As a general rule we have used words that were current at the time rather than their modern and gender-free equivalents. For example, we have retained the term day-boys. After the coming of co-education in 1971, it has on occasion been unavoidable to distinguish between boys and girls but for the most part we have used gender-free terms such as pupils and latterly students.

The School has also had three names at various and sometimes overlapping times: Thame School, Lord Williams's Grammar School, and Lord Williams's School. All three are used as appropriate. We also shorten the name to 'School'.

How best to describe forms and year groups poses a problem because for most of the School's history, pupils were grouped as much by ability as by age, and there is no exact equivalence in the current system of Year 7 to Year 13 for secondary-age students. We have used whatever system was in operation at the time.

For the first three centuries the pupils were simply divided into two groups, one taught by the Master, the other by the Under-Master or Usher. When the School was re-founded, it adopted a simple numerical system, using Roman numerals: Forms I to VI. These were further subdivided into Upper and Lower, or 'a' and 'b' when numbers required it or a 'mezzanine' form added between them called 'Remove'. When the School lost its independence in 1947, it was obliged to adopt the national system of grouping pupils precisely by age, but to start with it retained its old numbering system, including the Without Form for boys up to the age of 11. This then left four forms for five year-groups when the statutory school leaving age was raised. Eventually, the School adopted the then current and more logical system of numbering forms and years from one to five: 'Fifth Form' or 'Fifth Year' and dividing the Sixth Form into Lower and Upper according to age.

Finally, the present system of numbering school years from the start of primary education was adopted in line with government requirements and runs from Year 7 to Year 13.

FORMATTING

This is not an academic paper but also due to formatting constraints we have not included footnotes. However, we have indicated key sources within the bibliography at the end of this volume.

In addition, there are some platform quirks that sometimes lead to spacing errors beyond our control, and the Amazon platform does some strange things such as highlighting only one author on a page. To underline: this is very much a joint effort.

FURTHER VOLUMES

Volume 2:

Whereas Volume 1 has adopted a predominantly chronological approach, Volume 2 is thematic. It provides more detail than is easily included in a chronological account of the school's enduring features. For example, for nearly its whole existence the School took in boarders and the boarding school played a major part its history. It also deals in greater detail than in the Volume 1 with those areas in which the School has excelled. Drama, music and sport are the obvious but not only examples. This will be published later in 2020.

Volume 3:

This is a revised reprint of *A Twentieth Century Chronicle.*

Volume 4:

We hope to publish a facsimile edition of the John Howard Brown's *A Short History of Thame School.*

Lord Williams of Burghfield Berkshire and Thame Oxfordshire
quartered, the arms of Williams; Azure, two organ pipes in saltire
the sinister surmounting the dexter, between four cross pattee, argent
and the arms of More; Argent, A Moorcock sable, combed + wattled, gules.
Crest; A Fish Weir

John S. Sermon 1999

PART 1: PRE-HISTORY AND ORIGINAL FOUNDATION

PROLOGUE: DEVELOPMENT OF SCHOOLS IN ENGLAND, AND THAME'S EARLY HISTORY

THE HISTORY OF SCHOOLS in England goes back to Roman times: Tactitus wrote that in AD78 schools were set up to 'romanise the sons of native chieftans.' Later this likely developed into a system where first reading and writing were taught, and then grammar and rhetoric. This, though, was confined to a small group: sons of officials, wealthier merchants, and perhaps some craftsmen and traders, and only in the major towns.

When the Romans left, so their institutions disintegrated and it was not until the sixth century that schools were re-established with the arrival of Augustine. He and his successors established two types of schools that were run by monastries and the handful of cathedrals: grammar schools to teach aspiring priests, and the song school where the sons of the wealthier were trained to sing in cathedral choirs.

The earliest grammar schools (*scolae grammaticales*) attached to cathedrals and monasteries were responsible for teaching Latin - the language of the church - to prepare these future priests and monks. This is why they are called grammar schools as the bulk of the curriculum covered the teaching of Latin grammar.

Other subjects required for religious work were occasionally added, including music and verse (for liturgy), astronomy and mathematics (for the church calendar) and law (for administration).

By the seventh century, schools could be found in Canterbury, York, Dorchester in Oxfordshire, Winchester, Hexham, Malmsbury, Lichfield, Hereford and Worcester.

Although these mainly catered for those who wanted to enter the priesthood, there is evidence that other pupils were admitted too. From what little is known of what was taught, it would appear that beyond Latin and grammar it could include rhetoric, law, poetry, arithmetic, music and the scriptures.

During the time of the Viking invasions in the ninth century, development of schools largely ceased but when Alfred came to the throne in 871, schools began to be re-introduced.

With the building of more parish churches in the tenth and eleventh century, there was the slow introduction of some form of rudimentary education given by the local priest to children in towns and villages.

However it was the Normans who opened up a new era in education; they refounded, reorganised and continued to found cathedrals and monasteries, and schools in these institutions became distinct activities. At the same time, secular schools i.e. those not part of a religious institution began to flourish.

By the twelfth century there were schools that taught reading, song, grammar, and higher studies. Some were the schools of the religious houses but also independent grammar schools for the public, ranging from well-organised bodies in towns to small, private, and temporary operations in villages and parish churches. Every cathedral was ordered to have a schoolmaster who could teach the 'clerks of the church and poor scholars freely.'

With the establishment of universities from the late twelfth century, grammar schools became the entry point with Latin forming the foundation of a trivium. This was comprised of three subjects: grammar, logic, and rhetoric. This study was preparatory for the quadrivium, which included geometry, arithmetic, astronomy, music. Combining the trivium and quadrivium produced the essence of university education. Pupils were usually educated in grammar schools up to the age of 14, after which they would look to universities and the church for further study.

By the end of the fourteenth century, schools were being endowed by wealthy benefactors so that the master could teach without charging fees. They became known as 'free schools.'

The fifteenth century was a time of plague and wars. This led to some of the established schools becoming moribund due to lack of teachers. However in other places, schools thrived. At Oxford, the grammar schools were attracting boys from all over England. In nearby Ewelme, a school was founded in 1437. Other schools were were founded in association with hospitals and almshouses.

Guilds were charitable organisations set-up to honour saints or festivals but also to provide good works for the local community, which sometimes included maintaining a school. In Oxfordshire, two Trinity Guilds were granted licences to open schools in Deddington in 1446, and Chipping Norton in 1451.

At the end of the fifteenth century and into the sixteenth, increasing wealth and a more settled political climate led to greater investment in education through the largess of individuals, particuluary in towns and cities. The number of chantry schools increased, and independent schools such as Eton (1440) and Winchester (albeit earlier in 1382) had been founded.

By the start of Henry VIII's reign in 1509 it has been estimated that in England there were 400 schools and this number increased over the course of his reign, mainly funded by the monies raised from the dissolution of the monastries. New cathedrals were established which were required to maintain a grammar school. Teaching was done by a master and an usher, and salaries were set at £20 and £10 respectively.

Further free schools were also established in Edward VI's reign (1547-1553) and parents were encouraged to either ensure their children had 'some learning' or to engage in 'some honest occupation.' All the remaining cathedrals that had not established a grammar school were ordered to provide one.

Today, around fifty of the schools that were founded between the sixth and fifteenth century still exist, with the oldest being The King's School, Canterbury founded in 597.

❋ ❋ ❋

It is only recently that Thame's long history stretching back to Neolithic times was confirmed when an enclosure and henge were excavated on rising land on the outskirts of the modern town (and opposite the School's Oxford Road site.) These have been dated to be six thousand years old.

The same site also revealed evidence of continued occupation from the Iron Age through the Roman and early Anglo-Saxon periods including Iron Age round houses and drove-way, a Roman agricultural settlement, and later Anglo Saxon buildings.

In 675, Wulfhere, the King of Mercia signed a charter at Thame, with his hand on an altar, indicating the presence of a church. The charter says, 'Confirmed by Wulfhere, king of the Mercians, for he both placed his hand on the altar in the residence which is called Thame and subscribed with the sign of the Holy Cross in his own hand.'

If there was a church there would have been a settlement, and the indications are that this was at the site of the current parish church of St Mary's, close to the River Thame but on land that rises above the flood plain.

The River Thame's name has several etymological alternatives: it could mean either 'dark' or 'spreading' water, the latter an apt description, one that still applies as can be seen yearly when the river floods the water meadows as it snakes around the town. Another suggestion is that comes from a Celtic word meaning 'gently flowing.' Also apt.

Why a particular place was chosen as a settlement in Anglo-Saxon times can be down to a number of factors - or sometimes for no other reason than a family group decided to stop and put down roots.

In Thame, it is likely this was because the river was easily forded here; the river too was a means of transportation to the River Thames at Dorchester, and then on to London. Water meadows provided rich soil for crops. It was also a place where two brooks joined the river, adding to the richness of the soil but also ensuring a plentiful supply of fish to eat, and water for crops and livestock across a broad area.

The ability to cross the river was critical and led to Thame being the crossing point for the road that went from Aylesbury to Wallingford. The road's importance has now disappeared but in the Anglo-Saxon period, Aylesbury was a significant market town to the extent that William the Conqueror took the manor for himself and it is listed as a royal manor in the

Domesday Book. Likewise Wallinford was equally important, had been fortified in the Anglo-Saxon period, could mint coins, and post-Conquest would have a castle of importance and was one of largest towns in England.

It is little known but today's Upper School lies adjacent to the road. Not the Oxford Road - as might be thought - but the muddy lane that eventually leads to Morton, and which was once well-known to cross-country runners. This carries on to Tetsworth and then on to Wallingford.

In 971, the *Anglo-Saxon Chronicle* records that Archbishop Oskytel died in Thame, possibly he lived here - though only for part of the year - or was visiting an abbey or other ecclesiastical domicile perhaps at Thame Park.

The town is mentioned in the Domesday Book but it was in the early twelfth century when it was significantly expanded eastwards, away from the settlement surrounding the church. The first market charter was granted in 1183, and a second in 1215 was granted by King John.

Once Thame expanded, the town could be divided into three distinct parts: Old Thame around the church, and dating back to at least the 8th century; New Thame, which grew up in the 12th and 13th centuries, and Priestend, which was a distinct settlement in its own right.

In the early thirteenth century the town benefited from the re-routing of the highway through the town's centre. This led to the building of shops and houses, and in turn this led to it increasing its importance as a place of trade. The town had its market cross, a market hall, gallows and stocks, and a population of around 1000. Crafts flourished in the town and Thame acquired a reputation for its glazing tradesmen and, because of the market and the road passing though, for providing plenty of establishments for refreshments.

[The glazier responsible for the Sacristy and choir windows in Merton College, Oxford was Master William de Thame, dated to the period 1307-11, making this the earliest surviving English glazing scheme that can be attributed to a named glazier. He was paid £9 2s 0d for his work. And on stylistic grounds, glass at a number of locations throughout the county (including Ashthall, Aston Rowant, and Dorchester) has been attributed to Master William. As noted above, Thame was home to a significant number of glaziers in the fourteenth century. The tax roll of 1327 lists four glaziers, John the glazier, Adam and another John, all living in New Thame, and a Henry the glazier in Old Thame.]

By the sixteenth century - and the start of the School's story - the town was important both as the centre of the rural economy in what we now call the Vale of Aylesbury, and as an eclesiastical centre. The main industry was sheep farming, which at one stage was the backbone of the whole of England's economic power. Lord Williams farmed sheep and left six large flocks in his will. As elsewhere, the sixteenth century was a period of great prosperity for all yeoman farmers in the Thame area, and Thame market and its tradesmen must have benefited from their prosperity. The number of wealthy merchant families was considerable for the size of the town. The Dormer, Quatremain families were the richest followed by the Daunce, Wells and Hesters.

CHAPTER 1: WHEN DID THE SCHOOL BEGIN?

THE INSPIRATION FOR THIS BOOK was to do something to mark the 450th anniversary of the start of teaching at the School. This immediately raised the question: when did teaching begin? A simple question but, as with much of the early history of Thame School, the answer is complicated. Anniversary celebrations are usually dated from 1559, the date of the School's endowment by Lord Williams in his Will. Earlier generations sometimes dated anniversaries from 1575 when the School's Statutes were issued. But teaching did not begin in 1559 as there was no building and no staff; by 1575, however, the School had already been in operation for probably five years - but it is worth exploring the various alternatives.

These are three. It is often thought that the earliest but least likely answer is 1567. Some have proposed this date on the basis of the statement in the 1575 Statutes that the first Master, Edward Harris, had been in the post for eight years. There is no reason to doubt that Harris was appointed in 1567 (see Chapter 4) but appointing the Master does not mean that the School as we know it began in that year, and it is definitely known that the school building was not built by then. Some grammar schools of the period did set up in buildings converted from a previous use, and this may have happened at Thame, but the very detailed prescriptions for the running of the School drafted by Williams's executors in consultation with the Warden and Fellows of New College strongly imply that they wanted to honour the founder and benefactor's intentions properly.

The school building was completed in 1569, and this has also been suggested as the date when the School started. This is somewhat more plausible but still unlikely; it takes time to move from a complete but empty school building to a fully functioning school. The Executors would have realised that masters of newly founded schools need time to get everything organised.

The final date, and by far the most likely, is 1570. Opening the School within a year of the building's completion is feasible and probable, but that this actually happened is confirmed by direct evidence in the form of a note in one copy of the Statutes stating that the School opened on 29th November 1570.

1570 therefore is beyond all reasonable doubt the year in which teaching at Thame School began in the new school building.

CHAPTER 2: A SCHOOL AT THAME BEFORE THAME SCHOOL?

HAVING REACHED THE REASONABLE CONCLUSION that the School started in 1570 there is strong circumstantial evidence for the existence of a chantry school at Thame before 1570 although so far no direct evidence has been found.

We are in good company as the *Victoria County History (VCH)* seems to think so:

> *It is improbable that so large a town as Thame had no endowed school before then [1570] and one was no doubt supported by the Guild of St. Christopher founded by Richard Quartermaine in 1447. In 1547 the priest was described by the commissioners as 'a man of honest behaviour and well learned.'*

Chantry schools were often endowed by a wealthy family and were attached to a church. AF Leach - an educationalist who wrote extensively in the nineteenth century about the history of education in England - claims that nine-tenths of the grammar schools set up in the mid-sixteenth century were continuations of pre-existing chantry schools.

The Quartermaine family were wealthy merchants who had been established in the Thame area for several centuries. During this time they had built-up significant holdings of land, and were prominent members of the local but untitled gentry. Richard, though, was the last of the line locally as he died leaving no heirs; his splendid tomb can be seen in St Mary's, Thame's parish church.

Returning to the *VCH*, it states that pre-Reformation eight schools were attached to chantries and hospitals in Oxfordshire, and they further go on to say that Thame School was 're-founded' by Lord Williams, suggesting that it had, for period of time, disappeared.

That said, the evidence is compelling that indeed the School did not disappear at all, and might mean that Edward Harris , the School's first Master was teaching in Thame before the establishment of the current school.

We have wrestled a little with the fact that in 1575 Harris was said to have been teaching for eight years, and antiquarian Anthony Wood described him as 'a man of Thame.'

If he had been teaching at the Guild (although no mention of a teacher has been found) then this accounts for the eight years, and also because he was a longer-time resident of Thame, this might have been what Wood was referring to. Furthermore, in the Statutes it says that the School had actually been started by Lord Williams in his lifetime. This may just be that the Executors were being over generous in their praise.

After being granted the Guild by Edward VI, Williams took over responsibilities in 1550, including paying for a priest to assist the vicar. It seems reasonable to assume that this would not be a full-time job and that this priest could also undertake teaching. (The vicar employed wardens and a parish clerk who were responsible for the day-to-day administration and running of the church and parish.) There is also a reference in a recent doctorate paper that says that Oxfordshire was known for having priests who also provided educational services.

Conjecture certainly, but as Williams was writing his Will it could be argued that he made the decision to properly establish a school rather than having it continue as part of the Guild.

The story is bound up with the Quartermaine foundation and

the events at the end of the reign of Henry VIII and start of Edward VI, 1546-1550. The national context is that it was a period of extreme governmental financial crisis as a result of Henry VIII's ruinously expensive and fruitless war against France and Protector Somerset's against Scotland. This resulted in debasement of the coinage, heavy taxation leading to widespread poverty, and some rebellion. Also, a renewed financial grab by the Crown on church property, specifically the chantries. Though it was also a period of religious turmoil, it was primarily economics rather than religious politics that affected Thame and other Oxfordshire towns.

The Chantries Act of 1545 was designed to bring to the Crown the revenue of all chantry foundations that were solely for the saying of masses, deemed heretical by kings Henry and Edward. Commissioners were appointed in February 1546. For Oxon, Northants, and Rutland these included, unsurprisingly, John Williams but also John Doyley, his cousin and ultimately one of his Executors, both officers of the Court of Augmentations, the main function of which was grabbing money for the Crown. The commissioners would have had local knowledge as well as a national role in recording details of Oxon chantries, including Thame.

Henry died in January 1547 before the process of sequestering chantry funds had got under way, but in November 1547 Edward (in reality the Privy Council headed by The Lord Protector, Edward Seymour, Earl of Somerset), still desperately short of funds, got parliament to pass a second Chantries Act. This was more draconian: taking all chantry revenues, with a few exceptions such as the universities, into the Crown's hands. Though the motives on the face of the Bill were superficially religious and altruistic: 'to convert Foundations to good and godly use in creating grammar schools...' the terms of reference for the second set of commissioners, again including Williams and Doyley, were explicitly to replenish the royal coffers.

The results of the commissioners' work were the 1548 Chantry certificates, which survive for parts of Oxfordshire, and part of Thame. The information they gathered was similar to the previous commission but included the name and academic standing of the (former) chantry priests and the number of 'houseling people' i.e. communicants in the town.

Though the Act's nominal intention was to increase the number of grammar schools, it seems to have had the reverse effect. Banbury School, thought to date from the reign of Henry III, 'perished' because its foundation contravened the other terms of the new Act. Chantry foundations often, but not invariably, included a schoolmaster, for example at Chipping Norton the foundation included 'a schoolmaster to teach the rudiments of grammar free to poor boys and scholars coming to the town from any part of the kingdom.'

There is no mention in Thame's Chantry certificate of a schoolmaster, nor in earlier documents relating to the Quartermaine foundation. However, Rose Graham, an expert on the subject, writes: 'There is no evidence that Thame was deprived of its schoolmaster when the endowment passed to John Williams...' and she goes on to describe his endowment - ten years later - of Thame School. So there is a strong implication that: firstly there was a schoolmaster at Thame prior to 1559, probably connected to the Quartermaine foundation, and secondly that Williams took over the funding of this person for the nine years from the letters patent grant of 1550 until he made his Will. Presumably he wanted to make sure that schooling carried on, this time under his own name, and with a secure foundation. Of course, it should also be remembered that in fact he was doing what the Chantry Act had said was its intention: to increase the number of grammar schools.

Most probably there was no dedicated school building, and

whatever form the teaching took was undertaken in the parish church. Some evidence for this comes from Harry Lupton's 1861 book on the history of Thame. Here he writes that in the chantry of St Christopher in the church, there was once 'a desk with books attached to it by chains.' This at least points to a form of teaching taking place here.

Who was the schoolmaster? Not Harris, at least until 1567, as he went straight from being a scholar at Winchester College to become a Fellow of New College. The most obvious candidate is Sir John Yonge, the former chantry priest and from 1550 assistant to the vicar. The Thame Chantry certificate describes him as: 'aged 40, of honest behaviour, well learned'. (Like Ofsted, the commissioners had a grade scale: 'mean as in average, learned, and well learned') so Yonge would have been well qualified to be a schoolmaster, and though the grant to Williams states his role as assisting the vicar, he would have had time to undertake some teaching.

(As an aside, the chantry certificate for Enford in Wiltshire reads: 'The said incumbent is a very honest poor man, and hath no other living but only this chantry, and a man right able to serve a cure and hath always occupied himself in teaching of children there.' This statement seems to imply that the incumbent was not officially a teacher but nevertheless performed that role. The situation may have been the same at Thame.)

Yonge's original salary was eight pounds two shillings and two pence per annum, reduced when he retired as chantry priest to a pension of six pounds.

Six pounds per annum compares unfavourably with the salary of Thame's schoolmasters from 1575. If Yonge was acting as schoolmaster as well as assistant priest he was poorly paid.

Yonge remains an elusive figure. He does not appear in the *Alumni Oxonienses* as one might expect of someone who was 'well learned'. It is tempting to believe that he was the son of a well-known John Yong of an earlier generation, from New-ton Longville Bucks, educated at Winchester and Fellow, later Warden, of New College. However, another John Yonge, almost certainly his son, born in the same village fits the dates, except that he died in 1545. If there were a Winchester/New College connection with Thame prior to 1559 that would help to explain why the Executors approached the New College Warden, particularly as Doyley would have been party to the terms of the return of the Chantry grant revenues to Thame via Williams.

A second candidate - mentioned in the *VCH* - is the poet William Forrest, a former monk of Thame Abbey, who the VCH says 'may have been appointed by Williams.' In terms of teaching he had the right credentials: educated at Oxford, appointed as a chaplain to Queen Mary, and a prolific poet.

Because the government's financial crisis continued there was yet another raid on ecclesiastical wealth, this time church plate and other movable goods such as crosses and even church bells as a result of yet another commission in 1551. Interestingly Williams was not a commissioner for Oxfordshire this time. Thame residents are recorded as being angry with the churchwardens for selling off most of the church's plate etc between 1549 and 1551. Records show (Rose Graham provides detail) that the great bell was sold off and melted down. It is probably to Williams's credit that at this time of excessive crown greed, he kept the almshouses - and probably the schooling - going.

During the reign of Mary (1553- 1558) no records have been found that relate to a school at Thame. During the succession crisis of 1553 in which the Protestant Lady Jane Grey rapidly lost her throne to the Catholic Mary, Williams as usual made the right call and raised troops from Oxfordshire in support of Mary's claim to the throne. His subsequent influential position at the court of Queen and her husband Philip of Spain probably allowed Thame life to carry on without major disruption, despite the government's return to a militant Catholic religious policy.

After Mary's death in 1558, Elizabeth's accession ushered in a period of religious compromise and relative quiet. The now ageing Williams may have begun to think about his legacy. Possibly it was John Doyley, who had been closely involved with William as a fellow officer at the Court of Augmentations and twice Commissioner for implementing the Chantry Acts, that suggested to Williams, now living in Wales, the need to make a more permanent and extensive provision for education in Thame.

If some form of teaching was being undertaken in Thame, it is unclear why it took the Executors so long to get started on implementing plans for Thame School after Williams' death. Possibly they needed to build up capital reserves from rents to pay for the acquisition of the plot and the building of the schoolhouse, and this we explore in Chapter 4. Presumably though, some kind of schooling continued from Yonge if he was still alive until the Executors appointed Harris in 1567.

Much of what is written in the foregoing paragraphs is both complex and necessarily speculative, based on slender evidence. A full, accurate account is unlikely ever to be possible. However, in summary, it is probable that there was a school in Thame in the later medieval period as schools are known to have existed in other, and smaller, Oxfordshire market towns. From the mid-15th century the most likely person who acted as schoolmaster was the priest of the St Christopher chantry endowed by the Quartermaine family. As a result of the Crown's financial crisis and the abolition of the chantries, some Oxfordshire schools were forced to close but, almost certainly thanks to John Williams and his cousin John Doyley, the revenues of the Quartermaine chantry were returned to their former charitable use of maintaining both the almshouse and some form of schooling in Thame.

Following Williams's death, the four Executors, Sir Walter Myldmay, Robert Doyley, John Doyley, and William Place, began active planning for a new school with a dedicated building. What the plans were and how they were implemented is described in more detail in Chapter 4.

* * *

The Executors

Before finishing this chapter it is worth briefly commenting on the four Executors named in Williams's Will. Robert and John Doyley were descended from Robert D'Oyly a Norman baron, whose title was established under William the Conqueror; this Robert had been responsible for building Oxford Castle within a decade of the Conquest.

John Doyley lived locally as he had acquired Chiselhampton and Merton manors. He was also related to Williams through marriage. John Dunkin in his 1823 book, *The history and antiquities in the Hundreds of Bullingdon and Ploughley,* wrote that Doyley 'lived in great reputation in his countrye for his sinceritie in religion, integritie in life, equitie in justice and hospitalitie.'

Robert Doyley was also local and was either the son of John or his brother - both were called Robert and there is no means possible to now distinguish between the two. Both Roberts, though, were to die in 1577 after they attended the assizes at Oxford, where 'there arose such a stench from the prisoners' bodies and clothes that it immediately infected the judge, jurors and almost everyone present'. About 300 are said to have died in this incident which has been put down to some fever caught during the trial of 'Rowland Jenkes, a saucy foul-mouthed Bookseller, for scandalous words uttered against the

Queen.'

Sir Walter Myldmay was the most distinguished of the four: a statesman, he served as Chancellor of the Exchequer to Queen Elizabeth I from 1566, and founded Emmanuel College, Cambridge in the 1580s.

Of William Place, all we know is that he was a 'gentleman of Ludgershall' in Buckinghamshire, and that in Williams's Will, he described him as 'my trusted servant' several times, and bequeathed him the manor of Brill, and a flock of sheep.

As is the same now, there was no legal duty for an executor named in a Will to take on or complete the task. It would appear that both Myldmay and Robert Doyley ceased acting as Executors during the 1560s, the former's decision understandable as he had been appointed Chancellor.

CHAPTER 3: WHO WAS JOHN WILLIAMS? (C.1500-1559)

IN THE FIRST HISTORY WRITTEN ABOUT THE SCHOOL, its author John Howard Brown paints Lord Williams as a benign Tudor gentleman whose life was devoted to doing good. Perhaps in the 1920s it was understandable that Howard Brown - and the Headmaster - wanted pupils to admire their School's founder rather than question his behaviour. After all, if they knew the truth it might then be more difficult to encourage pupils to gather reverentially around the founder's tomb in St Mary's.

Although his founding of the School should be much celebrated, a number of recent works have painted a more critical picture of the man. While the facts of his life are not in dispute, as with his mentor Thomas Cromwell, no clear consensus exists of what kind of a man he really was. We have therefore included two rather different accounts to complement Brown's rosy view.

Sometime between 1500 and 1503 John Williams was born in Burghfield, Berkshire. His Welsh ancestors came from a long line of gentry who held lands in Glamorgan, and whose family name was Morgan. It appears that this was changed in the 15th century to the anglicised Williams, a not uncommon practice, and which is reflected in the canting (punning) allusions of organ pipes in the Williams' coat of arms.

John Williams's father was also John. Born sometime between 1460 and 1470 in Glamorgan, little is known of his life other than Lee's *Dictionary of National Biography* notes he fought at

Bosworth with Henry VII.

However, we do know for certain that John Snr had been appointed a Sheriff of Oxfordshire in 1495, and that he died in 1508 when his son John was still a child.

John Snr married twice. His first marriage was to Margaret Smythe, who was an aunt to Thomas Cromwell. She died before any children were born. Second, he married Isobel (or Elizabeth) More, who bore him two sons, one of whom was John Jnr, and three daughters.

The marriage to Margaret Smythe was one of three connections between the Williams family and the family of Thomas Cromwell, a connection that was central to Williams's success in later life. Cromwell, as is well known, became the most powerful of Henry VIII's ministers in the 1530s, and his patronage undoubtedly helped John Jnr gain the lucrative positions he held at Court.

The second connection with Cromwell is that John Snr's brother, Morgan, married Katherine Cromwell, Thomas' sister. In other words, Katherine was an aunt through marriage of the young John Jnr and Thomas Cromwell an uncle. Morgan and Katherine had at least three sons, two of whom were later adopted by Thomas Cromwell. (These sons were therefore cousins of John Jnr.) One was Richard Williams (later taking the name of Cromwell) and when he died in 1545, he left a legacy of two of his best horses in his Will to John Williams Jnr.

The third but unproven connection is that Cromwell's wife Elizabeth had been married previously to a Thomas (or Richard) Williams but he had died leaving her a widow. Other than the surname there are no records that directly link this Williams to the John Williams family but it is a possibility.

In previous biographies, the strong links between the Williams and Cromwell families were not fully appreciated and hence only a tentative assumption was made that John Williams benefited from some advantageous kinship with Thomas Cromwell. We now know better. However, despite this clear connection, as there are no written records to substantiate the premise, we can only surmise that this relationship enabled John Williams to be first a retainer in Cromwell's household, and then a retainer to Cardinal Wolsey.

As noted earlier, Williams's father had died in 1508 leaving him fatherless at a young age – although despite much research it is still unknown when his mother died. What is clear is that Cromwell looked after his kith and kin, which is why, like Williams's cousins, he brought Williams into his household, and later arranged for him to be taken into Wolsey's household.

Williams' position on the periphery of the Court and a man with prospects led to a marriage in July 1524 to Elizabeth Bledlowe, a wealthy widow originally from Thame.

For the rest of Williams's life we turn to the biography written by Michael Beech, with some amendments and additions based on more recent research by ourselves and others.

❊ ❊ ❊

A Brief Life of John Williams, Baron Williams of Thame.

At the age of 26 Williams gained his first official office at Court. Again it would seem this came through the patronage of Thomas Cromwell, and a little later, he became Keeper of the King's Greyhound – a symbolic post that brought him status and 20 marks or £13.33, a handsome stipend in those days. It is of significance that a pair of greyhounds formed the supporters to Williams's coat of arms that survives on the School's crest.

At some point in the 1530s, and because of Elizabeth's local connections, they purchased the estate of Rycote a few miles west of Thame. This came with an imposing Tudor house, and a separate chapel that had been consecrated in 1449. Subsequently, but possibly not until 1540, Williams demolished the old house and rebuilt a magnificent family seat.

In 1535, he had played host to Cromwell's son Gregory when the latter spend the summer at Rycote. Gregory's tutor had written that the '...summer was spent in the services of the wild goddess Diana...' Clearly an enjoyable time had been had and Gregory himself had written to his father stating that he had enjoyed the 'hospitality of Williams.' In common with many other landowners, Williams was busy at this time enclosing his tenants' lands to create deer parks, hence the reference to the goddess Diana.

It is not known whether Williams was part of Cromwell's commission that in 1535 condemmed to death a cell of continental Anabaptists, twenty five of whom were burned at the stake but it was a particularly brutal act.

By 1536, he was sharing responsibilities with Cromwell in the office of Master or Treasurer of the King's Jewels, responsible for buying, selling, storing, cleaning and supplying them as the King required.

However, Cromwell was the senior member of this partnership and was in a position to give Williams instructions as can be seen from a note he sent Williams in September 1536, asking him and two others to investigate a mill belonging to Sir John Browne in Oxfordshire that was flooding and 'which doth annoye the Kinges other subjects.'

Williams became a Justice of the Peace for the city of Oxford and for the counties of Oxfordshire and Buckinghamshire, which bestowed on him status and influence in the region.

However, his main route to fame and fortune had begun in 1536 when Thomas Cromwell appointed him as one of six commissioners to look into the morals and financial affairs of the monasteries in England, an undertaking that gave him the opportunity to prove his loyalty to the Crown and also to profit from it. Subsequently he supervised the closure of hundreds of monasteries in a swathe of England, from East Anglia across to Winchester. Close to home, he was involved with the closure of Notley and Thame abbeys, and a little further afield Studley Priory where his own sister Joan was Prioress.

Along with his cousin Richard Cromwell and others sent from London by Henry, Williams was also involved with suppressing the short-lived Lincolnshire Rebellion in 1536. He wrote scathingly of the conspirators at the time, that he'd never seen anywhere 'such a sight of asses so unlike gentlemen the most part them be.'

Rewards came in October 1537 when he was invited to be present at the baptism of Henry's only legitimate son, Prince Edward, and later that month he was knighted by the King.

On 3rd January 1540 Williams is recorded as walking in a procession to Blackheath to celebrate the first meeting of Henry and his fourth wife, Anne, Princess of Cleves. The actual marriage occurred on 6th January, but Anne did not please the King (he called her 'a Flanders mare'). Henry blamed Thomas Cromwell for organising the marriage and because the latter was already falling out of favour with the King he paid for his mistake with his head.

With the fall of Cromwell and his execution in July 1540, Williams must have feared for his position at Court, but he was certainly reassured when, in August 1540 the Privy Council, the effective governing body of the realm under the King, met at Rycote. The bells of the church were rung as Henry passed through the town, and from the churchwarden's accounts it is known that the ringers were paid in 'ale for ringing when the King's grace came through the town.' Then Williams was elected to the 1541 Parliament by the 'shout' of other men of property in the county, as one of the two members for Oxford-shire.

By 1542 Williams was accepting grants of land from the Crown and accumulating large profits for himself from the sale of monastic property. Ultimately some of these accumulated lands particularly in and around Thame would provide the endowment that would establish the School. The granting of manors and lands was an acceptable form of payment for services to the Crown in those days, provided the profits were not such as to attract attention.

In 1544 he exchanged the office of Master of the King's Jewels for that of Treasurer of the Court of Augmentations, with a salary of £320 a year. This Court collected all the revenues from the rent and sale of lands and property of the 800 or so monastic houses taken over by Act of Parliament. The revenues which came to the Crown enabled Henry to be more independent of Parliament for financial grants and to conduct an expensive war with France, during which Williams was listed as the Captain of 12 archers and 40 armed men in 'The King's battle against the army of France.'

In 1549 religious changes and inflation had created such discontent that there were rebellions over much of the southern half of England.

Locally Williams had already fenced in confiscated common land for his own purposes, namely hunting and sheep farming, and so the rebels 'arose in great numbers and with great anger towards Sir John Williams, tore down the fences of Thame Park and killed all the deer. They then went to Rycote and killed all his deer there, drank their fill of ale, wine and beer, slaughtered and ate some sheep before moving on elsewhere.'

And where was John Williams when this happened? He and 79 other gentry from Berkshire, Bucks and Oxon had gathered in Windsor at a special council to determine who was to deal with the rebels - but also to be out of harm's way. The decision was taken to form a force under the leadership of Lord Grey of Wilton, and to hunt down the rebels.

From Thame and Rycote, the rebels moved north and west towards Chipping Norton but they were now harried and chased by Lord Grey who had 1500 men at his disposal. Many fled back to their villages and towns while others were slain on the spot. Two hundred rebels were taken prisoner, and those perceived as leaders were selected for public execution by hanging. Two rebel leaders, one of whom came from nearby Great Haseley and the other from Watlington, were selected for hanging in Oxford and Watlington, with two others in Thame itself. Not all of the four suffered this fate: William Bowlar from Watlington was eventually pardoned; Thomas Bowldry from Haseley was hung drawn and quartered, and the final fate of the two condemned to be executed in Thame is unknown.

However, in August 1549 when order had been restored, Williams wrote to the Privy Council reporting that some of the 'Catholic rebels' had been hanged, 'and their heads fastened to the walls' as an example to others. He may have been referring to the men in Thame or more broadly to the executions that took place in Oxford.

Why Williams Bowlar was pardoned is something of a mystery, and contrary to Somerset's usual policy of hanging the ringleaders but pardoning the remainder. Though there is no evidence, it is possible that Williams was responsible for obtaining the pardon as a way of winning back some support from local people.

Thame was one of the focal points of the rising and the

fact that 'two of the most seditious' were ordered to 'suffer at Thame' for their part in the Oxfordshire outbreak of 1549 suggests that the Crown 'may have had a special reason for choosing Thame as the place to stage a spectacle calculated to deter revolt' according to the historian Amanda Jones. The reason behind this was that Thame had suffered significant depopulation and enclosure and the local clergy as well as leading townspeople had no sympathy for the changes that had taken place. However, despite the rebellion being put down, the following year two men from Thame, Robert Johnson and Thomas Jackson, were identified as being ringleaders in yet another planned but ultimately unfulfilled insurrection.

After life had settled down Williams was one of many who blamed Somerset as a cause for the unrest as he was said to have encouraged the hopes of the discontented and then not taking firm enough measures to stamp out signs of rebellion.

In October 1549 Williams rode from London to Windsor with a small company of armed men to arrest Somerset, remove him from the King's presence and conduct him to the Tower of London where he was to be executed - but not before he had formally transferred back to Williams the Manor of Thame which Somerset had recently confiscated.

In October 1551 Williams was himself arrested for having paid out pensions from Augmentations to former monks without having first obtained the Council's permission, at a time when the Treasury was nearly empty. In April 1552 he was sent to the Fleet Prison but was soon given permission to receive members of his family and he was released in June. Nevertheless, the episode was a warning to Williams by Somerset's successor, the Duke of Northumberland, not to overstep his authority. The Duke also wanted to curry favour with the populace as Edward's health deteriorated and the prospect of putting his daughter-in-law, Lady Jane Grey, on the throne came closer.

When Edward died and Northumberland proclaimed the 16-year-old Jane, Queen, (for nine days only), Williams sent 6,000 troops to support Queen Mary's legitimate claim. He must have decided that it was more in his interest to desert Northumberland and join Catholic Mary, even though she might have been harbouring a grudge against him for having closed so many monasteries. Fortunately for Williams, his gamble paid off and Mary was to create him Baron Williams of Thame in 1553. A year later in 1554 she made him Lord Chamberlain of the Household of Prince Philip (later Philip II) of Spain, who arrived in England to marry the Queen in July 1554. The marriage took place at Winchester Cathedral and it can be assumed that Williams was present.

Towards the end of 1554, and into 1555, Mary was thought to be pregnant and would deliver an heir. Celebrations were held in London as the pregnancy proceeded. In Thame, a Whitsun Ale was organised by Williams to celebrate Philip and Mary's happy news. An ale was one name for such festive gatherings, others being May games, summer plays, summer games, Whitsun or feast. The event was held in and around the tithe barn adjacent to St Mary's Church, which was lavishly decorated for the occasion. A set of accounts show that two calves, and two sheep, and fish were purchased; a cook was taken on along with a helper, and the animals were roasted over an open fire. Of course much ale was also purchased, and a piper and a tabret or tabor (a snare drum) player were hired.

Unfortunately her ghastly gynaecological difficulties meant that her much awaited pregnancy turned out to be a delusion. If Mary had borne Philip Habsburg a son there would have been a Habsburg dynasty in England, as well as throughout Europe.

Williams was obliged to respond to the favour shown him by the Queen when, as High Steward of Oxford, he arranged, after a show-trial in St Mary's University Church, Oxford - at which he presided - for the public execution by burning of Bishops Ridley and Latimer in October 1555, and of ex-Archbishop Cranmer, the author of the Book of Common Prayer, five months later.

While these were horrific times the act by Williams to participate in the burnings should not be underestimated. This was a man who acted without compunction. Two hundred and eight four people were burned for their protestant convictions between 1555 and 1558 in a campaign organised by Mary, her husband Philip, courtiers, and bishops. This was one of the most intense persecutions in 16th century Europe.

Certainly, as a loyal servant of the Crown, Williams did not hesitate to carry out the Queen's orders to burn the Protestant Martyrs but it is not clear that this necessarily meant that Williams had turned back to Catholicism, nor that he had ever left it. Circumstantial evidence suggests that his personal religious views were conservative but that he was willing to 'bend with the wind', placing obedience to the monarchy above any religious conviction. In the very same year, the long-standing and vicious civil wars across the Channel had ended in the Peace of Augsburg that established the principle of *Cuius regio, eius religio* – roughly translated as 'citizens should follow the religion of their ruler', a formula with which Williams would probably have agreed.

That he combined duty with an element of compassion is suggested by the words ascribed to him and addressed to Bishop Latimer in the near contemporary print of the bishops' burning – 'I will remember your suit', that is he would look after some poor men and Latimer's sister as Latimer had requested. This compassion is reinforced by his lenient, even friendly treatment of the Protestant Elizabeth during the period when she was under arrest by her sister.

In 1556, Williams's first wife died - possibly of 'flu as a number of epidemics swept across the country at the tail end of the 1550s - and was buried in Rycote Chapel. He went on to marry Margaret, daughter of the first Baron Wentworth of Nettlestead. Queen Mary too died of 'flu in 1558, Philip's sort-of-reign as an English king came to an end, as he resigned and returned to Spain as a proper monarch.

Williams switched allegiances once again, and was one of 32 favoured Lords who accompanied the newly acclaimed Queen Elizabeth from Hatfield to London. Williams' relationship with Princess Elizabeth had started in May 1554 when he played host to her at Rycote, as she travelled, a prisoner, to Woodstock on the Queen's orders, and again when she returned to London, nearly a year later.

She quickly showed her gratitude by appointing him as Lord President of the Council of Wales and the Marches, but he was only in residence at Ludlow Castle for four months before he died at 10am on 14th October 1559. Following his death, the body was 'bowelled, trammelled and wrapped in Lynnen clothe' before being brought back to Thame on 28th October, where the coffin remained in Rycote's Great Chamber until he was buried on 15th November. Williams had specified in his Will that he wished to be buried in Thame church.

After the mourners had departed and returned to Rycote for dinner, Williams was interred in a vault underneath the chancel floor.

✽ ✽ ✽

In a summary of William's life, Felicity Heal of Jesus College, Oxford concludes that no matter how deviously Williams was able to survive he was clearly a man of energy and drive. While he was on the margins of historical significance and was more servant and bureaucrat to men who held the real power, he made things happen. On the other hand, he was clearly engaged in fraudulent activities and, as she described it, allowed money to stick to his fingers.

She concludes that he was a man of paradoxical nature. Energetic and a largely effective servant of the state, but probably corrupt; at one time he was deeply unpopular in Thame but then was able to lead a popular movement of local men to support Mary; he was conservative - read Catholic - in his religious views but managed to balance these dependent upon how the winds blew and should be admired for the political skills of a survivor. He was also deeply loyal to his family which, in those times, was not necessarily common.

Whether he was as generous in his endowments to the School as he could have been is another matter that will be commented on in later chapters.

CHAPTER 4: FROM CONCEPTION TO BIRTH, 1559-1570

WILLIAMS MADE HIS WILL on 8th March 1559 when he was already ill, bequeathing most of his property to his second wife and his two daughters Isabel and Margery from his first marriage, but leaving rental incomes to provide for the building and maintenance of a free Grammar School at Thame, and for the refurbishment of the almshouse in the town, but as the old saying goes: 'Rome was not built in a day'. It takes time for all ambitious projects to move from the initial idea to its realisation. Thame School, as it was always known in its early years, was no exception.

The outline plan needed to be drawn up: how large a building, how many pupils and so on? For the school building, a site had to be chosen, land acquired, a master mason appointed, builders employed, the building erected and suitably furnished for staff and pupils. A master and possibly an usher had to be appointed, no doubt assisted by servants. Materials for teaching and learning needed purchasing and, throughout the whole period, the progress of the works would have needed to be matched to the availability of finance. John Williams's endowment was primarily from property rents so spending would have to take account of when rents fell due and when capital was accumulated. The Executors would have been unable to borrow money from other bequests within the Will and pay it back later. (Sometimes it was the case with other endowments that a school was established through the bequest of a lump sum or by transferring assets that could be sold.)

Even so, to use a biological metaphor, the period of eleven

years gestation from conception to birth might seem long. However, it took twelve years from the Foundation Charter establishing Winchester College to the start of teaching, and the building of the school, admittedly a much grander project than Thame, took five years. In the late 16th century, Bampton Free Grammar School in Oxon took 20 years to come to fruition after a bequest was made in a Will; Charlbury, 12 years; Woodstock, 14 years. In short there is no evidence that suggests that Thame was unusual.

One of the most import factors likely to have lengthened the realisation of William's plans for a school was the sheer length and detail of his Will, running to some fifty pages in a modern transcription. Anyone who has ever acted as executor of even a fairly modest Will would be aware that it is a time-consuming and lengthy process.

Understandably, matters of property, together with 'goods and chattels' would be the Executors' first concern. All the transfers of Williams's many properties to his relations and the other legatees who were to become the new owners would require various legal transactions. Payments in cash and transfer of goods to legatees would also have to be organised. Buyers would need to be found for the properties and goods that were to be sold, for example to pay for his funeral and the subsequent erection of his tomb.

They Executors also had additional tasks such as the repair of the footpath between Oxford and Botley, and strengthening the bridge over the Thames along that path. They had much to do.

It is reasonable to suppose that all this would have taken the Executors at least a year. Williams himself, or the notaries who drew up his Will, recognised this fact as the Executors are specifically expected to complete carrying out the terms of the Will within a year 'and a further convenient time if they cannot sell the same so soon'. It is highly unlikely that they met the twelve month timeframe.

One example of this is illustrated by the fact that the Executors had to buy a plot of land for the school site, and this itself did not take place until 1562 as noted in *The Tamensian Quartercentenary Edition,* the land being purchased from Henry Norreys.

The capital cost of Thame School itself is unknown but the *VCH* for Oxfordshire noted that two examples of new school buildings elsewhere in Oxfordshire cost in the region of £100 plus. Both these buildings appear to be less substantial than the one in Thame. The School too had to have a garden laid out, and the expense of installing stained glass windows. By looking at the cost of labour and materials in the later accounts some guess can be made at the cost but it is only a guess. It is also based on the assumption that the building of the school took approximately one year to complete, though this seems reasonable for its size.

The estimated costs of labour are as follows:

- A carpenter, stonemason, tiler/iron work fixing, gardener for landscaping, and 3 labourers working for 317 days for one year i.e. having Sunday as a rest day. This comes to £103.

- The estimated cost for making and installing the stained glass and windows, including £10 wages for a glazier including materials: £40.

- Finally there is the cost of materials, likely to have been in the region of £100.

In total it is estimated that cost of building the School and laying out the garden was around £250.

The endowed rents were £45 per annum so to accumulate that sum would have taken around six years and on top of that was the cost of purchasing the land, and the cost of equipping the School.

[In terms of cross-referencing this cost the VCH states that the churchwardens spent £37 13s. 3d. in 1550 on paving the market-place round the market cross and in making a new causeway at Town's End. In the next year the wardens spent £48 17s. 2d. for digging and carting stone and gravel, possibly for the roads, and over £3 on paving the space round the common well. Over £33 was spent by the warden of Old Thame on materials and labour for the highway from Crendon Bridge past the Vicarage. In 1552 the way at Town's End towards London was mended for 10s. Lee states that the work continued and that a total of at least £120 was spent by 1560.]

It seems likely that the timeline was first to buy the land with accumulated monies from the rent and, as already noted, this happened in 1562. Being prudent executors, they would not start building work until they held a sufficient lump sum to cover the full cost. Another five years to accumulate the bulk of these monies would take until 1567, which was when Harris was appointed (see below). Detailed planning would then take place before that money would be spent and the building completed in 1569.

On top of all this the Executors had two further major tasks in Thame to complete: the refurbishment and re-endowment of the 15th century almshouse, which had fallen into disrepair, and the commissioning of Williams' tomb.

In accordance with the Will, the almshouse was to be 'enlarged and augmented', which appears to mean that the old almshouse was upgraded and at the same time some of the services needed for the School such as a water supply would also serve both buildings.

Williams' funeral took place on 15th November 1559 at St Mary's Church, Thame, and in his book *John Williams, Baron*

Williams of Thame, Michael J Beech says 'when the embalmed body had been lowered into its final resting place in the centre of the church, a highly elaborate carved effigy of Lord Williams was laid over it.'

Francis Steer, former archivist to New College Oxford, wrote that the effigy was attributed to Gerard Johnson (or Gereart Janseen to give him his Dutch name), the Elder. There is no original source quoted for this claim but it is thought it came from an attribution by Katharine Esdaile (née McDowall, 1881 – 1950), an art historian and expert on English sculpture. If correct, it would mean that the effigy would post-date 1568, when Johnson set up his studio in London and therefore could not have been put in place at the time of the funeral.

Indeed, some later date for the placing of the effigy and table-top tomb is indisputable as there would be no time to create something so elaborate between Williams' death and his burial a month later. This is further borne out by the fact that in his Will, it is noted that the cost of the tomb would be paid from the sale of the manor of Great Leistrop. (It was sold to the Executor, Walter Myldmay who already owned the nearby Apethorpe Hall. He in turn passed it on to his son, who in his own Will said the manor should be be sold to pay for his funeral costs.)

The Will would have first needed to be proved, then the manor sold and proceeds collected in order to release was would have been a not insubstantial amount of money to create the tomb. Costs of similar tombs would put the price at around £50, and would have needed some detailed logistics to be planned. Another source of early distraction for the Executors.

It is evident that detailed planning belongs to the latter half of the 1560s, most probably starting 1567 when the first Master, Edward Harris, was appointed. Harris's road to becoming Master is told in Chapter 6. The only part of his story relevant at this point is the date of his appointment. The addenda to the 1575 Statutes state that Harris 'has carried out his duties for the last eight years'. That dates his appointment to 1567 and strongly suggests that his duties went well beyond just teaching the boys to include a major part in planning the School and bringing it into fruition, a hypothesis further developed below. This is confirmed by the note in the Charity Commissioners' copy of the Statutes:

Anno domini 1570 pridie festo sancti Andrea apostoli, Edwardus Harris, Ludimagister Thamensis ante electus, in schola recens aedificata docendi munus auspicatus est.

On the day before the feast of St Andrew 1570, Edward Harris, who had previously been elected master, took up his office of teaching in the newly completed school.

There is a second confirmation from the inscription on his memorial in Thame church: it records that he gave thirty years of loyal and devoted service to the School and gives the date of his death as 1597.

Thame School was the first of the new-style grammar schools in Oxfordshire. The Executors were not educationalists; they needed advice on setting up a new school. We have their own testimony that, well before New College took over governing the school formally in 1575, though precisely when is unclear, they turned to New College for guidance. It is not known for certain why they chose New College though, as described earlier in Chapter 2 the link between Thame and New College may go back to the 1550s. (The John Yong connection.)

New College anyway was an obvious choice. Oxford is not far distant. New College had a long established 'feeder school' in Winchester College, with both school and college being 14th century foundations by William of Wykeham, bishop of Winchester. Winchester provided most of the College Fellows, who would have acquired the good classical school education - the 'New Learning' - that it was the grammar schools' mission to impart. Most importantly, Harris was a New College man.

As an alternative, the Executors might have turned to Magdalen College, whose own feeder school founded by another bishop of Winchester William Waynflete in 1480, and which was and remains close-by. Why they preferred New College to Magdalen is ultimately unknown; perhaps they or Williams had some other personal connection. William's Will contains the rather mysterious bequest of a £10 annuity to a certain George Williams (most likely a nephew) 'now [i.e. 1559] at Winchester School'. By the later 1560s this George would in all probability have been at New College.

At all events, it was the Warden and Senior Fellows of New College who from at least 1567, possibly earlier, were to play a major part in bringing Williams's conception of a school in Thame to birth; probably their most significant contribution being to provide of one of its former Fellows as the School's first Master.

Whatever the date of New College's first involvement, it was Harris's appointment in 1567 that began the period of active completion. Completing the furnishings and acquiring the appropriate range of Classical Latin authors and other necessary aids to teaching, canes (or 'rods') included, would probably have taken the remaining months before the School opened its doors to its pupils on Wednesday 29th November 1570.

CHAPTER 5: WHAT PART DID QUEEN ELIZABETH PLAY IN THAME SCHOOL'S FOUNDATION?

THE CONNECTION BETWEEN ELIZABETH I (1533 – 1603), Lord Williams and his family is strong and well documented whereas the evidence of her connection with the School is circumstantial and comes from a recent suggestion from the curator of Rycote Chapel that in some manner Elizabeth I opened the School, although the documentation supporting this has now disappeared. Nor, it must be said, is it part of the School's folklore. However, it is worth at least exploring these connections because it has highlighted that indeed at the very least Elizabeth had some connection with the early School.

Elizabeth's first visits to Williams's estate at Rycote were as a Princess, recently put under house arrest and close confinement by Queen Mary. These occurred in 1553, 1554, and 1555 when Williams was charged with joint custody of the Princess. As already noted in Chapter 3, Williams treated her with leniency and, after Elizabeth's ascension to the throne in 1558, Williams was in her favour, and this led to his appointment as Lord President of the Council of the Marches of Wales.

After she became Queen, Rycote became a regular halt on Elizabeth's royal progresses through her kingdom: she was a guest in 1566, 1568, 1570, 1575 and finally 1592. Progresses had a number of purposes: they allowed the Queen to be seen by her subjects, they were for leisure (albeit the Queen only stayed in most locations for a few days before moving on), and during the summer this was how the Court escaped the London heat and the increased incidence of disease. All the dates of her visits to Rycote were in the summer, and usually towards the end of August.

Progresses were formed by much of the Court, retainers, and servants, and hence were large affairs numbering several hundreds. When they arrived at a destination they made a significant impact locally not least as they consumed vast amounts of food, beer and ale. This in part explains why they kept moving as, rather like a plague of locusts, they soon consumed all the available local produce.

Of course, one of the Courtiers attending Elizabeth on the Progress was her Chancellor and Williams's Executor, Sir Walter Myldmay.

So why did Elizabeth visit Rycote at all after her ascension to the Crown and with John Williams now dead? One consideration is that even before her own visits, Rycote had enjoyed Tudor monarchy's patronage. The Privy Council was held there on 26th August 1540, and Henry VIII made a second visit a year later. Documentation held in the Bodleian Library noted that 'Henry's visit was to be the first in a long succession of royal visits to Rycote that would stretch to 1683.' In other words, it was a place favoured by the monarchy across a period of one hundred and fifty years or thereabouts.

A second consideration is that she had become friends with Williams's daughter Margery - as the two were of a similar age - when Elizabeth was taken under arrest to Rycote in the early 1550s. (This is a view held by Felicity Field.) However, this is only conjecture not least because the age of Margery is impossible to ascertain accurately as there are no precise dates for her birth. With some certainty we know that Williams married Elizabeth Edmonds (née Bledlowe) in 1524, and Margery was one of five children. The History of Parliament gives the date of birth for the oldest son to 1524-6 and as Margery was the youngest daughter it would appear reasonable to assume that she was born in the early 1530s; Elizabeth was born in 1533.

Margery would marry Henry Norreys (1525 – 1601) and after her father's death, Rycote passed to the two of them. The precise date of the marriage is also unknown although she and Henry were married by 1544. As the age of consent at that time was 12 for girls, and such marriage arrangements were made when the couple were even younger for various contractual reasons, it is perfectly possible for Margery if born around 1530 to be married at what to the modern eye appears to be a young age.

After Margery's marriage, because she was young she may have remained in her father's house. If she had moved in with her husband, they lived only a half day's ride away in his family seat at Wytham Abbey, Berkshire. It is more than possible that Lord Williams invited Margery to Rycote when the Princess was present particularly with the two being a similar age. Perhaps Margery could have been of some comfort to Elizabeth.

However, there was another reason for Elizabeth's closeness to the Norreys family and another reason why Margery - and her husband - might well have been invited to Rycote to be with the Princess. Henry Norreys's father (also named Henry Norreys) had been beheaded for supposedly carrying out an adulterous relationship with Anne Boleyn, Elizabeth's mother. We are unlikely ever to know whether the charge was true though in all probability it was trumped up but even if Elizabeth was not the love child of the first Henry Norreys she always honoured Norreys's memory, believing that he died 'in a noble cause and in the justification of her mother's innocence.'

But it is certain that Elizabeth and the Norreys family were friends. Elizabeth once wrote an affectionate letter to Margery, addressing her as 'My old crowe' – an unusual form of endearment to modern eyes but certainly something that would not appear in a letter from a monarch to anyone but a close friend.

At the time of Elizabeth's first visit when Queen, in 1566, Norreys had been appointed Ambassador to France and when she came to Rycote, on 6th September, she conferred on him a knighthood. Prior to her visit, she had spent several days in Oxford, left by the East Gate and rode to Rycote via the London Road over Shotover, through Wheatley, and had then taken the road to Rycote from what is now known as Milton Common.

Certainly on this visit it would not have been possible to visit the School as it did not exist (although the half-acre plot of land where the School would be built had been purchased from Henry Norreys) but it is possible that she did visit the tomb of Lord Williams at St Mary's to pray for his soul, although there is no specific evidence for this.

Her second visit to Rycote was made two years later. A letter in the Bodleian records the preparations for Elizabeth's visit in August 1568 when she stayed for several days. She had come from Bicester and possibly had followed the route from Bicester that went through Long Crendon and then down to Thame. (On the other hand, it should be noted that there was a shorter and at that time better established route via Brill, Ickford, Tiddington, and along Sandy Lane to Rycote. The former importance of this route is signalled by the fine double bridge over the Thame river and floodplain between Ickford and Tiddington, and a late 17th century county boundary stone, unique in Oxfordshire and rare for that period anywhere.)

Again, during her stay she may have ridden to St Mary's to pray at the tomb, particularly if this was the newly installed tabletop tomb. If so, she could have seen the School in its early stage of construction, and possibly she might have met Edward Harris. Sir Walter Myldmay would have a more specific interest. Even if he had relinquished his role as an Executor, no doubt he would want to know what progress had taken place.

Her visit in 1570 was across late August and early September. The diary of William Cecil records that 'the Queen's majesty Aug 30th at Rycotte'; she then stayed at Rycote not only on August 30th but also Sept 2nd, 6th and 7th.

Before she arrived at Rycote, she stayed at Wing and Eythrope. Almost certainly, to travel from these locations to Rycote she would have passed through Thame on the road that ran from Aylesbury.

Once again it could be possible that she saw the School, and although teaching in the new building would not have started, the building itself was complete.

Elizabeth also visited Rycote in October 1575, coming from Holton before continuing to Brabenham near High Wycombe. This year coincides with the issuing of Elizabeth's Letters Patent that granted permission for the executors of Williams's will to assign their duties to oversee and manage the school to New College. However, this was issued on 27th January 1575 and by the time of her visit, it is clear that the administration of the School had been fully handed over to New College. It should be noted too that Letters Patent were not usually signed by the monarch but by clerks in Westminster and that most grammar schools had Letters Patent, so those for Thame do not signify any special royal connection.

Although the month and day when the Statutes were issued are firmly established, it is possible that they were not actually issued in 1575 by modern reckoning even though the cover has 1575 on it. This is because in the Tudor period the New Year began in March not January. By Tudor reckoning therefore January 1575 would come at the end of the year beginning March 1575, and so by modern reckoning would be January 1576. However, from other evidence we know that the implementation of the Statutes began on 10th November 1575, not least because the School's accounts - signed off by the Warden and Fellows - start from the Michealmas Term 1575. Official documentation takes time to prepare and might well have followed a few months later, in what for us comes after the New Year.

Although the administration of the School was now the responsibility of New College, the Norreys family retained considerable influence on the School's management through having final say on the appointment of a headmaster. This in itself at least opens up the possibility that Henry, Margery and the Queen would have discussed the School and the new Statutes on her visit and that perhaps again this prompted a visit.

What is surprising is that Thame has no mention of the Queen and her vast party passing through the town. Records where they do exist from visits elsewhere show – not surprisingly – much merry-making and celebration. The Queen too was not averse to visiting market towns as it was an effective way to meet the people.

The most likely extant place for a written record to be found is in the Church Wardens' accounts for the parish church of St Mary's. However, while these record two earlier visits by Henry VIII, the pages for the years that Elizabeth would have passed through are incomplete or missing.

The final piece of an admittedly incomplete jigsaw is the presence of a Royal Coat of Arms in a window at the School. Howard Brown wrote, 'The east window contained the Royal Arms together with those of Lord Williams (organ pipes) and his mother More.'

This he had sourced from Anthony Wood's description:

> *Arms in the Windows of Thame School built by the Executors of Lord John Williams. At the upp' end in ye East window. France and Engl. quartered with supporters. Qu.*

Elizab. A rose g. with a crowne on it.

This describes the Royal Coat of Arms adopted by Elizabeth, a combination of the three lions passant guardant of England and the Fleurs de Lys of France with a Dragon and Lion support alongside a Tudor Rose with likely the crown of Edward the Confessor on top.

The note that the school building had a window decorated with the Royal Coat of Arms is important, and at least possibly indicates a visit by the Queen. Would the window have required the permission of the Queen? The answer is yes. Whether this coincides with a Royal visit in 1568 or 1570 or in 1575 it is impossible to know. So, without further evidence, we cannot conclude when the royal arms were glazed in the window, whether this was when the School was under construction in 1568-9 or at some later date after another visit.

In conclusion: we know that Rycote was one of the more frequent stops on the Royal Progress, clearly indicating that it was a favoured place for Elizabeth to visit. She was particularly close to the Norreys family and Margery, and she would have held favourable memories of Lord Williams.

We know that she passed through Thame on probably two occasions: in 1568 and 1570. On her other visits, if she did not pass through the town, she was no more than a thirty-minute horse-ride away. On the Progresses, she was accompanied by the Chancellor Sir Walter Myldmay, one of the Executors of Williams's Will.

With her affection for Margery and her late father, it could have been possible that she visited the church to pray at Williams's grave. Other records show that she did visit parish churches usually to take divine service. An argument against this is that she could have prayed for Williams's soul in the chapel at Rycote.

In 1570, she could have both prayed at Williams's tomb *and* seen the newly built School though not at a time when teaching had already begun.

It is possible that in 1575 while staying at Rycote and with the School now under the benevolent arm of New College - and with Norreys having a role - this could have prompted a visit to the School where teaching would now be in progress.

And although not part of the argument as it is long after the School opened, in 1592 Queen Elizabeth made one final stop at Rycote in October, slightly later than usual as the Court had moved from London temporarily because of the fear of the plague. Interestingly, a month earlier, Thame Fair had been cancelled because of fears of the plague.

Thus far, no records have been found (contemporary then or more recent now) that either record or indeed suggest that Elizabeth visited the School let alone performed some form of 'opening' ceremony. At best, it can be argued that circumstantial evidence suggests it is possible (not probable) Elizabeth made a visit during one of her Progresses and, by giving permission to have her coat of arms displayed in a window, demonstrated her connection with and support of the establishment.

CHAPTER 6: LIVING THROUGH 'INTERESTING TIMES' - HOW EDWARD HARRIS BECAME THAME SCHOOL'S FIRST MASTER.

HIDDEN AWAY IN THE CHOIR OF ST MARY'S CHURCH is a brass commemorating Edward Harris, supposedly the only early brass commemorating a headmaster. Harris appears as an august, dignified figure, accompanied by a laudatory inscription. All of which was no doubt a faithful description of Harris, who died in post in 1597 aged 63. But his road to becoming Master was not without its pitfalls, nor most likely was its eventual destination what he originally had in mind.

The first half of Harris's life coincided with the most turbulent religious and political period in England's history up to that time, second only to the Civil War that rent the country a century later. As the Chinese saying has it, these were indeed 'interesting times'. The date of Harris's birth in 1534 was also the year in which the Act of Supremacy was passed: making King Henry VIII rather than the Pope head of the English church, breaking with a tradition and a deeply held belief going back almost a thousand years and initiating the religious and political struggle for power between Protestant reformers and conservative Roman Catholics – 'papists' to their opponents.

1547, the date at which Harris was probably admitted as a scholar at 'Winchester School', also marks the apparent victory of the reformers on the accession of the young, Protestant-educated Edward VI. 1553, when Harris moved from Winchester to New College, witnessed the start of the staunchly Catholic Queen Mary's reign and by 1555 when he obtained his Fellowship, her Counter Reformation was in full swing.

The standard history books give much prominence to the extreme reformers and those at the apex of society who lost their lives during this turbulent period because of their religious or political beliefs: Thomas More, Queen Anne Boleyn, Thomas Cromwell and the 'Nine Days Queen' Lady Jane Grey amongst the most notable. Attention is also paid to the mass populist reaction to these 'interesting times', such as the Pilgrimage of Grace and the widespread popular uprisings in 1548/9. Less attention is given to the 'middling sort', the bulk of the population who were growing up and living during this period. Nevertheless, the constant political and religious turmoil affected everyone. No doubt the young Harris was little concerned about what was going on but this would have changed once he started his schooling.

Scholarship and religion were closely intertwined. Harris's teachers at Winchester would certainly have been affected by the religious changes, as would his university tutors and brother Fellows. How all this impacted on Harris's life and beliefs can only be guessed at. Most likely, as did the majority, he 'bent with the wind'. There is no evidence that he held extreme views, either Protestant or Catholic. There is one small piece of evidence that suggests he was being cautious. It was a requirement of the New College's statutes that all its Fellows took Holy Orders. Harris, however, petitioned the Warden to postpone this step, a request that was granted.

By the time that Elizabeth succeeded her sister in 1559, instituted her 'Middle Way' in religious matters and promised not to 'make windows into men's souls', it seemed that Harris had survived the 'interesting years' relatively unscathed. As Elizabeth's reign proceeded relatively smoothly, Harris settled into the comfortable and secure life of an Oxford University Fellow, a job – and a home - for life if that is what he desired.

It would be wrong, however, to idealise his life as a Fellow. If the reports are true - like Thomas Cromwell's monastic commissioners they were written by hostile witnesses - the Fellows were some way from leading sober lives of devoted scholarship. The report demanded that: 'the communal privy called the Longhouse' was to be cleaned. Senior fellows should not dawdle near the college gate after dinner 'spinning idle stories for a considerable time as a bad example for younger ones'. Women were banned from 'the buttery, any bedroom or any place within the College'. Members were forbidden to feed dogs or birds (think hawks rather than pigeons; the college statutes prohibited hunting). Most disturbingly, 'those who live in the upper bedrooms should not pour or throw out through the windows any water, urine, or any form of filth harming those below.'

Whether Harris was amongst the perpetrators or the victims of the unhygienic toilet practices remains unknown. If the former, he would no doubt have made sure that the boys of Thame School never heard about his youthful pranks.

This report was written in 1567 by Dr George Acland, who visited New College several times over a period of a year on behalf of the college's Visitor, Robert Thorne, Bishop of Winchester. Colleges were periodically subject to a Visitation. As New College had been founded by a bishop of Winchester, his successors held the role of Visitor *ex officio*. The Visitor had wide-ranging powers and Bishop Robert Horne used these to the full. Elizabeth may have been inclined to be tolerant; Horne was not. A zealous Protestant reformer, in exile during the reign of Mary, he returned at Elizabeth's accession to become a bishop in 1560. His mission in life was to root out papacy and, as zealots are, he or rather Acland his representative, found papists everywhere, nowhere more so than in New College during the 1566/7 Visitation. Many of the Fellows, Harris included, were considered far too papist and were consequently expelled from their fellowships. It is most unlikely that Harris was actually a papist, but in the eyes of the fanatical Acland and Horne his delay in taking Holy Orders was enough to convict him. At the age of 32, Harris was suddenly jobless and homeless.

But fortune smiled on him. Almost certainly it was around 1566/7 that Williams's Executors were looking for a Master for their new school and were seeking guidance from the Warden about setting it up. Who better than 'a man of Thame', a scholar of one of England's leading schools, a Master of Arts and Fellow of an Oxford College? For Harris this was a wonderful opportunity; not only another job and home for life, with a guaranteed salary, but the chance to shape, both literally and educationally, a new educational institution.

Almost certainly he accepted the post with alacrity. It is known for certain that he carried it out with enthusiasm and dedication for in 1575 in the School's Statutes the executors gave special privileges to 'Edward Harris, who has assisted us in an especial manner before all others with all his energies in forming this school for learning, even from his very childhood'.

The meaning of the last phrase is unclear. Presumably his 'childhood' refers to his education at Winchester, but otherwise this ringing endorsement of Harris's work, not only as a teacher but in the development of the School could hardly be clearer. As mentioned in Chapter 2, the reference in 1575 to being in post for eight years dates Harris's appointment to 1567, no more than a few months after the loss of his Fellowship.

Despite being no longer formally connected with New College, it is most likely that he remained in close touch with the Warden and those Fellows who had survived bishop Horne's Visitation. Though the incredibly detailed Statutes were ostensibly drawn up by the Executors with the advice of the Warden and Fellows, it seems that Harris had a considerable say in those parts that dealt specifically with how the School should be run. In fact, from the style of writing with its great number of historical and literary references, the conclusion that it was written by a scholar would seem reasonable. This is further underlined because on the handwritten copies of the Statutes, at the top of the first page, alongside an illustration of Queen Elizabeth, is an illustration of Harris with a cartouche that reads *Pedagogus.*

Some of the minute detail included in the additional regulations smacks of schoolmasterly discipline; for example the regulation that the boy sat nearest the schoolroom door should be responsible for shutting it, and in a responsible manner, not kicking it shut with his foot.

Fortune had smiled on Edward Harris and he repaid that good fortune in full by creating a popular and successful school.

CHAPTER 7: EARLY YEARS, EDUCATION, GOVERNANCE AND MANAGEMENT

HARRIS WAS INSTALLED AS HEADMASTER, the building finished and, from an indenture attached to the Statutes, we know as well the style of teaching as the Executors wrote: 'We wish briefly to advise the Master to follow, as nearly as he can, the method of teaching which he will know to be served at Winchester School (the womb from which he himself sprang, or his nurse if you will.)'

However, at least initially, he did not employ an usher. Indeed one was not taken on until 1575 as can seen from this comment in one of the indentures prepared for transfering oversight to New College.

'But since we are here incited with some sort of hope and expectation of a more abundant harvest in future it is possible that a greater number may come together to learn than one Schoolmaster can manage, to give attention to the education of them all and several...' A recommendation was made to appoint an Under-Master.

That the School got off to a slow start is perhaps unsurprising. After all, Thame was not a populous place, and it would take time to further build pupil numbers from those inherited from the chantry school.

In an earlier draft of this work, one chapter was headed 'The Winchester Connection'. This remained a relevant factor for the most of the School's history, especially during the first century when all of its headmasters were products of Winchester and New College. But, as stated in the Statute extracts above, it was not just the teachers and the original school motto 'Manners Makyth Man' but the 'style of teaching' that was imported.

Even at Winchester itself the precise meaning of this motto remains a matter of dispute. Its significance, however, lies in its nature rather than its exact meaning. Remarkably, it is in English not Latin, that was the universal language of education in medieval England. Only King Alfred had ever previously conceived of English (or Anglo-Saxon) as a medium for education. Secondly, it was entirely secular in an age when the Church had a monopoly of what we would consider as education, and all the more remarkable for being a bishop's choice. It is not always appreciated just how radical William of Wykeham was in his educational views.

The 'style of teaching' included not only pedagogy but the way in which pupils were grouped, by ability and achievement rather than by age. To those familiar with the modern concept of 'year groups' where the accident of a child's date of birth determines when schooling begins and which year group becomes home for at least the next eleven years, the Winchester system of grouping by ability may seem strange, but it survived at Lord Williams's Grammar School until the 20th century and only came to an end when the School lost its independent status after the Second World War.

[To briefly jump forwards 350 years, a unique set of data enables us to see that in 1921 the Winchester system for grouping by ability and achievement laid down in the Statutes was still in force. Except in the Sixth Form and Form Va, there was a gap of between three and five years between the youngest and oldest boy in a single form. In Form IV Hugh McRea just turned 11, sat alongside James Robinson two months over the age of 16. McRea would leave the School two years later, join the

Royal Navy and be awarded the King's Gold Medal as a cadet. This led on to a glittering career before he was killed in the 2nd World War.]

Returning to 16th century, what do we know of the style of teaching? Nothing directly about Thame Grammar School but it can be assumed that it followed the same methodologies that were common at the time.

From the early Middle Ages into the Renaissance proficiency in Latin was a mark of status, and, as already noted, the prime purpose of teaching at the School. It was taught using techniques that would be familiar to teachers today using singing, reciting dialogue and poetry, taking dictation and giving speeches. In other words pupils learned the language orally as well as through grammar and the translation of set texts.

It is thought that the use of drama was frequent, sometimes the whole texts would be acted out. This helped pupils connect to the language and was also an effective way to train the voice.

Singing was important too, particularly for young children who would learn words and phrases through the singing of psalms - and in school through the singing of the school hymn.

Harris continued in his role until 1597, and was followed by Richard Boucher, who was Headmaster for a further thirty years, meaning the School enjoyed the benefit and stability of just two headmasters for the first sixty years of its existence, both of whom appear to have been good teachers.

Under Harris' headmastership the School eventually flourished after its slow start. According to the *National Dictionary of Biography* and the 17[th-] century antiquarian Anthony Wood (himself a former pupil) at least three pupils went on to have a distinguished life: the judge Sir George Croke (1560-1641), the poet William Basse (d. 1653) of Moreton, and the rector Theophilus Higgons (1578 -1659).

[NB: where detailed biographies are easily found on-line, the authors have decided not to include lengthy discourses on former pupils.]

Pupils usually attended grammar schools from the age of seven or eight. Those who went on to university left at four-teen or fifteen; earlier for those who left to start work. In other words, pupils at Thame School were much younger than we would expect if applying modern day practices.

Those pupils who lived within the School's catchment area could easily attend as day-boys – though they had to get up early; teaching started at 6am. How many there were we do not know. Evidence from elsewhere indicates that the lowest strata of society did not send their sons to grammar schools but tradesmen and skilled artisans (and upwards) did, and that taking advantage of an education was becoming increasingly popular at this time.

At the start of the 17th century the catchment area had a population of some 800, rising to 1500 by the end of the 17th century. Those from further afield would have enrolled as boarders, and it is likely that there were boarders in the school from the start. (Details of the lives of boarders are given in Volume 2.)

The teaching hours would today seem onerous:

On ordinary days the Under Master shall go to the school to teach at 6am, while the Master shall enter about 7 o'clock both of them to perform their duty with proper attention until a suitable time for dinner [which was normally around 11am]. And when this is finished the former shall return to school at once at 1pm and the latter at 2pm. And neither of them shall leave in the winter before 5 o'clock and in the summer 6 o'clock.

In comparison to other schools in the County these hours seem particular long and it is a reasonable question as to whether they were strictly adhered to. Perhaps as the Master's salary was generous it was felt this was the best way to justify the expense. (A topic touched on later.)

As the aforementioned William Basse came from Moreton – and one assumes he was a day-boy - it appears likely that he was getting up at 5am, and not getting home until 7pm in the evening. However at least everyone had annual holidays of around 14 weeks.

Punishment was common, and often administered by the rod, though the Statutes laid out that 'One thing we have determined to forbid utterly, viz. That on no pretence whatsoever may a boy be struck or beaten or thumped either by a rod or by any other blow either on the face, eyes, ears, mouth, or any other part of the head.'

The day started and finished with prayers. The School was divided into classes – although all taught in the one room and the pupils sitting on long benches at a single table. The Master would sit on a dais teaching the older pupils, and once the School's roll had increased the Usher taught the younger ones. They were instructed in the 'making of verses and occasionally in writing a free flowing prose style...For acquiring such skill and dexterity the reading of Vigil...Horace, Ovid, Plautus, Lucan, and other principal poets.' They would spend 15 minutes before dinner reciting some chapter of the Old or New Testament, and attendance at church on Sunday was compulsory for boarders and those living in the parish of Thame.

* * *

Governance

Another stabilising force, and one already noted, was that in 1575, Queen Elizabeth by her letters patent, granted the Executors her royal licence so that they could hand oversight of the School to New College, Oxford. It is clear that even in its early years, the administration of the School had outgrown the ability of the Executors and they were deeply concerned that the School would flounder. Consequently they in their own words, 'have anxiously and seriously begun to think of substituting new guardianship from some source, and about drawing up certain statutes and ordinances, by which both the government of this school, and the profitable management attached to it might be carried out as uprightly as possible.'

A critical factor that finalised this decision was, as noted earlier, it is likely that two of the Executors gave up their roles during the 1560s, and one of the Executors, John Doyley, died in 1569 meaning that now it was left to William Place to manage the School. Undoubtedly too onerous a task for one man.

In addition, Place would have been concerned about the low number of pupils and so would have hoped that the prestige of being under the wing of New College might give greater credibility to the School's qualities.

As mentioned earlier there is no surviving evidence as to why New College was either chosen or why they agreed to take on the task. Harris, of course, was a former Fellow albeit one that had been expelled but as that was not of the New College's doing he likely held no animosity.

There is another reason too that suggests why New College was a willing and able partner: they had experience as they were already running their own New College School. This had been founded in 1379 as part of the foundation of the College to provide choristers who would take part in the services. By 1394, these choristers were being taught grammar, and by the early 17th century they had their own school room. New College had other relationships with schools through its formal ties with Winchester College, and Eton College, that dated back to 1444. In 1552 New College took on the administrative role for Bedford School, and just a few years after taking on the role at Thame, New College was assigned the same role for Adderbury Grammar School in the county.

It is also worth noting that most grammar schools came under the wing of an outside institution. This might be a town corporation (as was the case in nearby Wycombe), by London Guilds, a cathedral, but the most frequent was to have control vested in an Oxford or Cambridge college.

❈ ❈ ❈

Financial management

When the formal association began in 1575 a set of Statutes were written that laid out in some considerable detail how the School should be run. This introduced a major change from the wishes of Lord Williams, as set out in his Will:

> *I will and bequeath the rectories and parsonages of Brill, Oakley, Burstall (Boarstall) and Eastneston (Easton Neston in Northamptonshire) to mine executors for ever, to the intent that they, the survivor or survivors of them, shall within the same erect a Free School in the town of Thame, and to find and sustain with the profits thereof, a schoolmaster and an usher, for ever in such sort and time as my said executors shall think most convenient for the maintenance of the said School for ever.*

Williams's intention was to set up a free school and it is known that in the first few years of its existence this was the case not least because a brass plate over the front gate to the School announced (in Latin):

Whatever boy wishes to learn Latin Grammar, so that he may speak learnedly in the Roman tongue, if he will first learn to write, our School, built by the Williams family, will teach him for nothing.

This was reconfirmed in the Indenture that was prepared in early 1575 paving the way for New College to takeover the School's administration, 'forever uphold and matntayne a free grammar school for the free teaching and exercise of grammar...'

In the final Statutes this was changed so that free tuition was provided only for his relatives and the offspring of tenants of his property in Old and New Thame, and the nearby villages of Moreton, North Weston and Priest End. The parents of any boys not included within this definition had to pay to pay a shilling (5p) quarterly to the Master and sixpence (2.5p) to the Usher; in total tuition fees of six shillings annually.

Even for those times this was a modest amount. Establishing equivalents between and converting Tudor to modern money is fraught with difficulty, but around 1600, six shillings would buy a wheelbarrow, a coarse rug or a small kettle: relatively inexpensive items for all but the poorest. A labourer would typically earn from £5 per year, a tradesman from £10 and merchant from £100. So the tuition fees would represent around 15 per cent of a labourer's earnings, 8 per cent of a tradesman's, and less than 1 per cent of a merchant's.

The fees were, therefore, affordable for many people. In which case, why were the fees charged? It is most likely that this was at the insistence of New College, as the respect that the Executor(s) had for Williams is made clear in the introduction to the Statutes and it seems unlikely that they would, under their own volition, have made the change. But why would New College ask for the change? Possibly in the five years that teaching had been undertaken it was already apparent that the School could not survive on its endowment income alone. There were salaries to pay, and it became quickly clear that every year maintenance was required on the building and grounds. The costs of this is looked at in more detail later.

In addition to the tuition fees, every pupil, including those exempt from tuition fees, had to make further compulsory payments:

- Two pence a quarter toward cleaning the School (done at least twice a week), and 'for purchasing rods'.

- There was also an entrance fee of 'one drachma' intended as a book fund.

This all adds up to 13 shillings to be paid by each pupil annually.

It is also worth highlighting that the imposition of fees was not unusual in Oxfordshire.

At Burford in the 16th century, the fees were nominal for inhabitants of the town, the entrance charge being 4d. and quarterage 2d. Those living in the country had to pay 12d. and 6d., with the exception of the Wisdom scholars, four boys elected by the founder or his heirs, who only paid 4d. entrance.

Dorchester was founded in the mid-17th century and scholars from Dorchester and Overy were to pay 1s. entrance fee and no more. Strangers might be charged 1s. 6d. and 5s. quarterage.

At Witney in the mid-17th century, each scholar was to pay 2s. 6d. (1s. 6d. to the master, 1s. to the usher), but those whose parents were not assessed weekly for maintenance of the poor were to pay 1s.

So though not strictly free, the scale of fees for day-boys would be unlikely to deter any but the poorest families from attending the School and, in principle, anyone who was clever enough and had attained a reasonable level of literacy in English could become a pupil.

However, unlike some other charitable foundations such as Eton, there was no positive discrimination in favour of poor scholars. Williams's Will makes no reference to social class. The School's purpose was simply 'the education and bringing up of young children'. Where they came from and where they were in the social order were not specified.

On 1st August 1575, the Indenture was agreed between the Executors and the Warden and Fellows. The annual income for the School from the manors and parsonages of Brill, Oakley and Borstall was 'thirtye and six pound of good and lawfull money of England.' The amount of income from East Neston was unrecorded in the Indenture.

The Indenture also noted that the Executors had purchased further land, tenements and hereditaments (property) so Williams's wishes for both School and almshouse could be 'better and more sufficient accomplishment.' So again, the Executors had already concluded that the original rents were insufficient to cover the running costs of the School or at least did not leave much leeway for extraordinary items.

Those new properties that would contribute to the School's income were identified as being in 'Newe Thame': a property then in the occupation of Johane Robothome, a widow, and a second property in the occupation of Thomas Symeon.

The first accounts for the School date from 1575 and they record the School's income as follows:

- Receipts for the Manor and Parsonage of Brill, Oakley and Borstall: £36
- Eastington Parsonage: £4
- New Thame from Thomas Symon: 120s (or £5)
- New Thame (JR): 42s

In total the School's total annual endowment income was in the region of £46 and, according to the historian Monroe Stowe, a level that would appear to be in the upper quarter of endowment income in this period.

His research showed that in the Elizabethan era, grammar schools that derived income from rents could expect to receive between £10 and £45. He also concluded that rents were the better way for schools to receive income rather than from annuities. In other words, financially Thame School should have been on a secure footing.

This is generally borne out by the level of endowments received by other schools within Oxfordshire and recorded in the *Victoria County History*. So for example Steeple Aston received £10 in rents; Williamscott Free School received £13. On the other hand, Charlbury Free Grammar had an annuity of £60 coming from rents, and Witney earned £50.

Many of the other schools in Oxfordshire were also beneficiaries of sometimes substantial lump sum endowments and gifts left in Wills and so the picture is more complex. Certainly, there is no record of Thame School subsequently receiving further lump-sum income in this way. This was to prove crucial in the School's later history.

As anyone who studies this period knows, disputes about lands and rents were always coming to the courts. The School was no exception. In the 1580s the rights of the School to the lands and income from Oakley was challenged by the Dyrham family, who claimed ownership and argued that they did not have to pay rents. The resulting tangle of arguments was heard at the Exchequer Court, which at first found in favour of Sir John Dyrham. The trustees of Thame School retaliated with their own Chancery case, arguing that the rectory of Oakley was coterminous with the rectory of Brill and encompassed the entire forest area. This time the court found against Sir John

Dyrham.

CHAPTER 8: APPOINTING THE MASTERS AND USHERS

THE SURVIVING EVIDENCE for the history of the School across the 17th and 18th centuries is thin and patchy. Most of it comes from the New College archives and is concerned with two main topics: the appointment of Masters, and the financial accounts. A comprehensive history of the School can only therefore be written in terms of its Masters and, to a lesser degree, financial matters.

The Statutes make it quite clear how the Masters were to be appointed and what age and academic qualifications they needed. In summary, the Warden and nine Senior Fellows of New College were to put forward two names from amongst the Fellows from which the heirs, or as it turned out, often the heiresses, of Lord Williams to the barony and ownership of Rycote Park, the Norreys family were to choose one. Later evidence suggests that their choice was largely a formality: the current head of the family would choose the College's preferred candidate. No evidence has survived to suggest that Williams's heirs ever ignored the College's recommendation, though on one occasion they initially chose the wrong one.

The process by which the Warden and Fellows chose the two names to be put forward or 'presented' was, at least superficially, democratic. Each Fellow wrote two names on a voting slip and, in theory at least, the names of the two candidates who topped the poll went forward. For a number of elections these voting slips still survive in the New College archives and the story that they appear to tell is that from the choice of the third Master in 1627 onwards, the election process was 'managed' to ensure that the Fellows were unanimous in the names they put forward to the Norreys heirs.

The College could not choose just anyone. The Statutes laid down that the candidates must have had a BA degree for at least eight years, or an MA, and that they should be between the ages of 26 and 60. For the most part the College Fellows observed these rules, though on occasion they 'bent' them for reasons that are understandable.

The first two masters were in their mid-thirties when appointed and regarded the appointment as a job for life – literally: both Harris and Boucher died 'in harness'.

* * *

The appointment of the first two Masters

Though the appointment of the first Master, Robert Harris, about 1567, pre-dated the formalisation of the procedure laid down in the School's Statutes, it is probable that what occurred in his appointment created the precedent for what became enshrined in the Statutes. Harris had been a Fellow of New College as described earlier. He was almost certainly the choice of Warden Culpeper, who had been advising Williams's Executors from the very early days, probably supported by the senior Fellows. It is our assumption that Williams's daughter Margery, would have wanted to take an interest in the new school that Williams had endowed and to have the right to make the final choice. In practice, given the low legal status of women during the Tudor and Stuart period, it appears that it was the male spouse of Williams's female descendants who formally made the choice.

No first-hand account survives of what happened when Harris died in 1597 and was succeeded by Richard Boucher, but from later evidence it is probable that the College followed the election procedure in putting forward two names for Henry Norreys to choose. The name of the unsuccessful candidate is not known. Boucher was about 36 when he succeeded Harris, a Fellow of New College since 1583 and a Bachelor of Civil Law since 1589.

* * *

Appointing and dismissing the ushers

The appointment of ushers was the prerogative of the Master who was instructed in the Statutes to make his choice on the Sunday following any vacancy. He would then announce his decision in the southern transept of Thame church before 'the churchwarden and six, at least, of the gravest inhabitants of the town.'

Dismissing the usher, however, was the prerogative of the Warden and two senior Fellows, after he had been reported three times to the Fellows for 'neglect of duty'. There is only one known example of an usher being dismissed and in this instance the procedure laid down in the statutes was followed. However, ushers seem to have come and gone remarkably quickly at certain periods. It is noticeable that many of them were young graduates and had just been awarded their BA degree. For them the post of usher, though lowly paid, was a 'first step on the ladder' but they would have been keen to move on to some more lucrative employment. Some in fact climbed quite high later in their career. Whereas the masters and runners-up were nearly always New College graduates, the ushers had graduated from various colleges and halls.

* * *

Early 17th century elections

Remarkably, there was a gap of three generations before the Norreys family were called upon again to confirm the election of the next Master, Hugh Evans. It fell to Henry's great grand-daughter and sole heiress Elizabeth, Baroness Norreys in her own right, or her husband Edward Wray, to make the choice – eventually - of Hugh Evans in 1627. The story of the Norreys family's turbulent history in the thirty years between the elections is told in Chapter 10 where part of the story is related. The full story can be found in the Bodleian website on Rycote.

The surviving evidence for the 1627 appointment, in the shape of the voting slips, reveals the inner workings of the election process. In the first round of voting seven names were proposed but with no consensus as to the preferred candidates. As stated earlier, the Statutes lay down that two candidates should be chosen by the Warden and nine senior Fellows, 'senior' being defined by the date of admission as Fellow. However, only three of those who voted in the first round were definitely Fellows of the College, and one more possibly; only nine rather than ten votes were cast (unless one slip got lost).

In the second round the voting was virtually unanimous with every Fellow voting for the same pair, differing only in their first preference, but Hugh Evans emerged as first preference by the substantial majority of 8 to 2 against his rival Edward Hyde, and was the Warden's first choice. Only two of those who voted in the first round voted again: Warden Pincke as might be expected, and Samuel Gardner who is not listed as Fellow. Again, those listed as Fellows were in a minority – only two for certain. What exactly happened between the two rounds and why an almost completely different set of Fellows voted on the second occasion can only be speculation. It is tempting to believe that between the two votes the Warden canvassed and lobbied all the Fellows - and possibly other members of the College - until he found nine who were willing to vote for the same two candidates.

Evans became Master in 1627 at the age of 29. Though they could not have known it at the time, Elizabeth and Edward would have done better to have chosen Hyde, as Evans died young after four years in post while Hyde had a distinguished clerical career, eventually becoming Bishop of Salisbury. This was the first known occasion but not the last when the runner-up was more successful than the man appointed to be Master.

The 1631 election was more efficiently if less democratically conducted than four years earlier. The nominees, William Burt and William Haydock, were the unanimously recommended candidates. Once again, it was Elizabeth and Edward who chose the former. Burt was a late developer but 'fast-track' appointment. He matriculated at New College in 1627 at the relatively advanced age of 22, but obtained his BA two years later and his MA two years after that, which qualified him academically. He was just old enough at 26 when appointed Master to meet the age requirement of the Statutes.

The circumstances surrounding the aftermath of Burt's appointment generated considerable correspondence. From all accounts, Burt was a highly competent and probably ambitious scholar and academic, who having resigned as Master of Thame School was later appointed Headmaster and then Warden of Winchester College. At the time of his appointment to Thame School in January 1631 he was highly regarded by the then New College Warden Pincke as his 'worthy friend'.

The success of these Masters will be looked at in detail in the next chapter.

CHAPTER 9: THE EARLY SEVENTEENTH CENTURY – MASTERS, SCHOLARS, PROMINENT PUPILS, AND EXPENSES

BY WAY OF INTRODUCTION, this can be seen as an era of high achievement, sufficient teaching resources, and regular maintenance of the building. Suffice to say that this also coincided with a flourishing of grammar school education nationally.

Into the first decades of the 17th century the School continued to prosper under the headmasterships of Richard Boucher, Hugh Evans and William Burt. As early as 1610 it is described as 'a very faire schoole' by Camden in his *Britain*, and it was producing a notable list of scholars who went on to have some significance in the country. The most notable was John Hampden but also judges and statesmen such as Lord Chief Justice Holt, Mr Speaker Lenthall, and Arthur Goodwin MP.

Bishops such as Henry King and Dr Fell; scholars such as Edward Pocock and Anthony Wood; dramatists included Shakerley Marmion and Sir George Etherege, and poets such as Edmund Waller were also pupils in these early years.

Yet Thame was not the only school in the county. Across Oxfordshire at this time, grammar schools included Adderbury Grammar School, Steeple Aston Grammar School, St. John's Hospital School, Banbury, Bampton Free Grammar School, Bicester School, Burford Grammar School, Charlbury

Free Grammar School, Chipping Norton Grammar School, Deddington Grammar School, Dorchester Free Grammar School, Ewelme Grammar School, Henley Grammar School, Magdalen College Grammar School, Nixon's Free Grammar School in Oxford, Watlington Free Grammar School, Williamscot Free School, Witney Grammar School, Woodstock Free Grammar School. All were doing well and producing able pupils.

Indeed, as noted at the start of the chapter, this was a prosperous time for grammar schools with 142 being established in England between 1603 and 1649. Lawrence Stone in his paper *The Educational Revolution in England, 1560-1640* says there was 'an astonishing expansion of education between 1560 and 1640.' The reasons, he wrote, were clear: a demand for lay administrators and professionals; children were seen less as a piece of property and more as an individual; the 'middle class' could see that social changes were happening and that an education would help their children take advantage of these. Most importantly the economy was growing, and this middle class was increasing in numbers and wealth.

Richard Boucher was Headmaster for thirty years until 1627, when he died in Thame. He had been born in Handborough, and his tenure at the School had coincided with Elizabeth, James I and Charles I sitting on the throne. In his will he left land in the village to his brother. Other goods were left to people who he knew in Thame, as he remained unmarried. He also left a generous £4 to the church. On his monument in St Mary's Church it refers to his mild rule 'sparing the rod' in order to better attract his pupils to learning. The monument also invited his pupils to weep because their master would not return to them.

✳ ✳ ✳

Finances

In this period, the school was on a secure financial footing as it could accommodate up to 100 pupils. However the roll was more likely to have beeen between 40-60 as this was the average school size calculated by Monroe Stowe, and matches other estimates that can be deduced from the accounts. If, for example, the roll was fifty, then this would mean that an additional £50 plus was received from pupil fees, slightly more than the income gained from rents.

Responsibility for the running and administration of both the School and the almshouse was given to the Master, who was also responsible for preparing the accounts. At least until the mid-18th century, two separate sets of accounts were prepared for each foundation to ensure that income and expenditure were properly allocated, and it would appear that the Master was meticulous in this.

The accounts would usually run from November to November - and often 10th November - matching the date when New College became responsible for the School's administration. These would be presented to the Warden and three other senior Fellows some time later in November along with any monies that had accrued but had not been spent. The Master would be paid a separate fee for the preparation of the accounts, and his expenses for travelling to Oxford would be reimbursed too.

Ultimately though, as the Statutes made clear, it was the Warden of New College who was required to ensure that the School's buildings, garden and orchard were kept in good repair.

As already explained, income for the School came from various property and land rents, while expenditure came in two forms.

The first was fixed outgoings including salaries for the master and usher, and the cost of maintaining Williams's tomb. The Master was paid £26 13s 4p, split across four payments annually. Howard Brown in his history of the school records that Monroe Stowe had calculated the national average for a schoolmaster was £16, so this was a generous salary.

Comparisons with other masters's salaries recorded in the *VCH* bear this out: Adderbury £20, Steeple Aston £10 increased to £20 in the 17th century; Charlbury £40 (but in the late 17 century); Deddington £13 6s; Dorchester £20; Lady Elizabeth Periam's School in Henley £20; Watlington £10; Witney £30 in the 17th century.

The Usher was paid £13 6s 8p. This again was generous and above Monroe Stowe's national average, which was around £10.

The tomb of Lord Williams had to be maintained, and for this a sum of eight shillings was paid annually to the Clerk of the Parish Church. Although the precise task were not spelt out, most likely it was to clean and dust the tomb, and in particular the effigies that would have accumulated a sooty coating from the many candles burnt in the church.

A sum of four shillings was paid to the man responsible for the maintenance of the water course that ran into the privy. (This man was to be chosen from one of the inhabitants of the almshouse.)

In total, the School had to pay £40 11s 12d for these fixed costs, a sum just under the annual rental income.

The second group of expenditure was for extraordinary items. These were unplanned, most often related to the maintenance and repair of the School's buildings, garden and orchard, and which varied from one year to the next. It was believed that the cost of repairs would be adequately covered by the rental income and fees, and hence the Master was instructed that they should be carried out in a timely manner.

In the early accounts, all expenditure is itemised down to the number of nails purchased, and who was paid for what specific work.

One of the striking features is the amount of work that needed to be carried out to maintain the school. In particular, in every year work was done on replacing or repairing roof tiles, woodwork and flooring within the school, and repairs to the windows. With the woodwork it would appear that this was down to wear and tear that would be associated with everyday normal life in the school, despite the Statutes laying down strict rules about the behaviour of boys. For example:

> *Neither shall the pupils be allowed to play handball beneath the court-yard or to amuse themselves in any other way there lest the glass windows should be injured, or some public injury committed. In the School itself, it shall be utterly forbidden to play at that childish sport of hurling up and down, or throwing or flying in the air, or flinging either hand-balls or books or inkstands, or pens, or hats or caps or pegs or any other material belonging to the school, which may injures or deface in any way the windows or walls or ceilings.*

* * *

Expenditure 1605 - 1611

The accounts for 1605 are worth recording in some detail as they are indicative of the type of work that had to be carried out every year.

John Groome (or Greene), a joiner, is named in a number of items, for example he was paid for the provision of oak boards, oak sleepers, and oak posts. Also he repaired the Gallery, a recent addition within the schoolroom to create extra space.

John Groome has been well researched not least by Antony Buxton, and published in his *Domestic Culture in Early Modern England*. He was not only a tradesman in the town but also owned some twelve acres of land where he grew crops. (Found in an inventory when his assets were recorded after his death in 1624.) This same inventory showed that he owned a lathe for turning, indicating that he also made furniture as well as undertaking joinery; this is supported by an item in the 1605 accounts for the repair of the school tables.

He was not the only carpenter working on the School's fabric: at other times Mssrs Howley, Hayborne and Alnutt were also employed. Parish records show that at least two Alnutt families lived in Thame during this period; Howley is more likely a misspelling and was Howlett; Hayborne is also found in the parish records including a William and a Thomas. Clearly carpentry was a trade in much demand, although this should be of no surprise.

Two glaziers, Olyffe and Paule Audley, provided services. Olyffe maybe the William Olyffe who died in Thame in 1616. Paule Audley may be the Paule Audley buried in Thame in 1606 and if so died shortly after being paid.

The windows had to be repaired and cleaned inside and out of accumulated soot and grime. In one record they were said to have been scoured. (The need for natural light in the School was critical of course.) The School had two large stained-glass windows as well as clear glass. As highlighted previously the stained-glass in the East Window contained the Royal Arms of Queen Elizabeth I and the arms of Lord Williams, and the second window on the north side of the school room had various arms of the Williams, More and the Wenman families.

The ironwork too had to be repaired from time to time, and the repairs were carried out by a Henry Shreeve (sometimes spelt Sheriffe), a local blacksmith who can be found in the Parish records when his daughter was baptised in April 1606.

The School possessed a clock, an essential item as it regulated the school day. Hence it had to be maintained in perfect working order, and each year's accounts would record a sum for this. In 1605, 'Corbett's man' was paid 3s 3d for amending the clock, and he also replaced door locks and provided new keys. (This seemed to be another regular item, which suggested that perhaps the Master thought it prudent to change the locks every year.)

The water system was crucial and this was extracted from a cistern using a pump. The pump mechanism needed to be repaired regularly most likely because it was made from iron, perishable wood and leather. New paving had to be provided for the 'children's privy' suggesting that there was a separate privy for adults.

Another re-occurring task was the repair or replacement of roof tiles. In 1605 (and for sometime thereafter) a Mr Burton undertook this work and there are items for his labour. (Burton was a reasonably common name in Thame in the early 1600s.) In later years there are payments for tiles, ridge tiles, gutter tiles, and special roofing nails including lathe nails.

Bricks, tiles and lime often came from Brill where a brick and tile making industry using the local clay could be found on the hill. However, roof tiles could have been fashioned from the Portland Limestone also quarried in the village and used as local building material. In a later entry, it was noted that gravel was brought from the (Long) Crendon pits.

In 1609 an additional sum was paid to William Weste for bringing the gravel from the street into the courtyard using a wheelbarrow, for which he was paid 6d.

In terms of the cost of labour, the daily rates in the first two decades of the 17th century were:

- Howley (Carpenter): 1s. By 1622 the rate had gone up to 1s and 4d.
- Sones (Mason): 1s.
- Burton (Tiler): 1s, although in 1610 he was paid 1s 2d for a day's work.
- A Labourer: 8d. In 1610 another labourer was paid 10d for a day's work; and in 1616, 10d was once again noted as the daily rate for a labourer.

Other items purchased at this time included lime (most likely used in the privy), bricks, gravel, and whyte earth. (Witchert or wychett, meaning white earth was the name given to a building material that was locally found at Haddenham, Long Crendon, and other Buckinghamshire villages. This is a subsoil of decayed Portland limestone, which would be mixed with water and chopped straw to produce a walling material. This was laid in layers usually on a stone foundation.)

The provider of bricks was Mr Ballowe - although we cannot be sure if it is always the same one, as there appeared to be several Ballowe families in Thame at this time:

1605: 6d paid to Mr Ballowe for bricks.
1606: He was paid for some lyme.
1616: A Mr Ballowe was paid for oak boards.
1622: Mr Ballow supplied a 'pecke more' (of roof nails).

This might well have been William Ballowe who was also responsible for funding the brass plaque that commemorates the first Headmaster Edward Harris, and commissioned around 1600. Ballowe is described by Brown as 'merchant and some-time churchwarden' so here is someone with the wealth of a merchant, some interest in religion and education, possibly the parent of a pupil of Harris's at Thame School.

(The Ballowe family were long established as the name had been first recorded in the area in the early 1400s when John

Bollour was mentioned as a juror in a Court of Inquisition. The National Archives hold the Will of William Ballowe alias Raffe, Mercer of Thame, Oxfordshire and which is dated 1570.)

All the names in the accounts appear to be Thame-based craftsmen as either the full name or surnames appear in the Thame Parish registers over this period. One other example is Cornelius Carden who was paid 9d for repairing the locks in 1609. His burial is recorded in Thame in June 1617.

Over a short span of years, a number of different names crop up as being responsible for repairing or maintaining the all-important clock. These include Corbett (1605) and Thomas Keene (1609, 1611). Keene was possibly the recusant among the fourteen people presented by the churchwardens between 1606 and 1609 for not coming to church or not receiving com-munion at Easter.

The School had its own garden and orchard. Payments for weeding first appeared in 1610 and 1611 to 'Mother (Agnes) Roger', and for repairing the garden wall.

In these years, the average total annual repair bill was in the region of 20-30 shillings.

✳ ✳ ✳

Books

The first record of a book being bought for the school appears in 1612: Delrio his *Commetaryes upon Seneca*. This was bought in London for 13s and sent to Thame at a cost of 6d. This was written by the Antwerp Jesuit, Martin Antonio del Rio (1551–1608) in 1593. That a book written by a Catholic was con-sidered desirable reading for pupils during a period of strong anti-Catholic feeling following the 1605 Gunpowder Plot sug-gests that Boucher was either tolerant in matters of religion or hankered after the 'Old Order'.

Then in 1616 the School had to purchase a new binding for Cooper's *Dictionary and Livy.* This cost 6s plus 8d for taking them to Oxford (the local centre for bookbinding) and returning to Thame. The author, Thomas Cooper, also spelled Couper, was born c.1517 in Oxford and died April 29th 1594 in Winchester. The Dictionary was in fact a thesaurus and was first published in 1565.

In the same year, Edward Swifte was paid 6d for installing two chains for books. Another six chains were ordered a year later in 1617 at a cost of 3s, and these again were provided by Edward Swifte. Two years later he was buried in St Mary's churchyard. Chain libraries were quite common at this period for larger and more expensive books, which were far too valuable to be left loose on shelves or desks.

Six books were bought in 1621 at a cost of 5s, although the record says 'paid towards the buying of books' suggesting, perhaps, that this was a contribution not the total cost.

Elsewhere in the accounts for the same year there is a separate record of 16s for buying another copy of Cooper's *Dictionary* as it had been damaged; the same amount was paid for the *Chillades of Erasmus*; and finally two Latin lexicons: the *Lexicon Graeco-Latinum* by Johann Scapula, and the *Calepine Lexicon* first printed in 1502. These two were purchased for 37s. The next year, a further three chains were purchased for these books.

From this, it would appear that school books were costing in the range of 14s to 19s annually. The titles of these books underline the fact that the main purpose of grammar schools was to educate pupils in the Classics, requiring key classical texts and dictionaries of various kinds.

It is likely that other books studied included the Catechism, the

Psalter, the Book of Common Prayer and, of course, the Bible.

In 1619, 6s was paid for a new ledger of accounts and another 2s for a bag to keep it in. This entry indicates that there was every intention to continue producing detailed accounts and to keep the ledger in good condition.

* * *

Expenditure 1611 – 1640

The ledger for 1611 is informative as the cost per unit of items is spelt out e.g.

- 100 tiles @ 19d.

- A bushel (about 56 lb weight) of lime cost 5d.

- 50 oak boards for flooring 5s 6d.

As noted previously, work had to be done on the water system every year: repairing the cistern, repairing the ball-cock mechanism, cleaning the well and water-course, re-leading the pump, and using soda to clean the pipework were among the tasks carried out. The cost of repairs varied from year to year: in 1612 it was 23s 8d, but in 1617 it was the lesser amount of 14s 9d.

In addition the all important water-course that ran outside the School also had to be cleaned and kept in good repair.

The windows had to be cleaned annually as already noted and, in November 1619, they had to be repaired at a cost of 2s 3d following heavy wind. (That was after a sum of 3s 6d had been paid a couple of months earlier for general repairs to the windows. It is wondered whether that in fact this was down to pupil damage and the explanation of a heavy wind an euphemism.)

In 1619 too, it was noted that the School paid for the repair of the scholars' seats in the chancel of the church.

In 1621, the all-important pump was rebuilt requiring wood (in fact it is described as a 'tree'), leather, ironwork and nails. In total, the cost for materials and labour was 30s, a not insignificant sum. And once again the windows had to be repaired as they had been 'brokyn with the wynde.'

In 1623 extensive work was carried out on the School, not least on replacing part of the roof, which took several men a weeks work; the annual bill that previously had run between 20-30s had now increased substantially to £5 0s 14d. The following year it had decreased to a more normal 12s 1d.

One of the men mentioned in the accounts was Humfry Jemnot for providing two bushels of lime. (Centuries later, before the School's swimming pool was built, boys from the school would swim in the River Thame at a bathing place called Jemmot's Hole as the family had remained as well established farmers in the area.)

In 1626 there is the first specific mention of stone being dug and transported to Thame for repairs on the building. Where it was dug from is not detailed but as it was carried locally this would be either Crendon or Brill.

However, in 1628, over £5 was spent on repairs, and as this coincided with the arrival of a new headmaster, Hugh Evans, it suggests that he wanted to ensure the building was in good shape at the beginning of his tenure.

One final observation worth noting is that clearly these administrative matters and overseeing the maintenance of the School (and the almshouse) would have taken up some quite considerable time on top of the Master's teaching duties.

✻ ✻ ✻

The Iles affair 1631-33

Evans was not long for the School: he died suddenly in the very first days of 1631 aged thirty-one.

William Burt was appointed in 1631 and appears to have been ruthless in maintaining high academic standards. He had inherited from Evans an Usher called John Ives. The two clearly did not get on. Burt accused Iles of a series of misdemeanors, set out in a lengthy document written by Burt and sent to the Warden. Amongst Ives's alleged failings were: leaving the School without permission, flinging a letter at Burt 'in contempt', paying money to obtain his post, being drunk in the 'Lyon', and at School 'one Tuesday'. (The Lion or Red Lion was a public house in the centre of the town.) Worst of all, Ives's relationship with the pupils seems to have been appalling. 'By his indiscreet demeanour he made himself contemptible to his scholars', and they refused to be taught by him.

The nature of Ives's reaction to these charges was typified by the complaint that he brought in clubs to the School under his gown.

Ives was summoned to New College for a meeting with the Warden and was summarily suspended. He received a formal letter to this effect from Warden Pincke and the senior Fellows in September 1632. The Ives family fought back however. Pincke received a letter from Ives's wife complaining that she and her children were being reduced to poverty. It is evident from a letter that Warden Pincke wrote to Elizabeth Wray that Ives's claim that he had been suspended without warning was unfounded as he had previously received many warnings about his behaviour even before Burt was appointed. Nevertheless, perhaps in consequence of the impending poverty of the Iles family, Pincke undertook to reinstate Ives if he could be satisfied about the Usher's future behaviour.

But it seems that Ives remained unrepentant or that Burt was determined that he must go, as a new Usher, Thomas Gilbert, was appointed in 1633. He too only lasted one year. Whether he resigned or was dismissed is unclear. He is described as a 'non-conformist' so may have disagreed with Burt on religious matters, though Wood states that Burt was more friendly to the Parliamentarian soldiers billeted in the School during the Civil War than the Royalists. The third Usher in three years, John Furness, took up the post in 1634.

* * *

Fluctuating numbers and continuing expenses, c. 1630-1640

An examination of the accounts over this period reveals for the first time the number of scholars who were at the School in the first half of the seventeenth century. From the 1630s onwards, a new item appeared, an admission fee of 4d per scholar. This sum does not match any noted in the 1575 Statutes, which further suggests that it was Burt who introduced this.

Based on the monies received divided by 4d, the number of admissions fluctuated considerably from year to year. In 1632 it was a mere 9, affected possibly by Ives's incompetence and poor behaviour. Perhaps due to his enforced departure and to Burt's growing reputation as a teacher, there was a dramatic jump to 37 in the following year and this number remained consistent during the mid-1630s until the end of the decade when the figure halved, probably because of the political turbulence and uncertainty prior to the outbreak of the civil war. By 1641, the number had fallen to 10 scholars.

By year:

- 1632: Sum received from scholars for their admission equalled 3s. Although it was not noted, this was made up of individual payments of 4d. Hence this would indicate the admission of only 9 scholars.

- 1634-5: 37 scholars paid 12s 4d.

- 1635-6: 35 scholars paid the 4d.

- 1635-6: 20 scholars. Admissions fees totalled 6s 8d.

- 1636-37: 35 scholars paid a total of 11s 8d.

- 1637-8: 38 scholars paid 12s 8d.

- 1638-9: admissions had declined to 18 scholars for unknown reasons.

- 1639-40: 18 scholars remained at the School.

- 1640-41: this had declined further to 15 scholars.

- 1641-42: Only 3s 4d was received this year, yet a further significant drop as this represents 10 scholars.

In 1631-32 another round of more expensive repairs was carried out, and the bill came to over £4. From then onwards this became the more typical annual expenditure.

One of the extraordinary items that year was the purchase of a canvas for Lord Williams's tomb, which was fitted around it by a tailor. This was used to keep off dust and grime and to reduce accidental damage: the canvas cost 7s 6d and the fitting 3d.

This same year the knot garden had to be repaired and the roses staked, confirming that a formal garden was laid out behind the School. A year later, 250 privet sets were purchased suggesting that it had now been decided to completely replant the garden.

The garden required weeding of course. In 1634 this was carried out over thirty days. We also learn that new wire was needed for the rosemary; that Bernard the gardener was paid for grafting and pruning trees at 6s 10d, and that the garden walks were re-gravelled. The following year, another gardener called Smith spent five days rooting up old trees and planting new ones. On another occasion he and Bernard pulled up the old hedges and planted new ones. Goodwife Pedley was weeding and across one year she spent forty days weeding, cutting hedges, and trimming the rosemary.

In 1636 a payment was made for the carriage of dung for the rosemary, a task that took two days.

From all this we can conclude that the garden was well tended and an important feature. In fact during this period, the annual cost of the garden's maintenance was in the range of £1 - £3 a year. It also suggests that there was some form of local nursery that could supply plants, shrubs and trees in bulk. (Currently, the published literature on the development of commercial nurseries in seventeenth century England is sparse.)

Also in 1636, 14s 4d was paid to J Green for making wooden hooks where the scholars could hang their hats.

The cumulative conclusion gained from these detailed accounts is that the masters and New College acted diligently during the early 17th century to ensure that the School was well resourced, and its building and grounds properly maintained.

✽ ✽ ✽

Civil war disruption

The town and surrounding area were perhaps surprisingly militant in this period. There was opposition to the unpopular measures introduced by Charles I: in 1628 the town's inhabitants refused to billet soldiers, and many of the gentry of the neighbourhood were opposed to arbitrary taxation. Among the 40 in Oxfordshire who refused to pay ship-money in 1636 was Sir Francis Wenman of Thame Park, and the bailiff of Thame hundred refused to have anything to do with its collection. The most famous dissident was John Hampden. In 1637, he was prosecuted by the Crown in a test case to confirm the legality of Ship Money.

This led to an escalation in tensions between monarchy and Parliament. As Charles could not be deposed, the only way of dealing with him was through military victory. When the First English Civil War began in 1642, Hampden was appointed to the Committee of Safety and became a key figure in the conflict.

The decline in the number of scholars from a high of 38 down to 10 at the end of the 1630s, continued apace so that by 1642-3 it had dropped to three. Whilst the reasons for the numbers dropping in the late 1630s are speculative, the sharp decline in the 1640s was almost certainly due to the fact that Thame was on the front line in the civil war. Nevertheless, it was not the most dangerous place in Oxfordshire and in 1643-44 the number rose to 10 scholars and remained at that level for the next few years.

- 1644-45: 2s 8d (8 scholars).

- 1645-46 3s 8d (11 scholars).

- 1646-47 3s (9 scholars).

The state of Thame at this time is known for some certainty because at this time the antiquarian Antony Wood was a pupil at the School. His family lived in Oxford and because it was expected that the Parliamentarians would attack the city, his mother sent him and his brother to Thame where they stayed in the vicarage with Hennant family. (Elizabeth (née Petty) the vicar's wife, was related to the Wood family.)

Wood wrote of this time:

...The Vicar and his wife were alwais more kind to the parl. soldiers or rebells, than to the cavaliers, as his master W. Burt and his wife were...but as to the Usher Dav: Thomas, a proper stout Welshman I alwaies took him to be a good loyalist, as indeed he was.'

However, while Thame might have been deemed safer than Oxford in 1643, a typhus and dysentery epidemic in the town that year resulted in 189 burials, 136 of them between July and early September, about four times the normal annual number, and representing about one-ninth of Thame's population. Such diseases were often the consequence of living in a war zone and garrison town

Howard Brown transcribes, at some length, Wood's account of life in Thame over the course of the civil war. It should be briefly noted too that Lord Williams's family were, through marriage, ancestral to Oliver Cromwell.

Our brief account comes from the *VCH*:

During the civil war there was again fighting in the town's streets. Thame's position on the Aylesbury-Oxford road at a distance of only 14 miles from the city and its importance as a market meant that both royalist and parliamentary forces were interested in controlling it and were constantly skirmishing in the neighbourhood.

Early in 1643 attempts were made by the parliamentary forces to obtain a permanent footing in Thame as part of their plan of controlling Oxford. Their companies were reported in the town in March and on 10 June Essex took up his headquarters there. John Hampden, mortally wounded at the Battle of Chalgrove Field, died at Thame.

The reverse at Chalgrove and other successful royalist attacks in the neighbourhood forced Essex to withdraw to Aylesbury in July. In August the royalists were commandeering all the fat cattle bought by London butchers at Thame market; in October they were planning to 'fetch away' all the cattle and stop the passage of provisions to Aylesbury; in January 1644 Prince Rupert made the town his base for an attack on Aylesbury and royalist forces appear to have remained in Thame until the spring of 1645.

With the king again at Oxford in November 1645 after his defeat at Naseby, the parliamentarians decided to occupy Thame in force in preparation for an attack on Oxford and so as to prevent the city from drawing on the Thame area for supplies.

A 'great party' of troops under Col. Greaves was quartered in the town, and in December two regiments under Col. Whalley were sent from Fairfax's army to tighten the parliamentary grip.

Already as a result of the occupation the town had suffered the raid led by Col. William Legge in September 1645, so graphically described by Anthony Wood. In June 1646 the operations against Oxford ended in the surrender of the garrison, and Wood recorded that on the same day many of the king's foot came into Thame to lay down their arms.

It is worth underlining that the School's illustrious John Hampden died in Thame during the civil war. In a battle at Chalgrove, one of his own pistols exploded in his hand causing wounds that, a few days later, would kill him. (More details regarding his death can be found in Volume 2 of this history.)

In 1647 Burt resigned. He had been Master for 16 years, still only in his early forties, but his last five years had been difficult because of the serious disruptions caused by the civil war.

Because Thame had been a war zone, the School may have temporarily ceased to operate. We know from Burt's petition to Warden Stringer in 1648 that he claimed reimbursement of the financial losses he had incurred as a result of the war. He refers to 'the dissipation of all his scholars upon the access of the army, general infection of the whole town, for a long time the school shut quite up, sometime turned into a hospital, sometime into a court of guard, sometime into a garrison'. The number of scholars detailed earlier shows that Burt was somewhat exaggerating the disruption; Wood refers to boarders living in the Vicarage and fraternising with the Roundhead soldiers billeted there. Though Burt did suffer some financial loss owing to the reduced number of scholar payments, there's no suggestion that he did not receive his full salary, which came from the endowments, a salary still above average in comparison with similar schools.

By 1647 Burt may have felt that he had enough of Thame. He took 'early retirement', or rather an extended sabbatical, becoming vicar of the tiny and almost depopulated parish of Wheatfield a few miles south of Thame, before returning to teaching as Headmaster of Winchester in 1653.

CHAPTER 10: THE LATER SEVENTEENTH CENTURY – CONTROVERSY, RENOVATION AND PLURALISM

WILLIAM AYLIFFE SUCCEDED BURT IN 1647. The exact date of the School's fifth headmaster's birth is unknown but it was probably around 1620 as he was admitted to Winchester College in 1632. He would therefore have been about 27 when he succeeded Burt in 1647 but of only one year's standing as a Bachelor of Civil Law, which should strictly have disqualified him. However, at that difficult time, the Warden and Fellows were probably not too concerned about rigid adherence to the Statutes. Given that the state of the School in 1647 was most probably poor, with few pupils and the buildings in bad condition after their use by the military, New College was probably glad that anyone was willing to take on the job.

Thomas Ellwood (1639-1713) was a pupil during Ayliffe's time as was Sir John Holt, a Lord Chief Justice. Elwood was a Quaker, a friend of John Milton's and had followed his brother to the School. In his autobiography he makes mention of his school days:

> At this School (i.e. Lord Williams' school at Thame) . . . I
> profited apace; having then a natural Propensity to Learn-
> ing; so that at the first reading over of my Lesson, I com-
> monly made myself Master of it . . . Had I been continued at
> this School, and in due time preferred to an higher; I might
> in Likelihood have been a Scholar: for I was observed to

have a Genius apt to learn.

But my Father having…accepted the Office of a Justice of the Peace, (which was no way Beneficial, but merely Honorary, and every way Expensive) and put himself into a Port and Course of Living agreeable thereunto . . . found it needful to retrench his Expences elsewhere; the Hurt of which fell upon me. For he . . . took me from School, to save the Charge of Maintaining me there; which was somewhat like plucking green Fruit from the Tree, and laying it by, before it was come to its due Ripeness; which will thenceforth shrink and wither, and lose that little Juice and Relish which it began to have.

Even so it fared with me. For … in a little time, I began to lose that little Learning I had acquired at School; so . . . that I could not have read, far less have understood a Sentence in Latin. Which I was so sensible of, that I warily avoided reading to others, even in an English book, lest, if I should meet with a Latin Word, I should shame my self, by mispronouncing it. . . . (Nevertheless I was not) rightly sensible of my Loss therein, until I came amongst the Quakers. But then I both saw my Loss, and lamented it, and applyed myself with utmost Diligence, at all leasure times to recover it.

The penultimate paragraph dispenses of the notion that the Free School in Thame was in fact free.

After eight years in post Ayliffe seems to have had a dramatic mid-life crisis. In 1655, at the age of about 35, he resigned to take up a living as Vicar of Ambrosden near Bicester, marry a young wife, lose his mind and, not long after, his life by jumping naked out of a window.

❊ ❊ ❊

The mystery of Beeston

According to the Revd. F G Lee, who wrote a history of St Mary's church, the town and the School (and published in 1883), Ayliffe's successor was Henry Beeston, appointed in May 1655. Lee gives no source for this appointment and all the surviving evidence strongly suggests that he was never appointed. Howard Brown in his *Short History* followed Lee in including Beeston in his list of Masters but the old boards listing the masters do not include him.

Beeston was the son-in-law of William Burt, at that time Headmaster of Winchester College, who might well therefore have tried to procure the master's post for his daughter's husband. However, during 1655 Beeston was a Fellow of New College drawing his weekly battels (living expenses) from the College, and there is no record of his absence. Harry Lupton, in his history of Thame published in 1861, does not mention Beeston, nor does Anthony Wood, who provides the story of Ayliffe's bizarre demise and would have been well informed about events at that time.

The voting slips that refer to choosing a successor to Ayliffe make no mention of Beeston. The votes are unanimously for Hugh Willis and George Crake (or Croke). The letter from Edward Wray to the Warden choosing Willis is dated January 1655 and both the bonds signed by Willis are endorsed '1655'. Together this evidence appears to be conclusive proof that Beeston was never Master of Thame School, but there is a snag. Until 1752 the new year started on 25th March, so 'January 1655' was by modern reckoning or 'New Style' (N.S.) January 1656. Since Willis would only have signed his bonds shortly after Wray had confirmed his election, these would also have been in N.S. 1656.

The precise date of Ayliffe's resignation is unknown. It is therefore theoretically possible that if Ayliffe resigned in March or

April 1655, Beeston could have acted as Master from May until Willis's election in January 1656, but there is no evidence for this other than Lee's statement two centuries later, and the speculation that Burt was attempting to support his son-in-law's candidacy. It is highly probable therefore that Ayliffe's successor was Willis not Beeston.

Willis was about 30 on his appointment. He had not taken his BCL degree until the previous year, although it was eight years since he had matriculated. Disruptions to his academic career may have caused the College to ignore the fact that he did not strictly meet the Statutes' academic requirements.

* * *

Religious controversy and family rivalry

Now responsible for signing off the Warden's recommendation were Bridget Wray and her father William Wray.

William's wife Elizabeth Wray (née Norreys) had inherited Rycote as the sole daughter and legitimate heir of Francis Norreys ; then she married Wray but he had died in 1645. That it was Bridget's father, Edward Wray, now in his 60s rather than Bridget herself or her new husband Montague Bertie who once again appointed the next Master is puzzling. Probably it was Wray's unrivalled experience of appointing masters that caused the Warden to write to him rather than Bertie.

But there is another possible reason that requires us to back-track half a century. In the early 1600s the Norreys and Bertie families were bitter enemies. As in the chapter about Queen Elizabeth's possible links with the School, the story of Francis Norreys's life and his feud with Robert Bertie, amongst many others, is peripheral to the main stream of the School's history. But it is too good a story to pass up and perhaps still remained in the mind of the Warden a generation later when he wrote to

Edward Wray.

Francis Norreys, born in 1579, succeeded his grandfather as 2nd Baron in 1601, his own father having died when he was still a baby. This may partly explain his hot temper and intemperate behaviour. His marriage to Bridget daughter of Edward de Vere, 17th Earl of Oxford and niece of the king's chief adviser Robert Cecil was a political coup but a personal disaster. By his high-handed behaviour he managed to make enemies of most of his well connected relations and his own pregnant wife, who fled from the family home to take refuge in Cope Castle, where she miscarried. Norreys held Bridget responsible for the breakdown of the marriage and threatened to disinherit their only surviving child Elizabeth.

Amongst all his other quarrels Norreys engaged in a long-running feud with the Bertie family. It came to a head in a Bath churchyard in September 1615 when Norreys killed a servant of Robert Bertie, 14th Baron Willoughby, during an altercation. Norreys was subsequently found guilty of manslaughter but obtained a royal pardon. King James was notorious for having favourites, and it seems that Norreys was one of them, for the King not only pardoned but also promoted him, in January 1621 creating him Viscount Thame and Earl of Berkshire.

In no way deterred by his lucky escape from deserved punishment and his subsequent promotion, within a month Norreys's temper got him into further trouble. On 16th February he was committed to the Fleet Prison for striking Lord Scrope in the House of Lords whilst the Prince of Wales was in attendance. He had reacted violently after Lord Scrope had clumsily stepped through a doorway before him. Once again, Norreys was able to play the 'get out of gaol (almost) free' card. His incarceration lasted no more than a few days. On 19th February he submitted a written apology to the Lords. The apology was accepted and he was summoned to the House to kneel before the Prince and to be reconciled with Lord Scrope.

Less than a year later, however, his nemesis finally caught up with him. On 29th January 1622, he shot himself with a crossbow at Rycote and died of wounds two days later. His estates and the right to choose Thame School's Master passed to his daughter Elizabeth, Baroness Norreys, who earlier had secretly married Edward Wray instead of her father's choice, the brother of the Duke of Buckingham, the king's chief favourite.

Attempted suicide is the generally accepted cause of his death, but no copy of the coroner's inquest has survived and in 2014 a comment was placed on the Bodleian Library's website, on which this Norreys saga is based, that the gamekeeper who found him was due to be dismissed, along with a conspiracy theory related to Norreys's 'enormous wealth'. (It is tempting to conclude that this was very first Midsomer Murder!)

Wild speculation aside, it is quite clear that of all Williams's Norreys heirs, Francis Norreys was the worst qualified to choose a suitable Master for Thame School. Luckily for the School, his early demise and Boucher's long tenure meant that he was never called upon to make that choice. It is inconceivable that the people of Thame, the School's pupils and the Warden and Fellows of New College were unaware of Norreys's extraordinary behaviour but there is no evidence that the reputation of the School's patron had any adverse effect on the School at the time.

Returning now to the appointment of Willis in 1655 during the Commonwealth period. It would have been controversial in a town such as Thame where there were many non-conformists and supporters of Parliament, for he was a known Royalist. In 1648, as a recently appointed Fellow of New College, he had refused to perjure himself by taking an oath of allegiance to the Parliamentary Visitors. After the Puritans desecrated Lord Williams's tomb, he rescued and looked after one of the brass tablets attached to it.

As the Commonwealth with its religious and political upheavals drew to a close and it became likely that the monarchy would be restored in the person of Charles II, a period of renovation began, at least in terms of the School's fabric and equipment. In 1659, there is a record of an itemised bill for some extensive work that was carried out over a continuous period of seven weeks by stone masons. And in 1660, a new 'clocke' with an alarm was bought at a cost of £3; and a further £11 16s 9d was spent on repairing the walls belonging to 'ye schoole and Almes House'.

That these repairs and improvements were significant is revealed in the 1661 record of a visitation to Thame by Michael Woodward, Warden of New College:

> I went to visit the school of Thame where I viewed all the buildings of the school and almshouse there, with the walls and outhouses: which were all safe and in good repair, being lately mended, lathed and tiled I went also and saw the Lord Williams his tomb in the church of Thame, that is very much mangled and broken. I resolved to speak unto Mr Jackson the stonecutter to mend it if he had such materials.

He also noted that soldiers had stolen the canvas that had been wrapped around the tomb, and he resolved to have it replaced.

The repairs to the tomb were undertaken but not by Jackson who had quoted £32 14s but by the sculptor William Bryde, who was paid £20 in June 1662 for the replacement of the hands, the ledge (plinth), and the unicorn and greyhound at the feet of the figures. These were then painted and gilded by Richard Hawkins at a cost of £13 6s 2d - and he was paid in May 1663 - almost a year later.

A separate expense of £10 was paid for the gilding of Lord

Williams and Elizabeth and the many coats of arms around the tomb – all done in 'oyle'. Hawkins also repainted and gilded the railings around the tomb. The tomb once again was a colourful centrepiece in the chancel.

[Richard Hawkins (1611–1699) was a heraldic painter and 'paynte stayner', and Mayor of Oxford 1689-90. Hawkins was employed as a painter by Anthony Wood and was also his friend. Wood records that on 3rd September 1667 he paid three shillings to "Hawkins the painter for painting the chamber and window", and on 23rd December 1669 four shillings for drawing his arms on vellum. Hawkins was obviously an expert on coats of arms, as twice Wood wrote in his diary 'Quaere Mr Hawkins' when he was uncertain about someone's arms. In 1668/9 Hawkins was paid £19 12s. for painting work he did in the Divinity School.]

✽ ✽ ✽

Pluralism, part-time teachers and short-lived ushers

Eight years after his appointment as Master, Hugh Willis became Vicar of Thame, the first to hold both posts. Ayliffe had resigned when he took up his ecclesiastic living; Willis did not. The fact that he could find time to add church to educational duties and the administration of the School and almshouse suggests few(er) pupils and a dwindling Anglican congregation.

One pupil was his son Francis Willis, who was born in the Vicarage, educated at the Grammar School and in due course entered Winchester College in 1675 before ultimately graduating from New College. During his life he was recognised as being an author and poet of distinction, and a renowned physician.

The period following the civil war is often seen as one of decline for grammar schools generally, and Thame was no exception. The poor found the fees unaffordable. The rich and influential chose to send their sons to either larger schools or to use private tutors not least because the education provided by grammar schools was becoming increasingly redundant. Knowledge of Latin and the classics was unnecessary as Latin was no longer the obligatory language of religion or the professions. The grammar schools were slow to adapt, sometimes because they were bound by the terms of their statutes - as was possibly the case at Thame - and to change them required a legal process to be undertaken.

Thame's occupations were still dominated by agriculture, traders such as bakers, butchers and innkeepers, and semi-skilled and skilled trades, such as blacksmiths, glaziers, gun-smiths. Professional occupations made up less than 10 per cent of the workforce.

In 1691, G. Miege stated in his book *The New State of England* that the Tuesday market in Thame was 'eminent chiefly for the buying of cattle, which makes it much frequented by graziers and butchers from London and other parts.' However, agricultural trades did not require a grounding in Latin.

In 1661 Willis was criticised by Warden Woodward for housing his family in the School's lodgings, contrary to the Statutes. That there was room for his family indicates there were also few boarders. During the Commonwealth period, the appointment of a Royalist as Master would not have encouraged local non-conformist families nor nearby Parliamentarian gentry to have their sons educated at Thame.

Willis's time as Master imitated Burt's in the frequency with which his ushers changed. The name of the usher that Willis inherited from Ayliffe is unknown, but in April 1659 Daniel Ballowe took up the post. The connection of the merchant branch of the Ballowe family with the School has already been described in an earlier chapter. Daniel, however, came from the academic rather than the commercial branch. His elder brother Thomas and his father William both had distinguished academic careers, the latter perhaps also as a spy or under-cover agent as he is stated to be 'in the service of the Lord Chancellor' in 1605, the year of the Gunpowder Plot when Robert Cecil is known to have run a string of secret agents sniffing out Catholic plotters.

Daniel seems to have been a good deal less successful. He gained his MA degree at Oriel College Oxford in 1636 but his subsequent career is unknown. By 1659 he was 44: Usher would seem a rather lowly post at that stage of his life. For whatever reason, his tenure probably lasted less than a year as another Usher, Thomas Fowkes, was probably appointed in 1659. Fowkes's bond is undated but annotated 1659 by a later hand. (It is tempting to believe he was an ancestor of the notorious 19th century Master, Thomas Fookes.)

For certain, both Ballowe and Fowkes had left the post by November 1660. Fowkes's departure was to return to his Fellowship at Cambridge from which he had been expelled in 1649. He was certainly over-qualified for the usher's post but during the anti-royalist period of the Commonwealth was glad no doubt to have found employment even if the pay was poor and there were few pupils to teach.

William Collins, who succeeded Fowkes, lasted a mere two years and was replaced by Richard Bourne. The reason for these rapid changes may be that Hugh Willis was proving a hard taskmaster, but the example of Fowkes suggests the possibility that the political and religious upheavals around the time of the Restoration played a part. Willis and his various ushers may have held different religious views.

✳ ✳ ✳

The Berties succeed the Norreys's

Willis's 20-year service as Master ended in 1675. New College offered Thomas Hugh Middleton and Anthony Rouse. James Bertie, signing himself as 'Norreys', confirmed the former from his residence at Wytham not Rycote. James Bertie, who had succeeded his father in 1666, was the first male Norreys for several generations to inherit the barony, later becoming Earl of Abingdon.

Middleton, (born about 1644, matric 1663, BA 1667, MA 1670/71) followed Willis's precedent in having more than one job but took pluralism to new heights. He was vicar of Chesterton from 1675-67, vicar of Long Crendon from 1682, and Wilsford, Wiltshire from 1684. Perhaps it was the stress of three jobs and all the travelling that hastened his relatively early death aged 50 in 1694 while still in post. Lee states that a marble monument to him could be found in the choir at St Mary's: 'Thomas Middleton, Master of Thame School, obit April 22 1694' but a recent search has been unable to locate it.

No records survive for the nomination or confirmation of Middleton's successor, Henry Bruges appointed in 1694, aged 25 or 26, BA 1691/2, MA 1697, who once again did not strictly meet the Statutes' qualifications at the time of his appointment. He was the son of Robert Bruges of Winchester.

He served as Master for a lengthy 33 years, and during his latter years was also Vicar of Pitchcott in Bucks.

Next to nothing is known about the School during Bruges' time other than Thomas Phillips, who had been born in Ickford, and who became a prominent Jesuit priest was said to have been a pupil. (However this may be a mistake and it was his great uncle William Joyner - who also wrote a book about Pole - who attended the School in the 1620s.) Of Bruges we know he was appointed a trustee of a Thame charity that distributed new clothing to the poor of the town, the money coming from a property called the Blue Man.

He married and had three children, Henry (who later studied at Corpus Christi), Katherine and Suzanne. We also know from a letter from his son to New College that he died, still in post, May 1727. He was buried in St Mary's on 6th May, and the entry for his burial can be seen in the parish records as the Reverend Henry Bruges.

His Will is also available and from it we can see that he was a man of independent means: he owned land near Southampton that he left to his son. Suzanne, his daughter inherited four hundred pounds immediately, and a further one hundred pounds to be paid after the birth of her first child; she also inherited a bedstead, a silk quilt, flaxen sheets, blankets, and half of his 'pewter copper.'

CHAPTER 11: THE EIGHTEENTH CENTURY- DECLINE

DURING THE 16TH AND EARLY PART OF THE 17TH CENTURY, Lord Williams's School had a history of educating scholars who went on to have significant national influence. In that sense, it had an impact that was greater than would be expected. It was, after all, a small rural grammar school in an area that was dominated by an agricultural economy; and perched on the edge of the county meant a certain isolation from the administrative centre. It did not enjoy the advantages of being one of the great city grammar schools.

As noted in the previous chapter, grammar schools across the country suffered a period of decline in the latter half of the 17th century. The frequent changes of master in the early 18th century (three in quick succession between 1727 and 1729) would have not helped the School's fortunes.

In Oxfordshire, six grammar schools closed across the 18th century. In part this decline was put down to the salaries being insufficient to attract qualified masters, or the master had to take an ecclesiastical position, and then teach on a part-time basis, in order to earn a livable income – which was the case at Thame. Clearly not ideal when it came to attracting pupils. Whereas in the late 16th and early 17th century the master's and usher's salaries was sufficient to live on, encouraging the incumbents to regard the post as a job for life, during the 18th century the unchanged salaries were worth ever less in real terms.

Across the 18th century and into the early part of the 19th, the cost of living at least doubled; by the early 19th century the salary at Thame and other schools had become derisory and was about the same as an agricultural labourer's. This inevitably led to part-time, pluralist headmasters in many schools as well as dispensing with the usher, his salary being pocketed by the master.

An example comes from the nearby Royal Grammar School Wycombe. During the first half of the 18th century, Samuel Guise was appointed Headmaster as a part-time position and as lecturer or curate of the local parish church, for which he was paid an additional £10 per annum. He was then made vicar both of Thame and of Wycombe in 1711. He remained as vicar in Wycombe until his death in 1753. Meanwhile he retained his position as Headmaster, and also served for a time as chaplain to the Duke of Wharton. So his headmastership now became a minor source of income for a pluralist.

As at Wycombe so very largely, in Oxfordshire. The *Victoria County History* notes: 'a general decline set in in the 18th century, and we are forced to the conclusion that in Oxfordshire, at least, the main cause was an insufficient supply of suitable headmasters, due very probably to the decreased value of the stipends.'

But there were exceptions. The *VCH* states that Adderbury Grammar School had a continuous existence, and New College when appointing masters throughout the 18th century increased the salary roughly inline with the rising cost of living.

The reason, at least in Thame, that salaries were not increased was because the rental income passed on to the School by New College remained largely constant over the years - apart from some minor variations - but most critically did not increase significantly over this 250-year period from the £40 per annum that had been the income from the first year of the School's existence.

The consequence of New College's failure to increase the masters' salary in line with inflation was evident from the second quarter of the 18th century. Bruges's successor William Lamplugh was quickly appointed, but equally quickly resigned. The reason for his brief stay is known: he had been made a better offer as Rector of Alton Barnes in Wiltshire. However, he was to die only ten years later.

New College acted quickly and forwarded two names, 'Mr Lamplugh, having had the good fortune to be preferred, the warden and nine senior fellows have nominated and elected Mr James Fussell and Mr Rice Price'. The Earl of Abingdon (the Norreys barony having been upgraded in 1682) acted with equal alacrity, and replied choosing Fussell. The College had responded to the rapid resignation with commendable speed and, in Fussell, had found a candidate who met all the requirements of the Statutes.

It seems rather hard on Charles Holford - who had been the second choice when Lampugh was appointed - that he was not re-nominated after Lamplugh resigned. This might imply that the second nominee, 'the runner up' was just a make-weight for the sake of complying with the Statutes rather than a serious candidate, but Holford looks to have been well qualified.

The runners up were again overlooked in a repeat performance less than two years later when Fussell resigned to become Vicar of Hardwicke. The College once again moved quickly to provide a successor, nominating Robert Wheeler, who signed his bond on 9th April 1729 - and tendered his resignation on 1st June. This time the reason for the precipitate resignation is unknown but possibly he moved to Somerset and became Rector of Dulverton.

So, for the third time in two years New College had to go

through the appointment process in a hurry. The College offered John Kipling and Mr Hutchinson to the Earl of Abingdon. New College may have run out of suitable candidates, for Kipling, aged about 35 on appointment, originally at Magdalen Hall but with a BA 1717/18 and MA 1720 from Christchurch, was the first nominee since the School's foundation in nearly two centuries not to be a New College graduate.

On 13th Abingdon confirmed 'Kiplin' [sic] as his choice and the following day Kipling signed his bond, ushering in a long period of stability, as he holds the record, at 39 years, for being the longest serving Master. On his arrival he had recently married Elizabeth Deeley at Towersey in 1729 but he was originally a man of the Midlands as he was born at Thatch Lee Farm, Middleton-in Teesdale in 1693.

New College's alacrity in dealing with the appointment of masters was not, seemingly, matched by its diligence in maintaining the School's fabric. The year of Lamplugh's appointment broadly coincides with the start of a period when detailed accounts are no longer kept. Though it is always dangerous to draw conclusions from negative evidence, and the records of the accounts may simply have been lost at some later date, the contrast between the meticulous accounting during most of the 17th century with the scrappy entries in the 18th century does suggest that New College was increasingly failing to honour its obligations. Other evidence, discussed below, supports this view.

Nevertheless, the bicentenary of the School's founding was celebrated in 1769 by the striking of silver medals.

There is nothing to suggest that Kipling's long tenure led to a golden age comparable to his 17th century predecessors Boucher or Burt. The only surviving document relating to his time as Master may imply the opposite. In a letter from Kipling to the Warden dated Sep 20th 1742 he writes that he will be 'sure to follow' the Warden's 'directions'. This suggests some back-sliding and possibly criticism from elsewhere as he also writes: 'You will know Sir John's answer, and perhaps in person'. The identity of 'Sir John' remains unclear. For sure it was not one of the Norreys/Bertie family as none of the Earls of Abingdon bears that name.

The adverse effects of pluralism grew ever greater. It was one thing to combine the role of master with a local living, quite another when these were further away. Kipling was perpetual curate of nearby Chearsley and but also vicar of Brize Norton, 30 miles west on the other side of Oxfordshire, an hour's drive today and probably the best part of a day's journey along 18th century roads. It seems likely therefore that Kipling was both an absentee vicar and an absentee master for much of the time, in contravention of the requirement in the Statutes that the master should not be away for more than one month per year in total. The Warden and Fellows were either unaware of this unsatisfactory situation or chose to turn a blind eye.

Nepotism is not necessarily a sign of decline but it is perhaps significant that on 3rd March 1756 John Kipling Jnr became Usher, a year after receiving his BA from Christchurch. (And of course it is possible that he had attended the School as a pupil.) Whether or not he was a committed and effective teacher is not known. He certainly chose not to follow an educational career. His time as Usher lasted eight years until 1762 when he was appointed to the Living of Midsomer Norton where he married Sarah Horton in 1765. He was later appointed to be Vicar of Staverton in Gloucestershire.

Kipling Snr died at Thame 1769 but was buried in the church at Chearsley. In his Will he left property including houses in Chinnor, Oxford and London to his wife, two sons John and Charles (who might well have also attended the School), and daughter-in-law Sarah.

The next two masters served 15 years between them. John Hook, though not strictly academically qualified on appointment, resigned in 1773 to take up the headmastership of the rather more prestigious and much better endowed Bedford School.

His successor William Cooke, also narrowly unqualified academically, added the post of Vicar of Worminghall in 1783. Both were former Fellows of New College. The lack of any surviving evidence suggests that the appointments were trouble-free, but the events that followed Cooke's departure and his later pluralism show that he did not take his job seriously and that the number of pupils had continued to decline.

The precise sequence of events from 1783 to 1786 is obscure. Howard Brown in his *Short History* states that Cooke resigned in 1783 when he became Vicar of Worminghall, in principle a more manageable six miles away, and he dates the appointment of his successor William Stratford to that year, writing that the date on the School's list of masters is incorrect. In fact, the error is Brown's, through repeating the similarly erroneous date in Lee's history, and his inference that the 'vacancy' at the School declared by the College's Visitors in 1786 was because Stratford was 'away from home' is also incorrect.

In fact, the absentee was Cooke not Stratford. What appears to have happened is as follows. When Cooke became Vicar of Worminghall, he did not resign but, at some point no later than early 1786, he did become an absentee master and handed over the teaching to the Usher, the Rev William Newborough. Newborough had been born in Oxford in 1746, and his father was the Reverend John Newborough. He had matriculated at Pembroke College in 1764, had obtained his BA in 1768 and a Fellow and MA in 1771 so he was well qualified to take over as *de facto* Master, though he was also pluralist. Besides his role at Thame, he was also a minister at Long Crendon.

It is certain that Cooke was 'away from home' in 1786 as a letter to Warden Oglander from J Davey dated 25th Feb 1786 states 'My friend Mr Newborough is in possession of the schoolhouse as Mr Cooke's representative and asks for his female servant to be there for a few days by way of airing after Innoculation. The house is a capacious one without a single scholar in it and without the most distant expectation of any.'

(J Davey might have been the Rev John Davey who was vicar at nearby Bledlow.)

This makes it absolutely clear that Cooke was non-resident and that there were no boarders. William Newborough may have continued to teach day-boys, as suggested by his letter of 22nd March, 1786 to the Warden stating that Cooke had appointed him as Usher, but not for long as he died in November 1787 and was buried in St Mary's churchyard.

It looks as though Cooke eventually gave up any pretence of teaching to write a book: '*A Political essay on the early part of education to which is prefixed an enquiry into the discipline of the Ancients with some observations on that of our public schools*, and authored by the Reverend William Coke M.A. Master of Thame School, Chaplain to the Most Honourable Marquis of Tweesdale, late Fellow of New College in Oxford, and Vicar of Worminhall in Buckinghamshire'.

As this was published in Oxford by the Clarendon Press in 1785, it is likely that he abandoned his teaching in 1783 or soon after. Interestingly among the subscribers was John Kipling Jnr.

* * *

A mistake put right

It seems that New College had been unaware of Cooke's absenteeism until alerted to it by the letter from Newborough. Belatedly it acted to deal with the situation. A Visitation was made on 21st March, 1786 the day after Newborough's letter arrived, and no doubt the reason for it, declaring a vacancy, in effect summarily dismissing the absent Cooke, who presumably had been continuing to draw his master's salary to that point.

On 23rd March the College authorities met to elect two candidates. On the same day Warden Oglander put forward two names, William Stratford and Benjamin Jeffries in a letter to Abingdon for him to choose. Either the letter was badly drafted or Abingdon did not read it properly as he chose Jeffries who was not the College's preferred candidate.

A no-doubt embarrassed Oglander wrote to Abingdon on 30th March explaining the misunderstanding, saying that he had delayed informing Jeffries of his inadvertent appointment. Abingdon's reply does not survive but he changed his choice as it was Stratford not Jeffries who finally became Master on 6th April and signed his bond in the same month.

Stratford was born around 1747, matriculated at Corpus Christi College in 1763, obtained his BA in 1768 and MA in 1770. He was therefore fully qualified for the post, though rather older on appointment than most of his predecessors.

The most apparently significant feature of the events of 1786 in relation to the way masters were appointed was the deviation from the procedures laid down in the Statutes. For the first time the appointment was made in effect by the college's Visitors rather than the Warden and nine Senior Fellows. However, the difference is more semantic than real as the Visitors were still Fellows.

* * *

The decline continues

Stratford was Master for 31 years, though like Kipling before him he did not restore the School's fortunes. Initially, he was keen to recruit more pupils, especially boarders, as is clear from the advertisement he placed in *Jackson's Oxford Journal* in early January 1798, offering lessons in 'Writing and arithmetic' and, more surprisingly, dancing.

This interesting advertisement shows that to flourish the School needed to broaden its curriculum from the traditional grammar school subjects of teaching the classics. Certainly, as stated in A.M.d'I.Oakeshott's PhD dissertation, across the eighteenth century, an increasing number of parents had decided that a strictly classical education was of little value.

Interestingly, Thame School was not the only school in town which now included Mrs Way's Boarding School, a girl's school run by Martha Bowler, and the Market House School for boys.

Jone's School was advertising in *Jackson's Oxford Journal* in 1800. It boarded boys and it too offered dancing lessons as well as English Grammar, Geography and 'every branch of education requisite to qualify them for trade.' The annual cost was 18 guineas with one guinea entrance fee. Two holidays a year were given of one month each in the summer and at Christmas.

We also know a little about the nature of the town too. Lord Torrington when he visited the town in 1785 described it as a 'mean, gloomy town.' As Gerald Clarke wrote in his *History of Thame,* 'in the 18th century, Thame was agricultural and provincial, perhaps even parochial…the tidal waves of the outside world rippled into this static, stable and self-centred society only slowly.' Not necessarily the environment that would attract boarders from a distance.

It is worth noting that when Thame School was stagnating, Britain was going through unprecedented social changes, and leading the world in scientific, engineering and agricultural innovations. All of this made the barest impact on the town bar a few improved turnpike roads and, in strong contrast to the seventeenth century, the School's pupils later made no significant contribution to national developments.

Events in Europe were proving to be volatile with Napoleon coming to power in France and going to war across Europe. In Thame (as elsewhere) a band of militia was raised in 1803 - and called the Loyal Thame Volunteers - to protect the town against a possible invasion. They were commanded by Major Wykham of Thame Park. The only Frenchmen, however, to invade Thame were the 100 or so prisoners on parole who were billeted in the town from 1805 until the end of the Napoleonic War.

Following Stratford's initial enthusiasm his health waned over the years. In a letter dated 11th March 1814 he gave good notice to the Warden of his resignation to take effect from the following September due to ill health: 'I have considered about having an Usher but it will not answer as the Expense will be too great.' One clear implication of the last clause is that Stratford had dispensed with the services of an usher. However the accounts for his last year as Master still show the Usher's salary being paid - along with his own - at a total cost of £40. In other words he was taking both salaries. (It should be noted that the School was not profitable on a yearly basis. The rents it was receiving were still just over £40 per annum but expenses that year were over £90, and the School was dipping into its reserves.)

As a comparison and in contrast to the rents that the School was receiving the average cost of farm rents at the time was around £1 per acre, which appears to be considerably more than what the School was charging. The Earl of Abingdon (at the time still a patron to the School) was charging £343 rent for a farm of 413 acres in Thame.

A paper written by Warden Gauntlett in 1794 revealed that for many years New College, despite repeated legal advice to the contrary, was paying only part of the endowed rents to the Master. It would appear that in fact New College had been raising the annual cost of the endowed properties' rents but only paying the School the same income it had received in the 1570s. The reason for this is unknown: perhaps they were withheld because of low pupil numbers but of course this would mean that the School had insufficient funds to invest in facilites or to increase the Master's salary to a level where he would be able to undertake only that role, and therefore increase the attractiveness of the School to prospective parents. Whatever the reason, New College was failing to carry out its duties.

Another reason Stratford complained about the expense may be related to a sharp increase in taxes that the School had to pay. Although the Window Tax had been introduced as early as 1696, it appears from the accounts that the School and almshouse were exempt for a period, but in 1800 it paid £10, and by 1811 this had increased to £26.

Nevertheless, it is difficult to believe that Stratford personally was in serious financial difficulty in 1814 as he had been Rector of Easington since 1773 and Rector of Holton since 1775.

It seems also that he had the rare distinction of holding the post of Master at two schools simultaneously: Thame School and Bedford School, though only for the year 1810-1811 at the latter. A plausible explanation for this rare occurrence is that he was chosen as a 'stop-gap 'master of Bedford on the death in office of Robert Hook, probably to avoid the promotion of the Under Master Charles Abbot, who on the very day that Hook died wrote to the Warden of New College with a 'memorial' or memorandum setting out the reasons why he should be appointed Hook's successor.

The appointment of Masters at Bedford was in the gift of New College. On the face of it Charles Abbot was a suitable candidate, educated at Winchester, with an MA from New College in 1788, a Fellow of the Linnean Society in 1793 and a distinguished botanist. However, aged 49, he may have been considered too old and in a series of complaining letters to the Warden he comes across as ultra-conservative, litigious and cantankerous.

Hook was 70 and in ill-health when he died. The College was likely looking for someone younger and more forward-looking than Abbott. The Mayor of Bedford, chairman of the Harpur Trust, the source of the School's endowments, was certainly very keen for the Bedford School to be modernised and improved. It seems that the preferred candidate was John Brereton, aged 29, a member of New College since 1801 but who had only gained his BCL degree in 1810 just in time to be suitably qualified to be Master. It is possible that he was not immediately ready to take over and the College therefore may have invited Stratford as an experienced stop-gap. Abbot did not get on well with Brereton; hardly surprising for someone who had been passed over in favour of a man 20 years his junior and a dedicated improver. One of Brereton's innovations was to take in boarders, hardly a radical move, but Abbot objected violently, refused to teach them and stated publicly in the presence of the whole School that they should not be there. Usher Iles's earlier misdemeanors at Thame seem quite mild by comparison.

However, there is no confirmation from primary sources that Stratford actually was a temporary Master of Bedford. At the most it would have been for two terms only as Hook died in November 1810 and correspondence between the Harpur Trust and New College indicates that no new appointment was made until January 1811 at the earliest. As with Henry Beeston in the 17th century, Stratford's time at Bedford may well be a myth.

Stratford resigned from Thame School in 1814 but he did not die in that year, despite the claim to that effect made by Lee and copied by Howard Brown. Had Lee taken the trouble to look at the parish registers of Holton he would have found the record of Stratford's burial some five years later on 27th September 1819. Unusually, the curate who made the entry originally recorded it as 11th September but later amended it. Perhaps the burial was postponed because, in the words of the parish register, Stratford was 'buried in the chancel under the Rectory Pew, south side, just under the south window' and this took time to organise.

CHAPTER 12: FURTHER DECLINE 1814-1841

THE DOCUMENTATION FOR THE NEXT HEADMASTER'S appointment is the most detailed in Thame School's history before the 1870s. All five candidates are named, together with their CVs, apart from the eventual winner, Timothy Tripp Lee, whose CV was probably already known to the Fellows as he had been a Fellow of Pembroke College since 1787 when he matriculated. He was born about 1770, gaining his BA in 1791 and had been Vicar of Thame since 1795. At the age of 44 he was by far the oldest candidate, and the only candidate for whom each of the nine senior Fellows voted is recorded.

The appointment reverted to the original procedures, with one notable exception: Lee actually applied for the post. Within five days of Stratford's resignation letter, he wrote to the Warden putting himself forward for master 'should you not find any members disposed to accept it'. This is probably a reference to the fact that he was not a Fellow of New College, though he had been educated at Winchester. As Vicar of Thame it is quite possible that Stratford would have acquainted him with his intention to retire or perhaps he had learnt of it from university contacts. At all events, he was able to get his application for the master's post in early.

There is an impression that in this instance 'who you know' rather than 'what you know' determined the decision, as in educational terms Lee was not the best qualified candidate. Thanks to the survival of the candidates' CVs it is evident that Mr J Evans was the best qualified through experience. At 29 he was about the right age, at that time curate at Woodstock but previously assistant teacher at Hurstmonceux School in Sussex which, after the death of the master, he managed for three-and-a-half years for the benefit of the widow and her children, one of whom eventually succeeded his father as master.

But various factors counted against him. He was not local to Thame nor Oxfordshire, nor even English, having been born in the remote parish of Dihewyd in West Wales, not that this had earlier been counted against his namesake Hugh Evans who was born in Harlech. Though he had been for five years at the university, he had not yet taken his BA degree at Magdalen Hall (later merged with Magdalen College).

There was no love lost between New College and Magdalen, and it is possible that the New College Fellows were not prepared to appoint someone from a rival college. He was not even short listed. The alternative candidate, as revealed in a letter to 'My Lord' on October 21st 1814 from Warden Gauntlett, was the Rev R C Fenton, curate of Dorton from Jesus College. No longer did the College act with alacrity. Though the new school term should have started in September when Stratford's resignation took effect, at least a three-week gap ensued before the College made its decision and another week elapsed before Abingdon's reply on October 27th.

So a vicar, whose ecclesiastical job should have been full-time, won over a man who had a good record as a teacher and acting headmaster. Unsurprisingly, the schooling remained of poor quality. Lee lived in the parish and in 1830 wrote that he had been there constantly for 35 years without a month's absence. Sometimes on Sundays he had to give several services, for two Sunday services were held in Thame and one in each of the three chapels, in Sydenham, Tetsworth, and Towersey. With eleven children to support he did not have the money to pay a regular curate.

It seems plausible that here was a man who, very understandably, could not cope with both his religious and educational duties. In addition, because of the lack of pupils - according to the Carlile's *Old Grammar Schools* - it would appear that like Stratford, he had dispensed with the services of an usher and, according to Brown, added the usher's salary salary to his own. It would also appear that the fee for boarding had risen from £20 in 1788 to 30 guineas but Carlisle wrote that 'there are seldom so many as six boys on the foundation at one time', a comment repeated in the 1828 *Thame Directory*. The charge of 30 guineas appears to be the norm at this time for schools in Oxfordshire. Higher fees but poor teaching was clearly not a recipe for success.

Carlisle also suggests that these were all under the age of twelve and that while in the past the pupils had used the *Eton Grammars*, they now used those of Valpy. (These were the Greek and Latin grammars written by Richard Valpy, 1754-1836.)

Although the documentation for Lee's appointment is extensive, it was this year that the accounts stopped being recorded, and no other written record of the School exists; yet another indication that New College no longer took seriously its responsibility for the school. We know from Harry Lupton's history that all the stained-glass windows had now disappeared, which he put down to miscreant behaviour by the pupils. Quite possibly true, but competent masters might well have prevented such behaviour or at least ensured that damage was repaired.

The educational health of Thame at this period compares unfavourably with other Oxfordshire grammar schools though few were thriving. Carlisle records that Watlington had 20 scholars, Woodstock 25, Chipping Norton 40 to 70; Dorchester between 9 and 15; Steeple Aston 50 to 70 – although that was because it taught all children of all ages from the parish and those adjoining. He obtained his information by writing to the schools and not all responded. In nearby Buckinghamshire, RGS Wycombe, like Thame, was on the verge of closure, as it too had no more than a handful of pupils, and it was said that it was 'useless as an institution and served no purpose for the town.'

The great public schools too were facing difficult times in the early part of the 19th century. In Richard Lawrence Archer's book, *Secondary Education in the Nineteenth Century* he records:

> *In the first three decades of the century the public schools were in a parlous state. Their low moral tone, their narrow classical curriculum, their poor intellectual results their roughness and bullying...were no longer tolerated.*

A further view presented by Henry Boddington (1813 - 1886) of brewery fame, who originally came from Thame, confirms the picture of near fatal decline. In his memoirs, he wrote:

> *Thame is famous for its endowed Grammar School. It may seem incredible when I state that during my youth hood and for many subsequent years not a boy received instruction there. The parson [Lee] took the endowment and not a jot did he do for the revenue received from it. This perversion lasted until very lately when an investigation was made, and since then an amendment has taken place – never could there be a more shameful perversion of funds, a perfect fraud. God forgive the perpetrators!*

It should be noted that Boddington did not attend the School itself but went to another private institution in Thame in the late 1820s. His memory of that place is vivid:

> *Our master Burnard was a cripple. He hobbled about with two sticks. His legs were positively shocking but his heads and arms were muscular and could strike with dreadful force. The flogging was dreadful. Cowardly boys with the*

first strokes of his cane would bawl out, 'Oh pray, sir,' and he then desisted.

I refused to cry out and as he exhausted himself he would exclaim, 'You diabolical villain, I will cut you to atoms.'

Oh, how he flogged me! Enough of this. I then thought, and my mind is unaltered, I thought he deserved hanging. I was the librarian, and if a book was found out of its place I was caned unmercifully. One day a quarto dictionary was found on the desk instead of being in its place. My punishment was fiercely savage. I was made to lie flat on my back on a school form, my hands raised over my head, the book laid on my chest. I was black in the face and almost gone when I was released. I was then ordered to stand on one leg when I tremulously put the other foot down to steady myself he jumped off his desk which was close to where I was set up, and oh, how he caned me!

Some of the educational choices in Thame in the early 19th century were bleak indeed: either no teaching in the Grammar School, or appalling physical abuse at a private school. Indeed Thame itself was bleak and therefore unsurprising that Boddington left to seek his fortune elsewhere. Due to changes in land ownership the number of people employed on the land fell and when the traveller Arthur Young visited Thame he commented on the town's 'very depressing poverty.'

It is also worth noting that life was brutal in this period, and that the physical punishments in schools should be seen against this backdrop. In 1821, two men from Thame were sentenced to death at the Oxford Assizes for stealing a lamb. Samuel North and William Drewitt had stolen the animal from William Badrick a local farmer. It was unruly too. Robert Hedges, an auctioneer in Thame, met with a serious accident that same year while celebrating the battle of Waterloo. He had been firing a rifle in the air and while reloading, it accidently fired again, shattered the ramrod in to several pieces which badly lacerated his left hand, arm, thigh as well as knocking out a number of teeth.

Thame was also infamous for bull-baiting (no doubt because of importance of cattle and the cattle market to the town's economy.) It was recorded in the early 1820s that the practice had been removed from the market place but still took place in adjacent fields.

In 1825 a report in Jackson's Oxford Journal described a bull-baiting scene in the town.

> *The baiting of the bull always takes place on the day after the Michaelmas fair; this day among the bull-baiting class is invariably spent in drunkeness and riot; they assemble in the morning to get themselves in high order for the longed-for sport. Some years back the poor beast was led through the town in such a state of exhaustion that every stimulus was required to urge it to move one leg before the other, its lacerated tongue protruding from its mouth panting for breath. A man seized the tongue of the unresisting animal and dragged its head to the ground.*

In 1826, the incidents of bull-baiting in Thame were mentioned in a House of Common's debate on cruelty to cattle.

This begs the question as to whether any respectable family would wish to send their sons for schooling in the town.

CHAPTER 13: COLLAPSE 1841-1872

THESE DIRE STRAITS were supposed to change with the appointment in January 1841 of the last Master of the unreformed school, Thomas Fookes, an appointment that was announced in the *Times* newspaper. He reinstated the position of Usher, now called a second master, when AR Venna of Jesus College was appointed in 1842. Later, he also appointed two more masters: Mr S Stratton-Watts and Mr Charles Schnride (from Paris) a teacher of modern languages. Fookes foresaw a new era, and to this end advertisements were placed in *Jackson's Oxford Journal* announcing that the School was open. He also placed advertisements in the *Times*:

> *The Head Master invites the attention of the public, particularly of gentlemen desirous of having their sons carefully prepared for Winchester or Eton, or for the Universities to this establishment. The terms are moderate, including instruction in classics, mathematics, modern languages and all branches of a superior general education, without extra charge.*

Change it did because in 1843 there were 9 day-pupils and 14 boarders; 1844, 8 day-pupils and 15 boarders and, in 1847, the registrations were 4 day pupils and 16 boarders. One of the pupils at this time was Frederick Lee, a son of the Vicar of Thame, and who went from the School to St Edmund's Hall, Oxford. Two other pupils from this period were Robert Warner Stone who had a distinguished career in the Army and rose to the rank of colonel, while William Musson was appointed Chaplin to Her Majesty's Forces in Hong Kong.

Additional buildings were added including a new kitchen and stables. Lupton notes that there was a productive walled garden, an ornamental garden, as well as a playground for the pupils. While not reaching the numbers seen in the early 17th century, the increase in numbers pointed to the possibility that the School was at the start of a revival.

Although the accounts do not exist, it is also likely that Fookes had been able to persuade New College to give him more of the endowed income, and clearly New College was now spending money on the School. The other significant change that helped revitalise the School's fortunes was the Grammar Schools Act of 1840 which made it lawful to use the endowment income for purposes other than the teaching of classical languages, although the change still required the consent of the schoolmaster. This released the grammar schools from the straightjacket of their statutes. Clearly Fookes assented to this.

Dr Thomas Broadley Fookes was born 1809 in Dartford, Kent, one of sixteen children. His father was an eminent barrister. In 1841 he arrived in Thame along with his wife Maria and three children – during their time in Thame another four were born. He had been educated at Winchester and then entered New College in 1828, aged 19; was a fellow 1828-34, B.A. 1833, B.C.L. & D.C.L. 1841. He met his wife in Oxford where her father was the Superior Beadle in Law at the university. However after their marriage, as Fellows were not allowed to take wives, he had to move out of College and was handed the curacy of a village in Kent. He was a man with a high academic reputation, a gifted musician and concert violinist to boot. On coming to Thame, he was also appointed the Curate of Stoke Talmage and Chaplain to Baroness Wenman.

Thanks to the reminiscences of Samuel Field, a pupil in the 1840s, we have some sense of what life at the School was like. Field was born in 1832 and his father owned a large farm outside Thame, although they lived on the High Street. He was one of eight children. By the time his memories were recorded, Field was an old man and they may not be entirely accurate. Nevertheless, from what we know from other sources, the picture he paints of Fooke's approach to education is likely to be substantially correct: a capable teacher but given to excessive and brutal punishment.

1843 I had just begun to learn Latin when I left Aylesbury but we [he and his brother Ben] were placed in the lowest form. Fookes was however too fond of sport and had besides too fiery a temper to make the school successful for long. He was a clever fisherman and very fond of driving his horses about. The Doctor was very severe on a stupid or idle boy. He would thrash them without mercy. I do not remember that he ever caned me but I have suffered from severe boxing on the ear. I have seen him often take a boy by the ear and lead him up the slope of his chair and send the boy rolling down to the floor by one box on the ear. Woolley [usher?] too was a savage fellow. He was not allowed the use of the cane. On one occasion he hit me on the head with the corner of his trencher cap [mortar board] and made my head bleed.

On another occasion, Field recalled:

A boy named Bell who once fought against a man in the cricket field who interfered with the game. I witnessed the fight and Bell had the best of it. He was caned by the Dr. in the presence of the whole school. I shall never forget the painful exhibition. Bell stood quite still with folded arms and never moved a muscle or uttered a sound while the Dr. thrashed him with all his might.

Around a year later, in 1844:

My brothers Spencer, Poole and Septimus were sent to Dr

Fookes' school around this time. He also received a prize from Fookes – Milton's Poems. After the prize-giving the Doctor called up my brother Ben and presented him with his old cane which was pretty well worn out by the work of the half year and Ben had been the best acquainted with it.

In 1846:

'I had progressed very well under Dr Fookes and personally had no cause to complain for I was never thrashed by him. My brother Poole, though an intelligent boy, was an inveterate gossip and not only neglected his own work but helped other to neglect their's. He frequently was caned and often in trouble with impositions. One day Poole had been very severely thrashed so that he was positively ill and at dinnertime he could not eat and looked the picture of misery. At last my mother broke the silence somewhat as follows: 'I must speak out. I am sure that poor boy has been beaten again by that inhuman Fookes. At this poor Poole began to whimper. He was examined and his little arms were found as Miss Squeers said "a mask of bruises". The flesh was broken in some places – he was at once taken in hand by my mother and, dinner finished, I was on my way to the school playground when my father called me back and being in a furious temper strode down to the school and had it out with the Headmaster, the result being that we were all taken away.

It was clear that Fookes' Christian beliefs did not stop him being a man of a violent manner. He gained a reputation in the town as someone who spent most of his time thrashing and expelling boys, playing the violin, and growing potatoes in the School's playground but, of course, a small town would thrive on such stories. This description appears in a number of books including Brown's *Short History*. Comparison with Boddington's early description of his experience at another Thame school indicates though that Fookes was not alone in combining competent teaching with excessive corporal punishment.

Yet, these were brutal times as we know from Dickens *et al.* Hangings were still public; and besides murder, people could be sent to the gallows for wounding, violent theft, arson, and sodomy. Courts could still order floggings for violent crimes. Transportation was common.

Nevertheless, Fookes's reputation for 'not sparing the rod' became well-known, and this probably explains why, across the 1850s, there was a steady decline in the number of pupils.

We know little else about school days at this time other than hints - to be found in Harry Lupton's history - of the attractions available to the pupils outside of school hours. Thame had many fairs but the one at Easter, which he called 'a pleasure fair,' when the local gentry would come to town in their carriages was particularly enjoyable. He writes also about being with a 'strong body of school-fellows in high glee around the bonfire and expending all their means in fireworks' on 5th November. And later he writes of 'four or five youngsters flattening their noses against that window and pointing with their fingers outside a shop for sweetmeats, and spread out before them are toffy, lollypops, bulls eyes, peppermint lozenges...'

He records too, a schoolboy prank: to take down the helmet that had once belonged to the Duke de Longueville, and which was now hanging in St Mary's Church. He had been captured by Sir John Clerke of North Weston during a battle that had been fought in France, early in Henry VIII's reign.

* * *

The death throes

Ten years after Fookes's arrival, the 1851 Census records the following present on the day the Census was taken: George Maudby an assistant master, Gustav Adolphus Weill styled as a Professor of Languages and born in Baden, and now only six boarding pupils: Duncan Robertson, born in Jamaica, George and Frederick Faber from the East Indies, and Richard Parker [most likely this was a transcript error and this was Richard Paxton] from High Wycombe. A descendant of Paxton contacted the school in 2018 and recounted that Paxton had lived at Green Hailey Farm, Princess Risborough, and that he had learnt Greek and Latin while at the School. This led in later life to him writing in both languages in his farm book.

The final two boarders were William and Walter Fookes, who were his brother's children. This brother was William Cacroft Fookes QC, a barrister, and the boys were aged 8 and 10 when sent to Thame.

In a series of reminiscences by Fookes's niece Isobel, she writes of visiting her uncle and his family who lived 'for years in the beautiful old house [the school house],' and how she 'spent many a happy time with them.' She describes him as man who enjoyed fishing, that he was a 'regular society man and very popular wherever he went.' She notes a visit by her and her uncle to Sir Thomas Bernard at Winchendon Priory where Sir Thomas played cello, and her uncle violin. He was fond of walking and would walk fifteen miles to Oxford to visit his wife's relations. It seems there was something of a Jekyll and Hyde about Fookes: out of the classroom a gifted, popular, even likeable figure; in the classroom a sadist.

The small number of boarders suggests that the terminal decline happened before 1851 as, while the Census would not have recorded day-boys and we have no idea whether it captured all the boarders, it is still indicative of numbers that at best had not grown to anywhere near the level needed to sustain the School. And presumably the two nephews were there as an act of charity by their father.

After 1847, Fookes failed to keep a record of registrations, which is indicative in itself of the state things. This lasted for ten years when in 1858 the Usher began to keep a record: in 1858 there were 8 boys on the book, all of them day-boys, the same number in 1859, 9 in 1860. Without boarders the School would have insufficient income to keep going.

According to accounts from the 1850s, conditions in the School were grim and its reputation at rock bottom. One long double desk ran the length of the dark, cold schoolroom across which two rows of schoolboys (if there were any) faced each other. In one corner was the usher's desk, where Barnes would sit and hear lessons. In other words the layout and fittings had remained largely unchanged since the School's foundation.

It was common for boys to be fetched out of School to do various jobs for their parents. Fookes was said to be never seen. With so few boys there were no games, but in any case the play area was now used by Fookes to grow those famous potatoes.

A contemporary letter in the recently launched *Thame Gazette* described the Grammar School as 'a richly endowed but comparatively useless Institution.' On another occasion, a reader wrote, 'The money goes not to educate the children of Thame but to provide a fine house and a sufficient income for some lucky fellow of New College.' (The master's salary was said to be now £200 per annum.)

By 1861, only Fookes and his wife, two children and three servants were living in the Grammar School. There were still no boarders; seven day-boys on the roll, dropping in 1862 to four, and to one in 1863 though briefly rising to seven in 1864. On the otherhand, advertisements in the *Thame Gazette* show that Fookes was holding public concerts in the schoolroom.

But things were looking up for Thame. The first trains came to the town in 1862 with four trains daily into London. In 1864, an extension to Oxford was completed. The railways had a positive impact: goods became cheaper, more produce could be both brought to Thame and carried away to the London markets. It was, though, still a town where agriculture dominated. Typical job advertisements at this time were for herdsmen, shepherds and wheelwrights, and many of the ads on the front page of the *Thame Gazette* were for products useful for farmers such as White Sheep Ointment, horse and cattle medicines, and something called Farmer's Friend.

In 1865, Fookes wrote a warm testimonial for one of the Field brothers:

> *Gentlemen*
> *Having been for a long time intimately acquainted with*
> *Mr Percival Field, both as a pupil at the school over which I*
> *presided, and also as a friend and neighbour, I have much*
> *pleasure in giving my testimony to his character and integ-*
> *rity. I have perfect confidence that in any employment he*
> *will be found diligent and throughly hard working.*

Percy Field had been expelled after he had endured a fearful beating after which he flung his text books at Fookes. However he had also been expelled from two other local schools. If he was an unruly child, he went on in later life to become a deeply respected member of the community in Thame.

In May 1866, the Taunton Assistant Commissioner, a Mr Fearon, convened a meeting in the Market Hall to find out what had happened to the School. In an earlier visit he had found only two boys on the register and only one present. This poor boy was examined for proficiency in reading, dictation and arithmetic and was found to be either bad or 'very bad.'

At the meeting, Fearon was told of 'the culpable mismanagement on part of the governors, combined with the total ineffi-ciency of the Master.' However, he also noted that the School was not alone in its sorry state though worse than most: Wit-ney Grammar boasted only 29 pupils and Burford 17, and he thought that endowed schools in smaller country towns did have a harder time to maintain numbers than their urban counterparts.

Fearon was one of a team who had travelled the country on behalf of a commission set by Lord Taunton to look at the state of the (mainly grammar) schools which lay between the great public schools (nine designated in the top tier with some twenty or so in a tier below) and those set up by the church or charities for children of the poor. The Government had recog-nised that in the industrial age schooling had to be improved - despite there being close to 800 endowed schools in various states of existence.

The Taunton Report concluded that in many of the endowed schools, 'the teaching was ineffective, and sometimes many of their resources were committed to teaching a few boys Latin. Many of them had ceased to be classical schools and had sunk to the level of poorly run elementary schools.' So Thame was not alone in its plight.

Specifically for Thame, Fearon reported that Fookes took no part in active teaching 'indeed in some years it can scarcely have been necessary that he should do so. Pupils were only learning reading, dictation and elementary arithmetic for which they add two guineas per annum to the master and one guinea to the usher.'

In 1867 and not for the first time, the services of an usher were dispensed with, which suggests that from that date no pupils were taught.

Despite the absence of pupils, Fookes continued to live in Thame and to draw his salary, but at some point during the next four years, probably after his wife died in 1867 and his children left home, he moved out of the School leaving it empty. In the 1871 Census, no boarders or masters were recorded living at the premises. Fookes was living in the alms-house along with four residents, and a servant. In the Census, he no longer gave his profession as a school master but a Clerk in Holy Orders.

Yet it was not just the School in a pitiful state - so was the parish church. The Rev J Prosser who was Vicar from 1841 - 1872 was said to be ineffective and the congregation dwindled. The sexton was reprimanded for drunkness in 1865, and on at least one occasion Prosser preached a sermon in his night shirt. Pigs were kept in a pen in the churchyard while a flock of 300 sheep grazed around the graves. A letter in the *Thame Gazette* in 1867 deplored 'the disgusting possibility of eating mutton fattened at the graves of our fathers.'

The whole town appeared to be in a sorry state. During this period, *Jackson's Oxford Journal* carried a weekly summary of cases that had been brought before the magistrates court. Usually they were charges of being drunk and disorderly, using threatening language, petty criminal damage, and a frequent number of cases of farmers or butchers selling bad meat.

In a calendar of public schools published in 1871, the entry for Thame mentions only Fookes as headmaster and fees of 3 guineas per annum. Yet it took four years after the last pupils left before the School closed.

Fookes retired to Hampstead on a pension of half his salary. Two years later, having moved to Clapham, he died and was buried in a single grave in Brompton Cemetery, his wife having been buried in Thame. Three of his sons had already emigrated to New Zealand, and one daughter to India.

It is clear that Fookes had made a good start after arriving at the School: he had secured the full endowment from New

College, overseen a building programme, recruited assistant masters, and increased the roll. On paper his qualifications were excellent. He came from a good background and had married well. Quite why it all went wrong is unknown. He clearly possessed a brutal, possibly sadistic, streak but it could be claimed that at the time this was not uncommon among school masters. Over the years he has been perhaps accused with little some malice and story has built upon story. Possibly he was not motivated by sadistic emotions but by an unwavering belief in 'spare the rod and spoil the child'. Obviously he took this to unacceptable extremes but through frustration at failing to get some of his pupils to learn rather than any deliberate desire to inflict pain. This may seem to be irrational behaviour by an obviously intelligent man but by no means unusual.

The final demise of the original foundation was also by no means only the fault of Fookes. As the Taunton Report concluded, much of the sorry state of endowed schools could be put down to the ineptitude of whatever body was overseeing the school.

> The interest felt by the governors or trustees, the care taken in appointing a master, the power of controlling him during his tenure of office, the ease or difficulty of removing him if he prove inefficient, are as different in different schools, as are the character and usefulness of the schools themselves. But while the proprietary school is framed to meet some felt want, and may be moulded till the want is met, the endowed school is in a large majority of cases hampered by obsolete or inflexible rules, and committed to the government of persons who are frequently unable or unwilling to give the requisite attention to its interests.

It is clear that New College was unfortunately one of these bodies that were not giving the 'requisite attention' to the School's health. From the somewhat rudimentary records it would appear that the Warden made no visitation to the School after 1861. Why? There is scant clue to this either. If they had paid attention then some corrective action could have been taken. Yet, does this unfairly malign the College? In the College's own history, we can read:

While not entirely a sybaritic, slothful backwater, New College was prevented by its medieval statutes from adapting to rising demand for university education. Having been the largest college by far in 1379, by 1800 it was one of the smallest, with at most 20 of the 70 fellows being undergraduates - all exclusively Wykehamist and dominated by 'Founder's Kin', real or pretended.

By the mid-19th century, Wykeham's statutes were out of step with the needs of higher education, and major reforms under new statutes in 1857 and 1883 started to create a recognisably modern college.

In other words it was not a thriving institution itself. Was that why it had withheld endowment income in the 18th and early part of the 19th century, using the funds instead to support the College in needy times? And in the middle of the 19th century was it focussed on sorting out its own problems, and so the issues in Thame were not a high priority?

The Commission report's comments about the superior quality of private schools applied to Thame. The decline in numbers was not just the result of Fookes's failure and New College's neglect. The School faced strong competition from local schools that had been established in previous decades to provide the kind of education considered more useful in an industrial age. In 1807 the Boarding School run by a Mr Jones was operating in Thame but the two most competitive were the Mansion House School that had opened in 1808, and the

Howard House School in 1841.

The Mansion House School on the High Street had been taken over by L. D. Hunt in the late 1830s, and extensive alterations were made which included new classrooms, boarding accommodation, two halls, a gymnasium, and swimming bath, facilities far superior to those offered by the old Grammar School.

The Mansion House School reopened as the Oxford County School in 1840. At the same time, the renamed Howard House Academy was teaching subjects such as history, geography, book-keeping, astronomy, land measuring, as well as more traditional subjects such as Latin and French. Pupils came from as far afield as Bicester.

In 1868 James William Marsh became the owner and headmaster of the Oxford County School, and the school was amalgamated with Howard House Academy. This new school offered instruction of a 'sound commercial character' and promised 'a practical commercial education'. Boys were prepared for the universities, the Civil Service, and especially for professional and business careers.

The combined schools continued to operate out of the Oxford County School's High Street premises 'warmed by hot water apparatus' and educated children between the ages of 6 to 18. It quickly gained a good reputation, took in around 150 pupils, and was noted for the annual charity banquet held for Thame's poor at Christmas.

The success of this institution had put paid to Fookes's claim that the reason he had no pupils was due to a declining population in the town. Indeed between 1801 and 1851 the population had increased from 2,100 to 3,200. The Commissioner had found that in 1866 the Oxford County School had 40 day-boys and 80 boarders and it was only 200 yards from the Grammar School. (He also noted that Aylesbury had 123 pupils, Wycombe 34 and Henley 129.)

It seemed in 1872 that the history of Thame School might finally come to an end, but the Taunton Commission's report, though highly critical of grammar schools, had recommended their reform not their abolition. It led to the passing of the Endowed Schools Act of 1869 that provided the machinery for a renaissance in grammar school education and which, eventually, was instrumental in bringing about the change needed at Thame; a change recognised nationally for, in a 1871 parliamentary debate supporting the extension of the 1869 Act, Sir John Lubbock mentioned the School to show just how necessary the original Act had been, 'At Thame, with an endowment of £300 a-year and two masters, there was only one scholar.'

For five years after the damning Commission report and the departure of the last pupils the governors did nothing. It was the Commissioners that finally took the initiative. In 1872, the Endowed Schools Commission stepped in and the governors were asked to close the Grammar School.

Phoenix-like, seven years later, a new Thame School was to arise from the ashes.

PART 2: THE SECOND FOUNDATION

CHAPTER 14: 1872-1879

IN THE 1870S NONE OF THOSE RESPONSIBLE for re-founding the School could envisage its long-term future; nor would they have been particularly concerned about it. Their concerns were more immediate; to re-establish the School and restore its badly damaged reputation. Both posed a considerable challenge.

The Endowed Schools Commission had been charged with re-organising such schools across the country, and by early 1873 they had produced an outline plan to open a new school in Thame. This proposed the establishment of a charitable trust headed by the Warden of New College, the Chairman of the Thame Poor Law Union Board of Guardians, assisted by ten governors.

At a rowdy Town Hall meeting in March 1873, Thame people came together to discuss the Endowed Schools Commissions Proposals. To summarise: there was much opposition. They wanted Thame to be able to elect four governors instead of two; they wanted Mr Wykeham and the Earl of Abingdon as *ex-officio* governors rather than co-optative. There was heated discussion about whether New College should now have anything to do with the School and instead its management should be left to the inhabitants of Thame. They objected to fees being set between £5 to £10 yearly, and instead suggested they should be between £4 and £6 at most. However even if parents were only charged 10s a quarter, it was thought this would exclude the children of labouring men who were earning 15s a week.

However it was also clear that there was little support for

schooling being free. One person said they were acquainted with the Scottish system and those receiving free education were the most difficult to manage and the most irregular in attendance.

Later in the meeting, the discussion began to contradict itself as there was argument over whether they needed a school such as the Grammar at all and might it be better to have a free lower and upper school. When someone shouted out 'The tradesmen of Thame don't want a boarding school' this was loudly clapped. It was then pointed out that Thame already had the National and British schools where pupils could be taught for twopence a week. (This was met with some 'hisses' from the audience.)

A later in the year, the Commissioners agreed to some of the points the townspeople had made: they increased the number of governors appointed by the town by one, and lowered the minimum tuition fees to £4.

The revised scheme did not meet with universal approval. It was still described in a letter sent to the *Thame Gazette*, as 'totally against the advantage which our townspeople in general ought to possess in the education of the rising generation,' and the fees proposed were considered 'too high to render any real service to the town, or to attract an adequate number of pupils.'

Another meeting was held in the Town Hall which drew the conclusion:

> *That in the opinion of this meeting the revised scheme...is very unsatisfactory; an Institution which by its benevolent founder, was intended to be a Free School, and was richly endowed by him for such purpose and at the present time having a yearly income of about £600, with a large accumulated capital not less than £8,000 or £10,000 the*

inhabitants consider that they are not being fairly dealt with...

Their numbers were largely correct and there remained an animosity towards the School that would linger for some time and into the first years of its new existence.

In 1874 the *Thame Gazette* commented while waiting for the scheme to be finally approved by Parliament:

Need we paint the deplorable picture of the empty school-house, not even at this time inhabited by a person to keep it clean, with a patrimony belonging to it so rich... Not a pupil has belonged to the school for years.

However in 1874 the Commission's scheme for the School's management was approved by Parliament. The charitable trust was formed, along with a new governing body formed of thirteen members including JW Marsh the proprietor of the rival Oxford County School. At this point, with the creation of this new governing body, New College's sole control ceased.

It was proposed that the school would take around 120 pupils including at least 60 boarders, with a seperate residence for the headmaster.

This led to the purchase of a new site on the Oxford Road at a cost of £1050, as it had been decided by the governors that the old site was unsuitable for the new school building – even though they had the opportunity to pull down the almshouse if they so wished. The *Thame Gazette* commented, 'in our opinion a more healthy or prettier spot could not be found in the entire neighbourhood.'

By 1876 the Oxford architect William Wilkinson had been engaged. His original plans were too costly and instead a rather sombre red-brick design was chosen with dressings of Bath stone, after the style of St Edward's School in Oxford that he had also designed.

Before work on the new school commenced in 1877 the Old School building was sold by auction to Mr PH Pearce for £1,710. He was later to open on the premises, a private school called the Old Grammar School. Also up for sale in a second auction was the Saracen's Head, which was described as comprising the inn, a garden, yard (with a pump and W.C.), and stabling, and the whole let at 'the extremely low rent of £17.'

Construction on the Oxford Road started with Messrs. Taylor and Grist of Aylesbury undertaking the work at a tender price of £6,095 – the money raised by the sale of government stock, the old school to Pearce, and a number of properties in Thame including the aforementioned inn, the Saracens Head.

The following appeared in the *Thame Gazette*:

> *The New Grammar School – since our last remarks relative to the erection of this pile, considerable progress has been made with the building, and for the information of those interested we may mentioned that the extent of the building proper will, we understand, be 200 feet by 160 feet, and it will stand in its own grounds of about 9 acres. There will be a well-planned master's residence, with all the necessary domestic offices; also separate and conveniently arranged apartments for a second resident master, a commodious schoolroom, classroom, dining hall and extensive, well-arranged and ventilated dormitories.*

> *The materials chiefly used in the building are a local red brick from the Hartwell brickworks and Bath stone, which harmonises exceedingly well; and we doubt not that when the whole is complete it will be a handsome and substantial structure.*

The location of the new school outside the town was also advantageous for the health of the pupils. In 1871 there were 16 deaths from scarlatina and Dr. Lee of Thame called in Dr. Buchanan. The latter found scarlatina decreasing, but reported most scathingly upon the sanitation of the town. There were no sewers, and no provision for excrement or refuse removal

The *VCH* wrote: Down both sides of the main street and in some bystreets ran roughly constructed open gutters, which received all manner of liquid house slop and other filth, notably washings from slaughter houses near the market. The gullies led into various ditches some of which ran into the Thame but most were stagnant.

[It would not be until 1900 that the town had a proper sewage system installed.]

However, within a year of a start being made, construction at the school was delayed temporarily when the workmen went on strike, hooting and throwing bricks at the clerk of works who had made himself unpopular by making what they believed were unfair complaints about their workmanship. This was quickly resolved.

That same year, five candidates were interviewed for the headmastership. George Plummer was appointed in November 1878 at an annual salary of £150 plus a capitation fee of between £2 and £4 per boy; this fee initially came to a total of £55. An allowance was made of £100 for the employment of assistant masters.

It had taken six years before the plan became reality. During that time the Oxford County School continuing to flourish, expanding with new buildings, and now had six resident masters, and two female teachers. Marsh had also opened a Preparatory Department for what he termed 'Little Boys' with fees of £8 per term and taught by a Certificated Mistress.

CHAPTER 15: A NEW BEGINNING 1879-1891

THAME SCHOOL REOPENED on 1st May 1879 on the Oxford Road site under the headmastership of George Plummer aged 32.

Plummer had been born in Penzance, Cornwall in 1847. His father was a beer merchant but other details of Plummer's early years are scant. We know he studied for a BA at London University and, by the age of 24 in 1871, he was already headmaster of Wellingborough Grammar School, a small school in the centre of the town. It had been founded in 1596 and, when Plummer was headmaster the roll was some twenty boarders and likely a lesser number of day boys. In short a small, market town school not dissimilar to Thame.

In 1873 he married Sarah Jane Pollard in Brighton, and a year later their first child was born, a boy who was given the name Edgar.

Plummer's appointment to Thame came just as Wellingborough was also moving into new larger buildings, on a 45-acre site on the edge of the town. Why he decided to leave at this pivotal point is unknown. Perhaps he believed that Wellingborough could not offer the same opportunity as Thame; difficult to understand as at Wellington was an established school with pupils, in a larger town with two railway stations, while Thame School was effectively starting from scratch.

But we do know that he hoped to achieve at Thame what the celebrated headmaster, Edward Thring, had achieved at Uppingham: to raise a small country grammar school to national importance. But as one of his first head boys would recall, Plummer was not a genius like Thring, just a very good teacher. (Whether a lack of 'genius' is a valid observation is open to question.)

Whatever Plummer's motives, he was stepping into the unknown with a weight of expectations on his shoulders.

Plummer was said to be a commanding figure with a large black beard. The latter is very evident in the photograph of him displayed in the present-day reception area at the school. His wife Sarah described him thus:

> *My husband was a very cheery and interesting companion...he was a good speaker and had a lovely voice. He was not a dandy but he was most careful and particular in his dress; nobody ever saw him untidy or slovenly and he always looked "well groomed" – his hands and nails were perfectly kept, this setting a good example worth copying to his boys...My husband was not short but being broad shouldered and inclined to be stout he did not look as tall as his height.*

Plummer, Sarah, and four children arrived at the School in early 1879, along with a number of pupils from Wellingborough who would now board at Thame. The School's roll in these first months is unknown, although forty has been claimed, and certainly by 1881 at least thirty five boarders were in residence.

Albert G Robinson - who was one of the pupils previously at Wellingborough - later wrote of the first few hours of the School's new existence:

> *The School buildings were brand new. The play shed was still unfinished. What afterwards became the Headmaster's garden was a tangle of green and weeds. There was no for-*

mal opening of any kind. We took our places, listened to a short speech by the Headmaster and were then gradually sorted into classes.

Plummer's wife Sarah was to write many years later:

We were both very fond of the school and took great pride in making it look its best. When we went to Thame it was just a building in a rough field, with the help of old Mr Walker, the florist, and James Rush our good gardener for twelve years, we saw everything planted and grow up, and when I left there was a flourishing fruit and vegetable garden, and lots of flowers in the beds around the house.

Annual fees for tuition of day boys were fixed at £6 while boarders paid an additional £35 which, by the middle of the decade, had risen to £42 per annum. The first assistant masters were Messrs. Mackenzie and King, with Mr RH Digby as a part-time music master. J Cole and HD Hodgson (who died the following year) were the first ever Head Boys; and J Harrison and Willey the first sports captains.

The year was divided into three terms of thirteen weeks each, and Plummer also organised the School into three sections: a Junior School, where pupils could be admitted at the age of 8; a Middle School, which was described as being for those whose ambition was to go into business; and an Upper School for those preparing to sit public examinations or to go to university.

In other words, the School had been organised into what we would still recognise as a modern institution that would endure little changed for nearly one hundred years.

One year later in 1880, the School's first cricket match was played on the newly levelled field: RSG High Wycombe was defeated by one run. (This is a fixture that continues to this day.) Masters were part of the teams and a boy called Crook 'made a lucky nineteen' for the School. A professional cricketer had been appointed to coach the team two days a week.

The Mercury, an eight-page school magazine, was published containing articles and stories, puzzles and gossip besides the usual school news. The price was rather high at 6d and the then editor Albert Robinson later recalled that 'there was always considerable difficulty in persuading boys to buy it.'

It was subtitled *The Chronicle of Thame Grammar School* and the first edition came out on Saturday 5th December with a request that boys should submit articles for the next edition that was due to be published at the end of January. They were advised that their submissions would remain anonymous. George Plummer had wrote an article on 'How we got our name' and two boys had described their adventures in the Far East, and a visit to the 'Factory of Krupps, of Essen.'

A rugby match was played against Linden House, a private school in Littlemore – Thame won but as Linden House was still a small school it was fairly noted that the opposition only had 'moderate capacity.'

Two years on, the 1881 Census records 35 pupils, all boarders. But as the Census was taken on a Sunday, the day-boys would have been listed at their home not at the School.

The Census only shows the place of birth and not where the boarders' families lived. A surprising number were local: Aylesbury, Long Crendon and Watlington for example. The furthest afield had been born in Turkey and Africa (the country unnamed), with others from the London area.

The two assistant masters teaching when the School opened had already moved on. Of the new assistants, we know only a little. Ivan Boynton was 22 and had been born locally in Watlington where his father was a GP. Boynton's appointment was only temporary as he later went to medical school and became a dental surgeon living in London. James Rochford was 27 and had been born in Ireland; and Christian Kortz who taught languages, while of Dutch heritage had been born in London. In a contemporary advertisement, Plummer wrote that there were 5 Assistant Master including a 'first class man from the University of Oxford for Mathematics.' This likely included two part-time assistants who came in to teach PE and music.

Boarders had to pay £14 per term, and the only extras were for optional Greek, German, and piano tuition. (NB: at the same time the Oxford County School was advertising their termly rates as £9 per term including books and laundress.)

In addition there was one House Maid, and four servants including James Rush the gardener.

Sarah Plummer wrote of this time:

> *We had a rather difficult first few years. Wellingborough was a large town with plenty of shops and we found Thame a very small place, only a few small shops and no competition so prices were high and supplies not good. We found it to our advantage to deal with a London store for most of the things we needed. Hence our unpopularity for a time. Afterwards I think we were forgiven and we had many kind friends.*

As noted in the previous chapter there was still a lingering anger from the townspeople, although Plummer in 1881 helped organise a concert in aid of the Parochial Band of Hope, and quickly established himself as someone who was willing to be involved with the town's affairs. A second concert was performed in 1882.

From one account by a pupil during the mid 1880s there were only about a dozen day-boys on the roll as many local boys who wanted a good education still went to the Oxford County School.

Half of the School's day-boys came not from Thame itself but from the neighbouring villages. However, during the later 1880s the roll increased only slowly if at all (though it is likely that it fluctuated from year to year.

In 1882, a report in *Jackson's Oxford Journal* of the School's prize-giving ceremony said that 55 boys were enrolled. In 1883 this had grown to 60 including boys from Abingdon, Aylesbury, Hastings, Kew, Leighton Buzzard, London, Oxford and Tring, as well as locally . In 1891, 56 were on the roll, of which 13 were day-boys. Down the road at the Oxford County School, the 1881 roll of 90 boarders including four teachers had almost halved ten years later to 48.

Stable numbers were matched by early academic success when Albert Robinson gained an open scholarship to Christ's College Cambridge, and William Eppstein to Corpus Christi. In fact a number of Plummer's pupils went on to be successful including William Church a highly regarded solicitor; Arthur Forbes became a judge and Resident in India; Wykes Gibbard rose to a Major General in the Army; Walter Burgess was a highly regarded ecclesiastical author, and Henry Mears had a distinguished career in the Civil Service, mostly spent in the Post Office, and ultimately was awarded an OBE.

Reflecting the School's rural location, Plummer also arranged that exams set by the Royal Agricultural Society could be taken and their scholarships applied for.

In 1884 soccer replaced rugger as the principal school sport, largely owing to the influence of a master Mr Buxton who had played for the newly formed Aston Villa. However the day-pupils played little active part in activities outside school hours – it was left to the boarders to fill the cricket and football teams – although this was to change gradually over the next few years.

Cricket absorbed much of the boys' energies in the summer as Plummer was just as happy to be on the pitch as in the class-room. One pupil wrote of, 'pleasant memories of long June and July afternoons of cricket – the small gathering of intent spectators, the white clad figures on the pitch, and beyond, the peaceful Oxfordshire landscape with the purple Chiltern Hills in the distance.'

They would also swim at Jemmett's Hole on the River Thame.

If daily work fell behind standard, the offenders were given a few hefty strokes on the hand by the Headmaster. Plum-mer was said to be generally a mild man but nonetheless was once summoned to the County Court for thrashing a day-boy, George Holloway.

Holloway presented his case for alleged assault. Plummer had accused him of rude behaviour towards a master when Hollo-way was playing cricket. He was then given the choice of either leaving the School or be thrashed. Holloway chose a thrashing. He was called into Plummer's study after which Plummer fas-tened the window, pulled the blinds down and locked the door. He took his gown off and told Holloway to take off his jacket. Plummer then struck him twelve times across the shoulders with his cane.

When Holloway returned home, he asked a servant to put some rags on his arms and shoulders. A witness, Dr Jones, said he had examined the boy and found six or seven weals on his back and bruises on his arms. The skin was broken, and Dr Jones said the blows were severe for someone of the boy's age.

Plummer won the case but the description of the beating sug-gests a facet of his character more akin to Fookes.

On the surface it seems unusual that a boy would bring a case against his headmaster but Holloway's late father had been a prominent solicitor in the town. Whether Holloway stayed on at School after losing his case is unknown but by aged 15 he had matriculated at Oxford University, and later became a schoolmaster living in the city.

Woodworking lessons were held in a nearby barn on Cox's Farm; two cottages on the farm were rented as living quarters for the assistant masters.

Bonfire night was always celebrated with a big fire, a barrel of tar in its centre, and a well-stuffed Guy atop; fireworks were bought by the boys from the ironmongers in town.

As there was no tuck shop, sweets were bought in Thame from Dunkin's, the confectioners on Corn Market or from May's, the boarders being allowed to shop once a week, no doubt still pressing their noses against the sweet shops' windows.

In 1885, the Plummer's suffered a blow when their eldest son Edgar fell seriously ill. The nature of the illness is unknown but come prize-giving the independent Examiner, the Rev H B George, Fellow of New College, said in his opening remarks, 'The impression which I derive from the whole examination, from the *viva voce* as well as from the papers, was that the boys were carefully taught, and that their performance as a whole was as good as could be reasonably expected, considering the circumstances.' This suggests that Edgar's illness had quite an effect across the entire School.

Sixty guests of the Headmaster had come to the School for the prize-giving and were giving luncheon. The ceremony itself started with a concert of music and the School's choir sang a number of pieces assisted by four singers from Magdalen College. Over the Plummer decade the number of talented singers and performers coming into the School from Oxford University increased, all organised by a Mr Franklin who was now in charge of music, and this can be said to be when the first shoots of the School's illustrious music capability appeared.

Prizes were awarded for Greek, Latin, Scripture, English, French, Mathematics, and Music as well as prizes for passing the Oxford Local Examination.

Plummer was able to attract around 20 to 25 new pupils annually, mainly boarders who were noted as coming from as wide a spread as London, Tring, Cirencester, Wolverhampton, Peterborough, and Plymouth. However he was having trouble keeping the boys beyond the age of fifteen and he often made appeals to parents to allow their sons to stay on for another year, hence the leavers tended to balance out the newcomers so that the School's roll did not grow substantially.

In 1888, the first Thame Show was held and the tradition of pupils enjoying a half day began. Plummer was much appreciated by the boys for his granting of surprise holidays and for some of his unorthodox ways: he would regularly declare the day before exams to be a holiday; he took boys to see Cup Ties in London; he would get the boarders together on wet Sundays and read stories to them.

Nicknames were *de rigueur*: Sharper, Sticky, Inky, Fatty, Nellie and Dollie, Bull, Tusky and Toddler were the stock-in-trade. One stunt was to ride down a series of steps on what was then known as a 'safety bike' with as big a series of bumps as possible. (Rovers, Premiers and Rudges were favoured makes.) Attempting to jump nearby Cuttle Brook was another craze. In hot summers, hurdles and sticks were used to make dens in the hedges at the side of the sports field. Another craze was putting coins on the rails at the level crossing for the trains to squash.

Sport continued to flourish; eventually the School was able to muster three cricket and three soccer teams. Opponents included some of the Oxford colleges such as Lincoln, Exeter, Worcester and Wadham, as well as RGS High Wycombe, Oxford High School and Abingdon High School. Football colours were originally half orange and half dark blue but these were changed first to shirts that were half red and half white, and then to dark blue shirts with the school badge. However there was no house system, nor any extra-curricular societies.

An interesting report appeared in Jackson's Oxford Journal, November 1890:

> *The celebration of the Fifth o' November took place on Wednesday last. An attempt at a 'guy' was paraded about the streets during the day, and early in the evening the customary fires and displays of fireworks took place on the grounds of Lord Williams's Grammar School and the Oxford County School. The proceedings however which took place later in the evening in the streets were anything but creditable to those who took part in them. Fireballs and lighted tar barrels were kicked about the streets at randon, and were followed by a hooting and reckless mob whose sole object not a rational celebration of the memorable Fifth, appeared to be a cowardly display of opposition to the police. The officers of the law and order, who were stationed at certain points in the streets were hooted, pelted at and submitted to treatment which, to say the least was disgraceful until past midnight.*

At December's Speech Day in 1890, Plummer said 'in no previous term had there been better health, better discipline, or better goodwill among the boys and masters.'

Sadly, only a few weeks later, on 8th January 1891, a boiler burst on the premises killing William John Ing aged 17, employed as a house porter. This came as a huge shock to Plummer; he paid for the funeral and also costs associated with the inquest that was held only a week later. (A transcription of the inquest can be found in Volume 2.)

It was claimed by Howard Brown that in this state of shock,

George Plummer died a few days later. However Plummer's widow refuted this many years later, 'I never considered that the shock was enough to cause his sudden illness and death.'

He did though die only two weeks after the accident on 23rd January, leaving behind his wife and four children: Edgar, George, Edith and Mary. He was buried with much pomp on the north side of St Mary's churchyard on 28th January, with the service being conducted by a former pupil from the early days, the 26 year-old Rev. John B Denchfield who was at that time a curate at St Jude's Camberwell - and by 1901 the vicar at St Luke's Church Bermondsey, where he remained until his death in 1925.

At Plummer's death, the School had grown to 57 boarders but still only 7 day-boys, a significant improvement from the period of decline but only fifty per cent of the building's capacity.

However, much had been achieved during Plummer's tenure: a syllabus covering seventeen subjects including four languages for example, although the syllabus had been laid down in the new statutes and was not Plummer's invention. However, his vaulting ambitions were never achieved. The endowment was small and no County Council or Government grants were then available. He had to borrow money to spend on the School as it was in debt from the very first day. The local people begrudged paying fees, and the existence of boarders continued to be resented in town. (These observations should be qualified by the thought that this was typical of townspeople wanting to find something to moan about.) The total number of boys was, in the end, too small to drive his ambitions.

It was said that he died both disillusioned and broken with little money left for his family. AG Robinson later wrote:

Before Plummer had been at Thame very long, it must

*have been clear to him that his ambitions could never be
realised. He died when he was not much over 40, leaving
his widow and children quite unprovided for. His old pupils
will always be grateful to him for what he did for them.
At the time of his headmastership the State was strangely
apathetic in regard to Secondary Education, and schools
which were trying to do work of value to the nation were left
to struggle on as best they could...Plummer was courageous
and self-sacrificing and who went on working hard though
life brought very little in the way of reward for his labour.*

Howard Brown provides a good account of Plummer's achievements and life during his twelve years as head, but his conclusions too are unduly negative and mirror Robinson's: 'He died,
while still a young man, disillusioned and broken.'

However Sarah Plummer disagreed with this assessment:

*I cannot think how the statement came that my husband
was a 'broken and disappointed man when he died.' His
was a most cheerful and hopeful disposition and we were
looking forward to the time when the debt on the school
buildings would be paid off and the governors would be able
to provide the extra classrooms and dormitories that were
necessary...I don't think Canon Robinson gave a fair impression of the School.*

After his book was published in 1927, Howard Brown realised
that he had misjudged Plummer and had been too swayed by
Robinson's point of view. In his *Additions and Corrections* published in May 1928, he provides a better balanced judgement.

*In spite of apparent failure, Plummer had much to look
back upon with satisfaction. He had found the school just
an empty building in a rough field; and within 12 years
had seen the grounds, gardens and fields got into order. The
number of day boys showed no sign of increasing, but the*

boarding accommodation was well filled; and a large pro-
portion of his pupils had, after university careers, reached
prominent positions in their various professions, while
their record on the athletic side was equally distinguished.
The School owes more than generally realised to his pioneer
labours.

Though Howard Brown was right to state that day-pupil numbers were not increasing, the three-to-one ratio between boarders and day-pupils was typical of grammar schools and minor public schools of the period, and not a problem. Given the difficulties of travelling every day to School beyond a comfortable cycling distance, even quite local families would make use of the boarding facilities for their sons. Furthermore, it was the boarders who brought in the bulk of the revenue. The health and continued existence of the School depended on maintaining or increasing boarding numbers rather than day-boys.

From Sarah Plummer's comment, it is also clear that the School was still paying off the debt from its re-founding, and the facilities that would allow it to expand had not come about. On the other hand, Plummer had certainly being successful in attracting pupils from across the UK as can be seen from the 1891 Census. The School's staff had also increased and there was now a cook, a matron, three housemaids, and three servants.

There is another factor too: because there was not a lot of money to spend on the School building, only one large classroom was built. While this could comfortably hold sixty to seventy pupils split into small teaching groups it did not make the School an immediately attractive place for parents to send their boys. To put this in some context, a new grammar school expecting a similar number of pupils (120), built in the same period on the edge of Stroud, a small town like Thame, was designed with six separate classrooms. They too had started with a similar building budget but having discovered it was insufficient the governors went out and raised more money. Plummer instead, compensated by using the dining hall but this was a make-do solution.

On 28th January 1891 the whole School attended Plummer's funeral and, as noted earlier, he was laid to rest on the north side of St Mary's churchyard. (Sadly today the grave appears lost.)

It is appropriate at this point to pause the narrative and consider the plight of the suddenly widowed Sarah Plummer. Her husband died, not only in office but during term-time. The School was rudderless, so in addition to all the stressful activities associated with bereavement and looking after her four no doubt traumatised teenage children, Sarah had to take over the School's running. The 1891 Census gives her occupation as schoolmistress, whereas ten years earlier no occupation is recorded. The Census was taken on 5th April a week after Easter, when 42 boarders were at still at the School, and so she had clearly taken over from her husband.

On 17th and 18th April an auction of goods belonging to George Plummer's estate was held at the School. These included furniture, 1500 books, linen, paintings, prints, dormitory fixtures and fittings, three pianos and a harmonium, a pony, a pony trap, lawn mowers, rollers, 29 hens, and the contents of the woodworking shop. This would underline that Plummer had invested his own money into goods for the School, and that understandably his wife wished that some of this be recouped.

Sarah's tenure continued until the end of the school year meaning she was head teacher for two terms, and although her tenure was short-lived she should, by rights, be included among the roll of head teachers, and recognised as the first of only two women in the role.

Following the appointment of Plummer's successor Benjamin Sharp, she left Thame, first to live in Hertfordshire and then

Essex, living on the pension that was ultimately provided by the Governors. She would outlive her husband by 45 years, not dying until 1935. She was buried not with her husband in Thame but at St Mary The Virgin, Lindsell, Essex.

Both of Plummer's sons were pupils at the School: one, Edgar, went on to become a doctor; George Seelie Plummer the second son, joined the Imperial Yeomanry and fought in the Boer War. He remained unmarried, and he and his mother shared the same house in Essex, as did one of the unmarried sisters. He died in 1928 while on a visit to Switzerland.

AG Robinson's Account of Life at the School

In this chapter Robinson has been quoted on a number of occasions and so it is worth adding here his full account of life at the School in those early days - remembering, of course, that his observations on Plummer have been disputed. This was published in the late 1920s.

'I have been asked to rummage in the recesses of my memory and to say what I can find time in regard to the re-opening of the School in 1879. I suppose this task has been assigned to me because I am probably the oldest of the boys who entered at that time. My recollection of what happened forty-seven years ago is not very reliable, but I will do my best.

It is well known to all friends of the School that in the early days of its history it produced men who in one way or another distinguished themselves. Among these were John Hampden of famous memory, Lord Chief Justice Holt, Anthony Wood the antiquary, and Dr. Fell, once Dean of Christ Church and afterwards Bishop of Oxford, whose name has been perpetuated in a well known rhyme. After their time the School failed to maintain its earlier reputation. It gradually dwindled away, and somewhere about 1870 it was closed. The income from the endowment accumulated, new buildings were erected, and on

May 1st, 1879 (I think I have got the date right), the School made a fresh start under the head mastership of Mr. George Plummer, M.A. He brought with him some eighteen of his old pupils, of whom I was one, and my younger brother, Augustus, now Vicar of Wantage, was another. These boys came for the most part from Northamptonshire. We arrived in the evening of a lovely spring day. For some reason we came by train to Aylesbury, where a brake from the Spread Eagle Hotel met us. I have still a clear recollection of our drive to Thame and of my first impressions of the place. The School buildings were brand new. The playshed (useful in wet weather, but certainly not beautiful) was still unfinished. The School field was a rough piece of ground, sloping down towards the railway. What afterwards became the Headmaster's garden was a wild tangle of rough grass and weeds.

On the day after our arrival school began. There was no formal opening of any kind. We took our places, listened to a short speech by the Headmaster, and were then gradually sorted into classes. During that first term there were some twenty-five boarders and about the same number of day boys, with three assistant masters so we were quite a small community. As I look back I realise what an awkward job the Headmaster must have had. The boys were of all sorts of ages, capacity and attainments. But all the same, from the outset the teaching was quite good. The Headmaster was young (somewhere about thirty, though his full beard made him look much older); he was ambitious and not afraid to see visions and dream dreams. His hope was to build up something on the lines of one of the older Public Schools, which was what our Founder had intended. Plummer used to speak to us sometimes of what Thring had succeeded in doing with a school of the same kind at Uppingham.

But Thring was a genius, a man of quite unusual power. Plummer was no genius. He was just a good teacher, with a great capacity for making boys work. Unfortunately he had few friends outside to back him. As the endowment was small, he borrowed money which he spent on the School, with results satisfactory to the boys, but in the end disastrous to himself. In those days there were no grants to be got from the Board of Education, and County Councils did not yet exist. Still, as I have already said, the teaching was good. Of the boys who were in the Sixth Form with me, some went to Cambridge, after winning open scholarships or exhibitions, and did creditably. One of them, Forbes, passed into the Indian Civil Service, then, as now, a distinction of some importance. I remember that I had excellent private coaching in mathematics, all at Plummer's expense. In those days at Thame, as elsewhere, hardly any science was taught, though a few of us learnt some field botany from one of the masters on the staff.

I was head of the School for three years. Among my contemporaries were WCH Church, who became a solicitor; Ralph H. Angier, who was partly French, and spoke French as easily as he did English and who became an engineer; WC Eppstein, afterwards Headmaster of Reading School; and AT Forbes, who was at Christ's College, Cambridge, before going out to India.

During the first summer after the reopening of the School we played cricket on the town ground. Later on part of the School field was levelled, but as the space was limited it was very easy to hit a boundary and very difficult to learn how to judge a catch in the deep field. A professional cricketer used to come over from Oxford to coach us on two days of the week. A few boys learnt to bat and bowl fairly well, but owing to the smallness of our ground we seldom made much of a show when we played matches away from home. Occasionally we played one of the smaller colleges at Oxford, when we generally got a good beating as reward for our presumption.

We played rugby football, but the School was too small to produce anything more than a team of very moderate capacity. A good deal of our energy went into School paper-chases. A favourite run was out to Princes Risborough and on to the Chiltern Hills. One of the remarkable things about the School in those days was the good health of the boys. I was never out of School for a single day, and during the whole of my time, to the best of my recollection, there was no case of serious illness.

We produced a School magazine, of which I was editor. I believe it came to an end soon after I left, and there was always considerable difficulty in persuading people to buy it. I am told that a copy of the first number has been lately discovered, but I hope for the sake of my own literary reputation that there will be no further discoveries of the same kind. We also ran a School tuck shop, a much easier and a more profitable undertaking,

There was always a man servant about the place, who did odd jobs for the School of various kinds. We played all sorts of tricks upon him, with the result that no one stayed very long. Whatever his name might be, we always called him Moses, but so far as I know there was no particular reason for doing so. I remember, too, that we were on very friendly terms with a dear old farmer called William Cox who lived just below the School, and from whom we used to buy eggs at sixteen for a shilling. On Sunday we attended the morning service at the parish church, and sat round the tomb of our founder in the chancel and in a vague sort of way we realised that it was our business to see that his hopes for the School were not frustrated. We boys only saw the members of the Governing Body at the annual prize-giving but have no doubt that they did their best for the School, but at that time their financial resources were very slender.

Before Plummer had been at Thame very long it must have become clear to him that his ambitions could never be realised. He died when he was not much over forty, leaving his widow and children quite unprovided for. His old pupils will always be grateful to him for what he did for them. At the time of his headmastership the State was strangely apathetic in regard to Secondary Education, and schools which were trying to do work of value to the nation were left to struggle on as best they could. I am glad to have this opportunity to give a small tribute to the memory of a man who was self-sacrificing and who went on working hard though life brought him little in the way of reward for his labour.

We lived a rough and tumble sort of life. When a school is in the making there are no traditions and no fixed rules. Socially we were a strange mixture, and every now and again there would be a furious row. But school life gradually took shape, and some of us received our first lessons in the important art of self-government, and were so fitted to take our place in that larger community life into which we passed when school days were over. Plummer certainly taught us not to be afraid of taking responsibility, to have the courage convictions and to be loyal members of the community in which we lived. Those are not bad things to learn, and a boy who learns them early in life is sure to have before him a career which is of some value to the neighbourhood in which he lives.'

❊ ❊ ❊

We also hold a second account of school life but this from an OT towards the end of Plummer's life.

'Reminiscences

Canon Robinson's notes dealt with the early '80's. I can add a few reminiscences of 1889-1890.

The School was then a much more highly organised community than it appears to have been in Canon Robinson's time. We had over fifty boarders and some twenty day boys: there were three cricket elevens and three football elevens (we played only soccer), but of course there were no Houses, nor did we have anything in the way of Camera Clubs, Natural History Societies, or a Cadet Corps. Mr. Plummer was a keen cricketer - cricket was in his blood - and the assistant masters (there were three resident) were also keen, and the general standard of play was good for a school of that size. We had regular 'rolling and netting' teams, whose job it was to go out before breakfast and see to the rolling of the pitches and the erection of nets. We played some of the Oxford Colleges including Lincoln, Exeter, Worcester and Wadham, amongst others and our visitors always expressed admiration for the pitches we prepared for them. There was a tradition that CB Fry once came over with a team from Wadham and was clean bowled by a boy named Endersby after making ten runs, but I do not know if this is true. [Charles Burgess Fry played for England at cricket and football, and turned out for the Barbarians too.]

We always had matches against Thame Club, who were too strong for us, and this led to the occasional importation of outside talent. Once we had a brother of one of the masters (Arthur J Skinner - who later moved to London to teach at Alleyn's, Dulwich), who was a demon bowler, and, with his help, we won that time. At another match we had two young Surrey professionals from Mitcham - probably obtained through the father of WA and AF Johnson, who lived at Mitcham. The names of these two pros. were Richardson and Sotherton: Richardson was a tall, dark young man, and I have always wondered if he was the famous Surrey bowler, Tom Richardson, of later years. Anyhow, he did not get many wickets, but made a few runs in a cheerful and enterprising style.
We played the Royal Grammar School, High Wycombe, Oxford High School, and Abingdon High School. The last was an enjoy-

able match, as we drove from Thame to Abingdon in a 'Spread Eagle' brake; our coachman was always a real Dickensian character whose name, I regret to say, I have forgotten. Mr. Plummer himself played occasionally: he was a fair bat, and bowled a slow round-arm round-the-wicket ball. He used to remind me a little of Dr WG Grace. He would trot up to the wicket, a big man, big black beard blowing each side of his face, so that the batsman would be a little puzzled by the deceptive lobbed-up ball that was delivered - he had been led to expect something very different.

Cricket seems to have absorbed all our energies and interest each summer term: I think that many an OT working in the city or going about his daily tasks at home or abroad, must have pleasant memories of long June and July afternoons of cricket - the small gathering of intent spectators, the white-clad figures on the pitch, and beyond, the peaceful Oxfordshire landscape with the purple Chiltern Hills in the distance.

We were fairly good at football, too, the chief stars' being BO Corbett (right wing; later an Oxford Soccer Blue) and HH Mears (full-back; later in the Civil Service XI). Football colours were originally an old-style jersey, half orange and half dark blue - very picturesque; later on, this was changed for shirts, half red and half white, and then we had dark blue shirts with the school badge on the left breast. For cricket, we had a striped blazer and cap - dark blue, a light blue, and chocolate.

Canon Robinson's memory must be a little at fault about the playing field. He speaks of it as sloping down to the railway line, but this should be to the lane that in those years was just as much of a morass in winter as I found it at the end of 1925! Old Mr. Cox's carts and cows used to cut it up then; nowadays the carts and cows may be different, but the owner's name is still, I think, Mr. Cox - a pleasant instance of continuity in a changing world.

Safety bicycles had begun to appear, and several boys had them. One of the favourite stunts was to ride down the three shallow steps at the end of the terrace with a series of glorious bumps - but those old solid and cushion-tyred Rovers and Premiers and Rudges' never seemed any the worse for this or kindred exploits.

Mr. Plummer had that great asset for a schoolmaster - personality - and had he lived he might have realised a good many of the ambitions of which Canon Robinson speaks. He was never afraid to do rather unorthodox things; e.g., the day before an important examination he would declare a holiday and take the boys concerned for a long ramble; or he would select a few boys and take them up to London to see a Cup-tie at the Oval - Preston North End v. West Bromwich Albion was one of these. And I remember very well how, late in the afternoon of a wet Sunday, when we were all noisy and restless, he gathered the whole school together in the schoolroom and for over an hour held us spell-bound with a reading from Great Expectations as much a tribute to his personality and influence as to the genius of the author.

He was a very good German scholar, and had devised his own method of teaching German, which was most successful. He was a good classical scholar as well, but I fancy his opinion was that a good grounding in modern languages would be more useful than the classics to the average boy who came to LWGS. There was no tuck shop at the school, but Dunkin (baker and confectioner) and May (sweetshop) supplied our wants. One of Dunkin's specialities was leathers - flat, round covered-in pies filled with gooseberries or rhubarb or some other fruit. They cost one penny each, and were very good and satisfying. Cherry turnovers were another dainty - they required to be eaten carefully so that the juice was not spilled down one's waistcoat.

Nicknames were universal - I suppose that every boy who entered the school acquired a nickname of some sort sooner or later (generally sooner), and very apt some of them were. The stock names, Sharper, Sticky, Inky, Fatty, and a girl's name or two - Nellie or Dolly - were always fitted to someone, whilst Boko, Bull, Tusky, Toddler, Eyes, etc., described some personal characteristic. Some of these nicknames, given in a boy's early school days, stuck to him long after he had left Thame. A clergyman named Bowley, who came over from Oxford to teach some special subject was immediately christened Holy Bowley, whilst a carpenter who held a class in woodworking was always Botcher.

These classes were held in a barn belonging to one of the cottages opposite Cox's farm; the School rented these cottages as quarters for two or three assistant masters. I cannot remember the odd job man Moses, of whom Canon Robinson speaks, but we had as gymnastic instructor a most excellent man named Sergt. Cleaver, who was always called Jickner - why, no one ever seemed to know. Later on, he went to Felsted School, where one of the assistant masters of about the same time also went; his name was GG Fraser.

As in Canon Robinson's time, we were a healthy lot, except for epidemics of mumps and measles. The sick room for occasional cases was on the north side of the house, close to the matron's room, and I recollect watching from the window several young foxes at play in the field on the other side of the road.

There were the usual crazes that start in schools for no particular reason and then die out. Once it was jumping Cuttlebrook on Sunday afternoons: someone usually fell in, and as we had our best clothes on there were minor rows about it. During one very hot summer it was the fashion to get hurdles and sticks, and with rugs to make dens down the hedges at the side of the field. We used to go in gangs of four or five, take books and little stores of tuck, and stay in the dens as long as we were allowed to. Another craze was putting knicknacks on the rails at the level crossing for the trains to squash. One boy once put a sovereign on the rail - it was decidedly flattened. Mr. Plummer heard about this, and finally gave the boy another sovereign and wore the squashed coin on his watch-chain.

One of our usual walks was to Scotsgrove Hill. Scotsgrove House was then occupied by Mr. Joseph Franklin - a real old-style gentleman farmer. The grounds of the residence were beautiful, and there were and no doubt still are some magnificent trees in them. Mr. Franklin was one of the School's Governors for many years, and was a familiar figure to several generations of Tamensians. November 5th was always celebrated by a big bonfire with a barrel of tar in it and a well-stuffed Guy,' and was a great event, for the junior boys at any rate. We saved up for weeks beforehand to buy fireworks, which were sold by the ironmongers - Ponting's or Kirby's were the proprietors. There was a tradition that 'roughs' from the town used to come up on bonfire nights looking for trouble. I believe there were a few encounters, but, as far as I know, nothing very serious.

CHAPTER 16: BENJAMIN SHARP 1891-1899

REPLACING PLUMMER was Benjamin Sharp, who had taught at Lancing, Bradfield, and Loretto before becoming head-master of Hawarden Grammar School. He was a graduate of Brasenose College, Oxford where he matriculated in 1871 with an Open Scholarship, obtained his BA in 1876 and an MA in 1878. He was also a talented oboe player and a believer in the importance of musical education in schools. He was appointed as the new headmaster in September 1891 at the age of 37, beating six other candidates who were interviewed by the governors in Thame Town Hall. Among the candidates was EP Guest, a teacher at the School, and RW Batho who had taught maths a few years earlier but was now teaching at St Paul's School in Kensington, London. In total, 90 applications had been received before it was reduced to seven.

Sharp arrived with his wife Alice (née Crick), and three children. Two more would be born while they lived in Thame. He was a Lancashire man, having been born in Warrington in 1853 but his father, a chemist and druggist, had been born in Oxford. By the time Sharp was 18, the family had moved to Ipswich where his father had established another retail business.

Sharp's headmastership was at best undistinguished, at worst potentially fatal to the future of the School. In his *Short History*, Brown devotes a mere nine lines to Sharp's eight years as Headmaster but expands on this in his continuing history chapters in *The Tamensian*. Howard Brown describes him as 'a soft voiced, smooth mannered man who 'saw difficulties' in every proposed innovation: an able scholar who had perhaps mistaken his vocation in becoming a schoolmaster' and this was reflected in the popular riddle 'Is B sharp A flat?' He was far from unique in resenting the visits of school inspectors but this hostility did not do him any favours. Like his predecessor and his successor, he had to cope with financial difficulties but with less success than either.

If the School was to remain financially solvent it had to overcome the inadequacy of the endowment fund and increase the numbers, from the eleven day boys and 47 boarders that were on the roll when he arrived.

In early 1891 Oxfordshire County Council (OCC) had been asked by the governors for a grant so they could increase the provision of science teaching. But in their first attempt to ascertain what they would be willing to pay, OCC had been thwarted because Plummer in their words 'was seriously ill and unavailable.' Fortuntely the next year, with Sharp at the helm, they agreed to pay £12 per quarter for the instruction of science. Burford Grammar School was awarded £37 per quarter; they were the only two grammar schools in the county to be granted money.

Unfortuntely Sharp struggled. (Although the sports teams were doing well under Mr Frazer, and Oxford Colleges were beaten in both cricket and soccer. One of the players, AL Corbett later gained an Oxford Blue playing soccer, and a place in England's national side.) Far from achieving growth, the numbers declined despite extensive advertising in *Jackson's Oxford Journal* year after year and in the national press including *The Times* and *The Guardian.* The Governors made efforts to economise, for example by reducing the salaries of assistant masters but the savings were not enough to balance the loss of income. They even reduced the fees for the younger boys so that they were now £2 per term for day-boys and £10 to £12 for boarders in the hope that this would be outweighed by increasing numbers. This had no impact either even though it was no more expensive than grammar schools of a similar size. Indeed in 1895, it was noted that boys were passing through the School rapidly - joining but not staying for too long. Nothing but outside aid could save the School.

The Bryce Commission Report of 1895 led to the establishment of the Board of Education, and the setting up of Local Education Authorities at the county level to 'supply or aid the supply of education other than elementary'. Subsequently, the Governors applied to the County Council for LWGS to become a School of Science. This would bring in extra revenue by way of a grant. True to form this was opposed by Sharp but the Governors over-ruled him. As a classicist, Sharp was opposed to new educational initiatives and particularly disliked science, which was in the process of becoming an accepted part of the curriculum. According to Brown, Sharp resented completing the reports that he had to make in order to receive the annual grants to help with teaching, and he could only foresee further work if LWGS became a School of Science.

Despite Sharp's opposition, the County Council made a grant of £650 to build science laboratories. Once built, they were opened in 1897 by Sir William Markeby, a Fellow of Balliol College, and Chairman of the Oxfordshire Technical Instruction Committee. Besides science facilities the accommodation included a 'manual' room for woodwork.

The rooms were only designed to accommodate some 16 boys at a time and became seriously overcrowded when numbers later increased. Of the School's first science master, FC Britten, and its woodwork instructor, RJ Escreet, little is known, though the work of the latter, to quote Howard Brown: 'was very favourably reported on while the teaching ability and technical skill of his successor, EF Lay 1899 to 1921 will be remembered with gratitude by many generations of Tamensians.'

As noted earlier the County Council were already paying for the services of science master but initially he was part-time and came into the School only one day a week. Further grants of £50 a year were used in part-payment of an art master, and for various pieces of equipment.

This support from the County Council led the Chairman of the Governors to remark in 1898 that 'in the near future Lord Williams's Grammar School might be more closely connected with the County Council who would supervise the school rather than the Charity Commisioners.' He thought this would be a step in the right direction.

The improvements to the curriculum failed to stem the fall in pupil numbers. The roll dropped to below 40. By 1899 the total number of pupils in the School had plummeted to 22. If the numbers dropped below 20, the County Council advised the Governors that they would cease paying any further grants. Said one member of the County Council, 'I was very disheartened to to find that the school of science was getting down below the limit which the Board of Education recognised. They would not recognise a school as a school of science with less than 22, and that school got below 20, and that became a very serious thing, because in wisdom the Board of Education paid high grants for that kind of education.'

In April 1899, the Governors 'considered it of advantage to the School that Mr Sharp should tender his resignation.' They resolved to give Sharp 'a satisfactory testimonial to his conduct.' Then, as now, headmasters were the whipping boys if numbers fell in independent schools.

He went to a housemastership at Reading School – taking 12 of the 22 pupils. He had brought the School close to extinction. Sharp is certainly open to criticism but not for taking the boarders with him. Though this might seem sharp practice today, that would be to misunderstand the respective roles of headmasters and boarding housemasters in 19th century independent schools.

In the large public boarding schools the housemasters were powerful 'barons', responsible for recruiting their own pupils, subject only to the pupils passing an, often nominal, entrance examination. Housemasters received a significant portion of the school fees in return for providing board and lodging. Headmasters were responsible for the school's academic provision. In smaller schools such as LWGS, the headmaster was also the housemaster and it was not unusual if he moved schools for him to take some boarders with him. Brown recounts how Plummer had done just that, bringing no less than 18 boarders with him from Wellingborough. So Sharp was certainly within his rights in removing the boarders but he would have been aware of the financial jeopardy in which he placed his successor.

A year after he left, the governors reimbursed Sharp for the not inconsiderable sum of £24, which he had personally spent on the Science School.

His later career was said to be undistinguished although in 1902 he wrote a paper on *The Neglect of Music in English Education* and gave lectures on the topic. One reviewer wrote that it 'was an interesting paper and much appreciated by the audience'. In1905 he was appointed as a Lieutenant by the Royal Engineer (Volunteers) to help run the school's cadet corps.

By 1911, he had left Reading School and was teaching music privately. He died in 1929, having spent his last few years in the Marlborough Nursing Home, Reading. He left a not inconsiderable £6473 14s 9d to one of his daughters, Alice, a spinster and music teacher, who had lived with him following his wife's death.

Sharp's reputation amongst contemporaries was not wholly

negative. The appreciation in the very first issue of *The Tamensian* was polite, brief although noticeably lacking in any reference to his achievements:

> *To Mr Sharp, who has so courteously presided over the School during the last eight years, may his new work be in every way a pleasure to him, and may he always retain a warm corner in his heart for Thame School, which will always be ready to welcome its old Chief of Staff.*

Indeed he seems to have remained on good terms with the School, for after he left - and a few years later - he was invited to attend an Old Tamensians's dinner where his successor was also present.

Quite why the School failed to thrive under Sharp is an interesting question. The Warden of New College remarked at a Speech Day in the early 1880s that the decline of the School prior to it being closed was due to the unsuitability of the 'old Winchester College system' to the wants of a grammar school in the 19th century. (As described in a previous chapter, this was only a partial truth; his predecessors' neglect of their governing duty had also played a major role.)

He went on to say that the School under Plummer now had a broader curriculum that 'afforded opportunity to all boys who could profit by a gain of knowledge of all the subjects taught in the best English schools.' Clearly, however, the provision of a more relevant curriculum, while moderately successful during Plummer's time had not ultimately led to a dramatic or sustained change in the School's fortunes.

The perilous state of LWGS at the end of the century was far from unique. In Thame, the County School too ran into difficulties during the last two decades of the 19th century. James Marsh who had founded the school died in 1883; his son JW Marsh who succeeded him committed suicide in 1888 because of financial difficulties. The school was then sold on to Thomas Gardner. As already mentioned, it was losing boarders at an unsustainable rate during the 1880s and, by the middle of the next decade, Gardner had left and set up a school in Weston-super-Mare. The new principals were named as CH Hulls and Son.

Secondary education as it is now defined was not compulsory during Sharp's headship. Pupils from Thame and the surrounding villages were required attend what was known as elementary schools until the age of 14: the British School and the National School in Thame, and various village schools, such as those in Chinnor and Long Crendon.

Most pupils were not sufficiently academic to attend a grammar school; the parents of others saw no need for their children to remain in education. Consequently, the pool of young teenage day-pupils continuing their schooling was small, which partly explains why so few day-pupils were admitted to LWGS in the late 19th century.

As for boarders, with improved transport, middle class parents could send their children anywhere across the country, so competition for boarders was not just between LWGS and local schools but with schools nationally, and this was as fierce as ever if not more so. In particular the big private (or public) independent schools were now well established and wealthy families were prepared to pay for their superior facilities. This was a decade when many under-funded small grammar schools, despite remedial action by the Taunton Committee, remained unattractive to parents.

Contemporary educationalists were aware of this situation. In 1895 James Bryce had been asked by the Government to relook at the state of the endowed schools. One of his conclusions was that despite the reforms of the last two decades, many grammar schools remained financially insecure, with some suffering fluctuating pupil numbers, while others were in a state of terminal decline. This was mainly, concluded Bryce, due to poverty within their catchment area, but other factors included geographical position, the inefficiency of some head-masters, and growing competition from the newly introduced higher grade schools.

The collapse of the grammar and private schools in Oxford-shire matched the national picture. Of the endowed schools that existed in Oxfordshire at a similar time to LWGS's founda-tion: Adderbury, Steeple Aston GS, Chipping Norton, Dorches-ter and Ewelme had been converted to elementary schools; St Johns Banbury, Bampton, Bicester, Charlbury, Nixon, Wat-lington, Williamscot and Woodstock had closed; only Burford, Henley, Magdalen College School, LWGS, and Witney remained open. In this context, Plummer's success in maintaining num-bers appears all the more creditable, and Sharp's failure to do so more explicable. It required considerable effort on the part of a grammar school headmaster in the 1890s to buck the trend. Sharp did not make that effort and when he departed a second collapse in thirty years seemed a real possibility.

It is not over-dramatic, therefore, to say that when the Rev. Alfred Edward Shaw was appointed Headmaster in 1899, aged 38, this was a final chance for LWGS. The challenge that faced Shaw was formidable: when he arrived, there were only six boarders and twelve day-boys.

On a final note before closing the century, pupils from Thame still went on to achieve success despite the issues that the School faced. In one of the classrooms, an honours board was mounted under a window to record some of the pupils who made a significant contribution at School, including academic and sporting. The list and their achievements in later life is below:

- Albert Gossage Robinson. Head Boy. Scholarship to Christ'

College, Cambridge. 22nd in list of those awarded First Class Honours in Mathematics at Cambridge. Entered the Church of England, and ultimately became Canon and Cathedral Treasurer at Winchester Cathedral.

- Ralph Haynes Angier. Construction engineer.

- William Henry Christian Church. Head Boy. Successful solicitor who practised in Newcastle upon Tyne.

- William Charles Eppstein. Head Boy. Scholarship to Corpus Christi, Cambridge. Entered the Church of England and became Rector of Lambourne but also taught and was headmaster of Reading School.

- T C Wykes (Thomas Wykes Gibbard). Head Boy. Durham University to read Medicine. Pioneer in treatment of syphilis. Major General in the British Army. After retirement Commissioner of the Royal Hospital Chelsea.

- Arthur Trevor Forbes. 1885 Christ' College, Cambridge. Selected into the elite government Indian Civil Service. Postmaster-General, Madras, Resident, and judge.

- Harold Kislingbury. Became a mercantile clerk after leaving school but died aged 29.

- John Schultes Dodwell. Head Boy. Farmer, and later hay merchant.
- William Charles Kislingbury. County cricketer. One of the founders of the OTA. He became a teacher.

- Edgar Curnow Plummer. London University (Medicine), and subsequently practised as a doctor.

- Henry Herbert Mears. Head Boy. City of London Imperial Volunteers (CIV) (Boer War 1899-1902), later awarded OBE for services to the Post Office

- John Arthur Mears. Head Boy. Chartered surveyor and estate agent.

- Arthur Vernon Kislingbury. Architect and surveyor

- Henry Herbert Dodwell. 1897 Exhibition studentship at St John's, Oxford (History). Professor of History and Culture of the British Dominions in Asia at the School of Oriental and African Studies.

- Walter Sydney Harris. Entered the Civil Service. Killed in the battle of Cambrai.

- George Ernest Shrimpton. One of the founders of the Old Tamensians's Association, and a solicitor.

- Sydney Robert Tanner. Head Boy. Chief Examiner, Inland Revenue.

CHAPTER 17. THE SHAW ERA 1899-1920

THE SOURCES FOR THE SHAW ERA ARE VOLUMINOUS. Both the admissions register and the School's magazine *The Tamensian* begin at the turn of the century, as does the staff register. In addition to the School archives, one author's connection by marriage with the Shaw family means that written, oral and photographic evidence about the family is available to supplement the more formal school records. The former provide the official history, the latter, together with *The Tamensian* and the memoirs of a teacher from Shaw's time, George Moss, provide a more informal glimpse of school life at the time.

❋ ❋ ❋

The Shaw family

Enter Alfred Edward Shaw – and family. It might be thought irrelevant in a school history to describe the headmaster's family. Not so in this case. Every member of the Shaw family played an important part in the School's history. Between them they provided three teachers, two pupils, the *de facto* head of the boarding house, and three OTs – the anomaly is explained below. The two boys, Donald Patrick and Edward Brian (known as Brian) were pupils who had distinguished school and later careers. Patrick was Head Boy for two years from 1905 to 1907. He gained a respectable degree at Oxford and proved a successful oarsman before following his father into the teaching profession as a master at the prestigious Westminster

School, from where he enlisted in 1914. His war career was truly remarkable and is recounted in a different chapter. He returned to teaching in 1919 and looked set for a glittering career as a schoolmaster but died of his war wounds in 1924.

Brian was extremely clever but wayward. While at LWGS he won a scholarship to Westminster School and completed his schooling there. His father wanted him to read 'Greats' (Classics) at Oxford so he elected instead to study mathematics at Cambridge. A brilliant shot, he captained the University Rifle team, left with a first-class degree, secured a much-coveted place in the elite Indian Civil Service and married the school doctor's elder daughter, almost as intelligent and as wayward as he was. Unsurprisingly, in this 'diamond cut diamond' situation, the marriage did not last for long and Brian's later career did not live up to its early promise.

The two girls, Margaret and Dorothy, both taught at LWGS, though only as what would now be termed supply teachers, and in the case of Margaret only briefly pre-university and for a short period in the spring of 1915 before a second spell at Oxford. She was a female version of Brian, equally bright and not a slave to convention. Having studied modern languages at St Hugh's Oxford from 1910-13, she gained the equivalent of a first-class degree in her finals with distinction in colloquial French. (Until 1920 the university did not recognise women's degrees.) After university she spent a year as an *assistante* in the École normale supérieure de jeunes filles, at Sèvres, returned to Oxford for a year on a Gilchrist Educational Scholarship, presumably to do research, and another year teaching at Bradford Grammar School before returning to Oxford for the third time as a tutor at St Hugh's.

She lived openly with a male colleague who was not her husband, resigned her post in protest at the College's ill treatment of another colleague, became one of Her Majesty's Inspectors of Schools, one of the very small number of formidable women inspectors, again resigned for reasons unknown and ended her educational career as a modern languages teacher at Repton independent school. Her academic career continued to flourish and she became a well-known translator of French poetry for Penguin Classics. Her obituary in St Hughes Chronicle read: 'Her warm heart and robust humour endeared her to her students, who valued her as a tutor and whose friendship with her lasted to the end of her days.'

The youngest child, Dorothy, though she lacked the brains of her older siblings, arguably had the greatest impact on the School's history in a variety of ways. Just six years old when the Shaw family arrived in Thame, she spent most of her youth in the 'private side' of the boarding house alongside the boarding boys. Debarred by her sex from being a pupil, she nevertheless seems to have been treated as an honorary boarder. *The Tamensian* for 1906 cryptically describes a school outing with 'a certain D Shaw'.

Dorothy's younger daughter Pam later described an incident in her mother's youth:

> *Dorothy was very pretty and (innocently) flirtatious. No doubt living in a house full of growing teenagers she was made a pet of. Her father found her sitting on the knees of an 'old boy' (not a boarder!). He promptly packed her off to boarding school.*

Like so many of the best stories, this one has suffered from Chinese Whispers over the years. Dorothy did indeed go to boarding school, St Elphin's in Darley Dale, a school for the daughters of clergy. However, she went as a sixth-former aged 16. If there is any truth of her sitting on the knees of an OT a couple of years older than her, it seems unlikely to have been an innocent flirtation.

Her absence from LWGS during term time for two years may

have helped her to gain credibility on her return in 1914 when she became a teacher of the youngest pupils and filled-in at various times later during for the war years for absent staff.

On 11th January 1917, aged 21, she married The Reverend Edward Arnold Fitch, 15 years her senior and at that time an army chaplain, who continued to serve after the war. Consequently, he and Dorothy spent much of their lives together abroad on various foreign postings but had returned to live in Taunton by 1939.

On her husband's death in 1965, Dorothy moved to London and re-established links with the School. Her daughter Pam drove her to several Thame reunions. Once again after some fifty years, she became well known in Thame. She was elected as the first female honorary Old Tamensian and attended the President's dinner in February 1976 as the oldest OT. She died in 1982, having witnessed a school that had grown from 22 to over 2000.

Shaw's wife Henrietta, Harriet to her family, also played a crucial role in the School. Not only did she have responsibility for looking after the boarders and running the boarding house, if family tradition is to be believed, she had an important role in calming her somewhat irascible husband. Shaw was undoubtedly a strict disciplinarian and a strong believer in the retributive importance of corporal punishment; he tended to over-react to incidents of relatively minor pupil misbehaviour. Shaw's granddaughter Hilary described how Henrietta prevented her husband from becoming a Fookes:

Shaw was very excitable and hot tempered. His wife was placid, warm-hearted and motherly, and she did her best to calm him down. She made him keep his cane, or birch, in a separate place [from his study] so that it took him some time to fetch it when he wanted to whack a boy, and this gave him time to calm down.

So Henrietta was not the formidable figure that she appears to be in the photographs. Rather, she was a kind of foster mother, particularly for those pupils who would seldom get to see their parents living in the far-flung corners of the British Empire. Some of them would spend the whole of the academic year in Thame, and only return home over the summer holidays; some might not return at all.

Initially, her task in running the boarding house would not have been onerous, with only six boarders to look after and with seven domestic staff to assist her, not including the governess who presumably looked after young Dorothy, but that was soon to change as recounted below. The evidence about the troubles and trials of running a boarding house described by Marion Goodall two generations later in Volume 2 would no doubt have applied equally to the challenges that Henrietta faced. Nevertheless, she had a life beyond being the wife of a head - and housemaster. Hilary described her as 'a strong personality, practical but with an Arts and Crafts bent. Her hobbies were woodcarving and embroidery.' An example of the latter, a handkerchief sachet, was presented by Hilary to Thame Museum in 2009.

✻ ✻ ✻

Dr Alfred E Shaw

And what of Alfred Edward, Edward to his family and the Reverend Shaw or later Dr Shaw to everyone else? First and foremost, he succeeded where Sharp had failed in similar circumstances. Almost the last words of Howard Brown's *Short History* read:

> *… on the arrival of the Reverend AE Shaw in 1899, there*

were but 22 boys, six of them boarders, and dormitory II was being used as a lumber room. Within a year, the numbers had increased to 72, half of them boarders.

The clue to Shaw's success lies in a characterisation that Howard Brown gives in his continuation history chapters some twenty years after Shaw left:

Shaw was a head of the old type, now almost extinct: an enthusiast who never spared himself where the School was concerned, and who in consequence performed himself many duties now generally left to the other masters: and above all an autocrat who liked to retain in his own hands control over all school activities.

So it was Shaw's energy, determination and willingness to 'go the extra mile' that enabled him to succeed in rescuing the School. In a sense, thousands of extra miles when it came to advertising for boarding pupils. Whereas Sharp had advertised in London papers with little success, Shaw placed advertisements in British papers overseas.

1900 was the high watermark of British imperialism and there were many ex-patriates in the distant corners of the Empire, such as the Malay States, who needed to find boarding schools for their growing children. The admissions register bears witness to Shaw's success in attracting boarders with this kind of family background.

British imperialism was also seen in another way. The first *Tamensian* magazine appeared in 1900 and echoes of the Boer War are frequent. A number of Old Boys were fighting in South Africa and the magazine, that initially appeared thrice yearly, celebrated victories such as the relief of Ladysmith. There was an appeal for subscriptions to Princess Christian's Fund for wounded sailors and soldiers, and the correspondence page had letters sent from serving Old Boys.

Though Howard Brown describes him as 'of the old type', Shaw was in many ways a mixture of the old and the new. Like most of his predecessors he was a Clerk in Holy Orders, ordained deacon in 1886 and priest in 1890, the last ordained headmaster. Like them, he too was a scholar though not a College Fellow, and his first degree and later doctorate were from London University not Oxford though he gained a second BA degree there in 1898 after studying at Worcester College, Oxford for four years.

Unlike many of his 18th and early 19th century predecessors he was neither a parish priest nor a pluralist. Nor was he on his second headship, at least not of a senior school, as were his two immediate predecessors. (After a crisis or scandal, it is common for governors to look for a 'safe pair of hands', someone who has already proved himself as a head. This is a sensible but not fool proof strategy; it had worked well enough with Plummer, but less well with Sharp.)

In appointing Shaw, the governors chose someone with a good track record as an assistant teacher. Born in 1860 and educated at Maidstone, he taught first at Maidstone High School, followed by Barnsley High School and the Moravian School near Manchester before becoming Headmaster of Weymouth College Lower School from 1885-95.

Shaw's educational philosophy was also a blend of old and new. He certainly was a believer in the classical grammar school education and in high academic standards, but he also had a broader though not an entirely comprehensive view of what a rounded education should include. By nature an intellectual, he favoured literary rather than artistic activities, founding and presiding over the Literary Society and supporting the *The Tamensian*, but musical activities were confined to concerts of then popular songs, art to drawing, and drama to end-of-term romps and burlesques.

Like many of his contemporary heads he subscribed to what, as a classicist, he would have termed *mens sana in corpore sano* – a healthy body in a healthy mind - but he valued physical education, both games and gymnastics, not just for exercising the body but for what would now be termed personal and social education: team spirit, sportsmanship and the like.

More unusually perhaps, he shared the opinion supported by many present-day educationalists that schooling should not become over-dominated by examinations. In 1901 *The Tamensian* reported his remarks on Speech Day:

> *In examination work perhaps the boys would agree with me that they have rather too much of it. Long ago a school year was divided into three terms; church, cricket, cram. Those good old days are past. We now have one term: cram, cram, cram. It begins in May and ends in July. During that time I think you are examined every week.*

❈ ❈ ❈

Increasing numbers; improving quality

The immediate challenge he faced in September 1899 was to increase pupil numbers; otherwise the school might be forced to close. The rapid increase in the first year from around twenty to over seventy was followed by a slight decline over the next five, the handful of new admissions smaller than the number leaving. Then the decline changed to renewed modest growth up to 1910, with a substantial increase in new admissions slightly exceeding the leavers. It seems likely that Shaw expended great effort at the start to recruit new pupils, but having met the challenge of sufficient quantity, turned his attention to improving quality and was content to maintain the numbers at around 70.

To some extent, Shaw was luckier than Sharp. Whereas the latter had to compete for both boarders and day-boys with the Oxford County School the latter abandoned boarding education in 1900, a few months after he arrived. The 1901 Census records its premises, the Mansion House, as unoccupied, implying that no staff nor pupils were resident there on the Sunday night before the Census was taken on 1st April. Thereafter, it stuttered on for a few years primarily as a prep school - as noted earlier, a school like Oxford House would rely on the income from boarders to keep it going.

Shaw also benefited from the the Education Act 1902 (Balfour Act). One of its provisions was to ensure that all the endowed grammar schools now received more grant-aid from LEAs assuming that they delivered a satisfactory level of education and that 25 per cent of admissions were free and given to boys from elementary schools.

Up to the academic year 1907/8 Shaw had proved far more successful in recruiting boarders than day-boys, although in part his success was due to a reduction in the fees so that boarders now paid between £36 - £39 per annum, lower than the £40-plus charged in Plummer's time. For example, in April 1906 there were 46 boarders and only 19 day-boys, little different from the numbers in Plummer's day. To build the numbers of day-boys, Shaw began to advertise in the *Thame Gazette*:

Lord Williams's Grammar School, Thame
School re-opened on Tuesday 18 September, 1906
Important improvements in equipment are being made during the vacation in the Lecture Rooms & in readiness for the coming term.
During the last four years 98 Certificates have been gained in the Oxford Local Examinations, including 30 Honours and several Distinctions.

He also had a further stroke of luck that changed the Grammar School's composition for the rest of its history. In January 1908, Oxford House finally closed, and the Girls Grammar School moved into its Mansion House premises. Local pupils in Oxford House and those in the elementary schools who wanted to move on to secondary education had no choice but to attend LWGS if they wanted to be day-boys.

Consequently, an unprecedently large number of day-boys admissions occurred at that time, six from Oxford House and ten from local elementary schools, a total of 19 for the academic year 1907-8, compared with two the previous year. From then on, day-boy admissions often outnumbered boarders. What it did do, for the first time for at least a century and perhaps longer, was to make LWGS once again a school *for* Thame as well as a school *in* Thame, bringing it back closer to its founder's original intentions.

Shaw's achievement at building numbers should not be underestimated. A report issued in 1906 by the Consultative Committee of the Board of Education stated that the majority of secondary schools, so far from fulfilling an urgent need for pupil places, had great difficulty in getting an adequate number or in keeping those they did attract for more than one or two years out of the four year course.

As previously pointed out, the substantial increase in the number of day-boys at LWGS made little difference to the financial health of the School: that depended on attracting enough boarders. A summary of fee income for the period from January 1907 to 1911 demonstrates this clearly. Tuition fees were calculated termly, occasionally half-termly, reflecting the fact that pupils often arrived and left at times other than the start of the school year.

In 1908 when the amount payable by each pupil was first recorded, the fee was £2 for all fee-paying pupils whether boarder or day-boy. This increased in 1911 to £3 3s. Conflating the termly figures, the income for the spring and summer terms of 1908 was £216 of which the boarders contributed £168 (77 per cent). In the following full academic year, 1908/9, the income was £340 of which the boarders contributed £230, (68 per cent). Given the sudden increase in the number of day-boys – 19 admissions during the year compared with 12 boarders, this disparity looks wrong. The explanation lies in the number of day-boys who paid no fees. Either they had free places or they had been awarded foundation scholarships, funded from the School's endowment.

The number of free places increased sharply from 3 in spring term 1908 to 11 a year later and 19 the year after that. Boarding admissions, after a slight dip in 1908/9, rose the following year to outnumber day-boys restoring the contribution of the boarders to the total fee income to around 75 per cent.

In terms of providing education of high quality, Shaw was quickly successful. By the early 20th century, regular inspections by His Majesty's Inspectors of Schools (HMI) were quite a feature of school life. Already in 1902 an HMI remarked: 'There was no school in the whole of the six counties to which he came with greater pleasure than Thame'. Three years later the HMI report stated: 'The work of the scholars is in a very satisfactory state and the system of teaching is sound and good. Very promising work is being done in Latin.'

Then, as now, a school that continued to maintain high standards was not much troubled by inspections. By the end of the Shaw era George Moss wrote: 'Occasionally, the Area Inspector visited. Dr Shaw merely introduced him to each master, and then marshalled him into his house for a quiet drink and a polite goodbye.'

Howard Brown paints a rather less rosy picture in terms of the relatively low numbers achieving external examination results. Exam statistics are notoriously difficult to interpret, but the limited numbers were more likely the result of the relatively short periods that many pupils spent at the school than of poor quality teaching. During almost the whole of the Shaw era, the minimum school-leaving age was 12, rising to 14 only in 1918.

* * *

Early days of sport

When Shaw arrived sports had been well-established since the opening of the new school. Football was the main ball game played and in 1900, the opponents included Watlington FC, St Mary's church, St Kenelms, Cuddesdon College, Oxford High School, Wycombe Grammar, St Edmund's Hall, Tetsworth, Royal Latin, Jesus College, and St Philip and St James.

Sports Day was a positive gala event with over sixty distinguished guests including the governors, dons from Oxford University, the clergy, and the upper echelons of local society. Stokenchurch brass band played music in the background. Besides the expected races ran over various distances there was a four-legged race, and a sack race. Afterwards tea was provided by Mrs Shaw. As the *Tamensian* noted, this was against a backdrop of golden clusters of laburnum, the pink bloom of may, and chestnut blossom; all 'toned with the deeper note of the rich green that spread before the eyes and climbed into the haze of the sunny Chiltens.' Halcyon days indeed.

Cricket games were played against Wycombe Grammar, Thame, Royal Latin, Oxford High School, Burford Grammar, and New College School. Unfortunately this was not a great season for the School and in 1900, the School was trounced, for example, by Burford who scored 143 runs against 18 from LWGS where 6 ducks were recorded.

The two final events of the school year were the Aquatic Sports (as it was called) held at Jemmett's Hole, and a tennis tournament.

* * *

How long did pupils stay at school?

The Forster Act of 1870 had provided free elementary education for all children aged 5 to 12, and ten years later attendance was made compulsory from age 5 to 10. By 1899, the school-leaving age was further raised to 12. The Education Act of 1902 created a new model of education with the establishment of grant-aided secondary schools. The number of pupils advancing to secondary education after the age of 11 and those who passed an exam could receive free education slowly increased. However by the time of the outbreak of the First World War, less than 5 per cent of 11-year olds attending elementary schools went on to secondary schools. In other words, most stayed at their elementary school until they left at the age of thirteen or fourteen.

Given the national picture it is no surprise that the number of terms pupils spent at the LWGS ranged widely. For the boarders admitted between 1908 and 1917 the number of resident terms ranged from 1 to 26. Almost half of these boarders stayed for less than two years: 20 only stayed for a mere three terms; another 25 stayed for less than six terms, and 9 for less than three complete school years, the minimum expected time before external examinations were taken. Only 26 stayed for the full five years or more that would now be the norm and a mere five left from the sixth form.

Whereas today pupils rarely leave secondary school mid-year, in the early 20th century this was much more common, particularly for those staying less than three years. Day-boys tended to stay longer but also on occasion left mid-year. So not only the relative lack of pupils reaching the examination forms but the constant comings and goings mid-year would have disrupted continuity of learning.

Most of the credit for the high standards that were achieved according to the inspectors goes to Shaw's own teaching. Incredible as it may now seem, Shaw taught almost half of the curriculum: English, French, History and Latin. Even with a full teaching load he can only have had time to teach the higher forms: IV, V and VI (roughly corresponding to Years 10-13, though in those days forms were determined more by achievement than age and the Sixth Form was tiny). The remaining subjects of the curriculum: mathematics, science, and geography, and the whole curriculum for the younger forms (I, II and III] was in the hands of three or four assistant teachers. What were then minor subjects: singing, drawing, woodwork and physical education, were the responsibility of visiting, part-time teachers or instructors. All the staff in one way or the other assisted with games, athletics and other out-of-school activities. The resident staff also had boarding house duties.

* * *

Staff and pupils

The details of staffing in Shaw's early years are difficult to determine because of gaps in the staff register but it is clear that the recruitment and retention of mathematics and science teachers, then as now, proved a struggle. From 1906 to 1913, there were five different maths/science teachers, staying for five terms at the most. In 1913, however, the problem eased on the arrival of John Howard Brown with a degree in chemistry.

He was to remain on the staff until the late 1940s apart from two terms absence on military service from 1918-1919.

Another teacher who became part of the establishment was George Moss, who arrived at the same time, in his memoirs noting that he had taken the train to Thame and then a horse cab from the station. Though Moss had a degree in history, he was appointed to teach geography as there already was a Senior Master, Edward Davies, who shared teaching history with Shaw. As Moss himself wrote in his account of his years at the school: 'In those days a teacher had to be prepared to teach almost any subject.' For Moss, this included Latin, art, PT and games.

For all this work, he was initially paid £100 annually plus free board. In his first term he received his first pay cheque only in December.

Shortly after Howard Brown arrived, he said that the outstanding event of the first autumn was the closure of the School due to a scarlet fever epidemic that had broken out in the town. Not that this stopped teaching. The boarders were kept in quarantine on the Oxford Road site, while day-boys were taught in the town hall. His other observations included that all classrooms were kept locked out of school hours, and each boy had a single desk. At this time of course, all lessons other than science were held in that classroom and boys did not move around. The School had no main drainage, no mains water supply nor electricity and was lit by gas.

The boarders' day started with half-an-hour's prep before breakfast, after school they would have games although if it was too dark they would walk to what were known as the Red Houses along Rycote Lane. Tea was served at 6pm and then evening prep from 7pm to 8.30pm followed by a light supper and bed. Howard Brown said that a feature of boarding house life that was much enjoyed then was the informal concerts, sing-songs, reading and dramatics that would take place on a Saturday evening. Howard Brown thought that the boys organised their leisure well, showed good initiative in amusing themselves, and there was a strong work ethic. His example of this was that boys in the spring and summer could be found on a Sunday afternoon or evening sitting around the cricket pavilion reading their English examination texts.

The staff, as is common in schools, can be broadly divided into stayers and movers. Both are needed for a school to be healthy, the former for stability, the latter for energy and new ideas. Because of their short stay, the contributions of the movers are often difficult to assess, but the best of them were able and ambitious young teachers, who both gave and learnt much for two or three years before moving on, often to a more senior post.

Shaw himself exemplified this before his arrival in Thame. Amongst his assistant staff Ernest Achey Loftus was a prime example. LWGS was his third school in six years and he only stayed at Thame for two years before moving to Palmer's School in Southend but *The Tamensian* makes it clear that he entered fully into the life of the School during that time. His later career included a distinguished war service, rising to the rank of Lieutenant Colonel, and headships of one junior and two senior schools. As already noted, Howard Brown was a stayer and, to a lesser extent, Moss. Mr Purnell too remained as a part-time teacher until his retirement more than two decades later.

Teaching was hard work. Moss recorded that they rarely had a free Saturday afternoon (lessons being taught in the morning) and if they did, which was roughly once a month, he would cycle to Oxford to shop and get a haircut. Later, he and Howard Brown acquired motorcycles which made transport much easier. Sundays, were said to involve as much duty as the other days.

In order to create a little bit of variety for the boarders, Moss and Howard Brown organised monthly music concerts on a Saturday evening. The senior boarders, as it was discovered, also had their own ways to create variety including storing a secret hoard of food under the floorboards of their dormitory.

Even the best of staff requires good 'raw material' if the school is to achieve high standards. Some of the boys that Shaw recruited, particularly some of the boarders, were both academically gifted and good all-rounders. Despite its limited numbers, the School performed well in its two major sports, cricket and football - with Oxford High then being the main rivals. One amusing tale is of a new boy who while preparing to put on his kit first took off his jacket, waistcoat, sweater, shirt, vest, and then a padding of Thermogene. Perhaps the School was very cold in those days.

Cultural and literary activities grew and flourished. All these developments and achievements are well documented in Thomas's *Chronicle* and the early issues of *The Tamensian*, requiring no further elaboration here. On all fronts the School was thriving – and then came the war. Shaw, his staff, and his family faced new challenges.

❊ ❊ ❊

The impact of the Great War

The impact of the war was relatively slight at first and only started to become noticeable during the academic year 1915/16; and it was by no means entirely negative. Until 1916 pupil numbers remained around 75, but the balance between boarders and day-boys changed. Before 1909 boarders were in the majority; after the closure of Oxford County School, day-boys outnumbered boarders by a significant amount. From 1916, however, the two were roughly in balance thanks to a sudden influx of boarders, reaching 50 for the first time. The overall numbers rose to between 90 and 110, and only briefly fell below 100 in Shaw's final years.

The war was at least partly responsible for the sudden increase in boarders. In the autumn of 1915, the government, concerned that the military were running out of soldiers, introduced the Derby Scheme, named after Kitchener's recruiting officer Edward Stanley Earl of Derby, to increase the number enlisting. Joining up was still voluntary but males between 18 and 40 were encouraged to 'attest' that they would enlist as needed and many did so immediately. Those that didn't were often shamed by receiving 'white feathers'. In some families where the fathers were lost to the forces, the parents realised the value of their sons being placed in the male environment of a boarding school. However, the Derby Scheme did not result in sufficient new recruits to balance the haemorrhaging in the armed forces caused by unprecedented casualties. Consequently, Kitchener introduced conscription which took effect from 2nd March 1916, resulting in yet more absent fathers and further boosting boarding numbers.

Another reason, slightly earlier in time, was the onset of the German Zeppelin raids on London and other cities starting in May 1915. By comparison with the Blitz of the Second World War, casualties were few but this was the first time since the Napoleonic era that a war had impacted on British civilians and on British soil so it caused some panic and encouraged parents to evacuate their children to schools in rural areas such as Thame. Brown refers to these boarders as 'bomb-dodgers', which later caused offence to some Old Tamensians, but at the time did not carry any negative meaning. However, the admissions register only includes four from the London area, and one from Auteuil in France but as noted later records were not faithfully kept at this time.

Such an increase in pupil numbers was obviously good news

financially but less so in other respects. Boarders needed to be fed and food was becoming increasingly scarce and expensive. Brown's description of the difficulties experienced by house staff at this time is also included in the chapter on boarding in Volume 2, but he also makes the point that, academically, more did not mean better.

Firstly, able and committed pupils, who would normally have stayed on, left early for the workforce to replace those who had enlisted. The registers provide only a partial example of this: John Edmund Rose was absent during the Spring and Summer terms of 1917 doing farm work at home. Howard Brown states that academic results therefore declined. It is not possible to confirm this from the admissions registers. Very few pupils stayed on into the Sixth Form and the proportion did not change during the war.

Of the remainder, some may have left who would normally have stayed on to take the Oxford Local Examinations, but a fair number of pupils who stayed for several years never progressed to the examination forms, so the evidence is inconclusive. Howard Brown also states – and one would have thought he should know as he had to teach them: 'a new type of boy began to enter the School – old, usually ignorant, and not infrequently idle, the result of the absence of fathers on military service, and of constant moving about from place to place'.

The register gives only slight support to the increased age of boys admitted during the war. Only 7 out of the 80 admissions between January 1915 and September 1917 were over the normal entry age of 11-13, and all of these were just 14, but these did all enter around 1916. It is possible that what Howard Brown was remembering when he wrote about the war years some two decades later related to the last two years of the war; or in retrospect the number of older and poorly motivated pupils had become exaggerated in his memory.

* * *

Recruiting and retaining staff

It might have been expected that the war would have had a devastating effect on the recruitment and retention of teachers but this was not so, at least not until near the end of the war, even though two key teachers, Brown and Moss were young men. The Military Service Act which introduced conscription exempted men in certain 'reserved occupations'. Teaching was one of these. Though teachers were free to waive their exemption and enlist, neither Howard Brown nor Moss chose to do this at least initially. Previously, both had, in Howard Brown's words, 'refused to attest' under the Derby Scheme, whether of their own volition or under pressure from Shaw is not known.

Others, however, did enlist. The part-time teacher of singing, Claud Collins joined up early in the war and was absent from January 1915 until September 1919. George Moss took over the singing. In February 1915, Edward Davies, the history teacher, followed Collins into the army, returning in the summer of 1919. Davies was replaced, but not by a historian. It would seem obvious that Moss, in view of the subject of his degree would have added history to his geography at this date, though strangely the staff register states 'History from 1921'. This entry was made in a different hand than Shaw's, most probably by the incoming head Walter Bye and may therefore have been merely an official confirmation what had been the actual situation for four years.

The age and the qualifications of the man who notionally replaced Davies reflected Shaw's growing difficulty in recruiting the kind of teachers he needed to maintain the School's high academic quality. John Page was 59, for a long time head of a private school. His qualification, gained at the age of 16, was 'London Inter-Arts', an external exam provided by the University of London. This barely qualified him to teach any subject in a grammar school. However, he was appointed to teach French, Latin and English, almost certainly to ease Shaw's teaching load of these subjects.

In the following two years no new staff were appointed but when on 29th June 1918 Howard Brown left finally to join the army, a crisis ensued. The least worst replacement that Shaw could find was George Ludwick. He had a degree from Cape Town - the subject is not recorded. He arrived, on probation, in May, presumably to understudy Howard Brown before the latter left. But he was a sick man from the start, having been discharged from the forces as medically totally unfit, and lasted only a month before collapsing, sadly dying a month later.

Shaw was therefore forced to find a replacement for the replacement, one Doris Bailey, with a science degree and aged 27, who stood in between 4th and the 25th July when term ended. Shaw had employed women teachers before, of course, but only his own family and mainly for junior forms. Doris Bailey was the first woman teacher of a major subject to senior boys. [Miss Bailey went on to have a distinguished teaching career, becoming headmistress of St Mary's School, Lytham.]

It was probably during Howard Brown's absence during the autumn term of 1918 when Moss found himself teaching mathematics. Whether anyone taught science during this term is doubtful. Over the next two years Shaw employed three more women and a man, all with limited qualifications, to teach Forms II and III.

The first appointment that Shaw was able to make of someone with appropriate degree qualifications and which proved long term was that of George Cooper to teach English and French, after the end of the war in January 1919. It must have come as an enormous relief to Shaw, and indeed to other staff, when Brown returned to teaching in the same term.

* * *

Illness and stress

As if the academic problems caused by poorly motivated pupils and absent staff were not enough, the pressures on Shaw and the School generally were exacerbated by successive years of ill health amongst the pupils which added to the difficulties of maintaining continuity of work and placed extra pressure on the boarding staff. These started with a scarlet fever epidemic in the autumn of 1913 already mentioned. This was followed by a series of spring term epidemics: the most serious of these the 'flu of February 1915, when at one time the attendance was reduced to 38; this was followed in March 1916 by chickenpox and by measles in 1917.

Despite Howard Brown's return, Shaw's last years had proved immensely stressful. The signs of strain are everywhere in the records. *The Tamensian*, usually published termly from 1899, first became annually, and then ceased publication altogether between December 1917 and December 1919.

The staff register for 1918-1920 also shows signs of deteriorating accuracy. Shaw in particular and the school generally, like the rest of the UK, were suffering from war weariness. Moss's comment about the visit of the HMI, quoted earlier, might be interpreted as not so much as a comment on the academic achievement of the school, as a compassionate understanding that Shaw was doing the best he could in difficult circumstances.

Whether the so-called Spanish Flu hit the School is unknown. However one victim was Viscount Bertie of Thame, a school governor, who died in 1919. His funeral took place at St Mary's church, and Shaw and many boys were in the congregation.

✳ ✳ ✳

Shaw's achievement

However, despite the trials and tribulations of Shaw's last few years, his twenty-one years as Head proved a great success, a fact formally recognized at the time of his death in the pages of *The Tamensian*. In strong contrast to the brief appreciation of Sharp, the September 1921 issue devoted four pages to Shaw, by three authors. 'DPS', almost certainly his son Donald, by then a housemaster a Westminster, provided a largely factual but nevertheless impressive catalogue of his achievements, including his scholarly and his wider educational work as chairman of the Oxfordshire Headmasters Association.

'GES', GE Shrimpton, a prominent Old Tamensian, wrote that Shaw 'won for himself an enduring place in the annals of the School. Under his touch the dry bones of textbook facts glowed with life and colour'. He refers to 'the graphic force of his history lectures and the genuine love for great literature with which he was inspired, and could so readily inspire others. The school lost a great headmaster when he retired; his Old Boys lost a true friend when he passed beyond the veil.'

'JHB', John Howard Brown's contribution, all the more persuasive for falling well short of hagiography, stated:

> *Added to an intellect of the highest order, and a quickness of thought, which at time made him impatient with those whose minds moved more slowly, Dr Shaw possessed an unequalled power of discipline, helped by a wonderful intuition as to when to expect trouble and who would be the ringleaders in it. His rules and regulations must often have seemed erratic to those who were unable, or who did not*

take the trouble, to see the purpose behind them; but many are now, though perhaps unconsciously, the gainers thereby.

Informally, George Moss, who like Howard Brown had known Shaw for seven years, stated succinctly in his memoirs: 'The Rev AE Shaw was one of the finest men I have ever met, a great scholar, a marvellous teacher and a real friend.' A century on from Shaw's retirement, these contemporary judgements still ring true, but with the advantage of being able to take a longer term view, it is clear that his main achievement lay in rescuing the School from near extinction, restoring its reputation, increasing its numbers and ensuring its future; in short, laying firm foundations on which later headmasters and principals could build with confidence.

Other headmasters may have achieved more in absolute terms, but Shaw's success in leaving the School in a much better place than he found it has never been exceeded. Yet recent generations seem to have forgotten Shaw's achievements. Unlike other prominent headmasters, Plummer and Goodall for example, no building is now named after him (although the cricket pavilion was - but more on this later) although one meeting room bears his name.

After Shaw retired in 1920 he went to live in Tunbridge Wells. Here he became actively involved with the Workers Educational Association but was unable to enjoy a much-deserved retirement as he died after a short illness on May 16th 1921. He was buried in Hawkenbury Cemetery, and the whole school 'was cast in gloom.' It was noted that his death at the early age of 61 was in part brought on by the supreme effort he made to keep the School going during the Great War.

※ ※ ※

The Old Tamensians's Association

It was in the Shaw era that an Old Boys association was established, first mooted as a means of maintaining the *esprit de corps* that existed at the School.

During the 1880s under Plummer there had been an Association of Old Boys but this had petered out. Now GE Shrimpton led the way and contacted the former Hon Sec of the old, Old Boys. He was warned 'If you found an Association, you may get some members, a few of them will pay their subscriptions fairly regularly, still fewer will attend dinners and functions, and you will never see or hear anything of the majority unless one occasionally calls at your office to see if you can oblige him with the loan of a fiver.'

Undaunted by this, on the 10th March 1908, eighteen old boys met at the Chinese Salon, Holborn Restaurant, London. They included Dr Shaw, three former masters, three of the four Kislingburys who had been at the School, four of the five Sims, GE Shrimpton of course, and EL Stroud.

The Holborn Restaurant, one of London's most famous at the time, was a favourite place for societies and groups to meet, and had been the meeting place for the first incarnation of the Old Boys. During the discussion it was agreed there were nearly 200 Old Boys who could be contacted and encouraged to join. It was also suggested that perhaps an Old Boys Freemasons Lodge be formed. Noted too was that the food, wine and cigars 'produced the appropriate spirit in the diners.'

In 1909 a second dinner was held at The Holborn and as the number of guests had swelled, showing at least some enthusiasm for the idea, it was resolved that an Old Tamensians's Association should be formed. (The term Old Tamensian applied to Old Boys had been in existence for many years and so it was natural that this should become the adopted name.) The first President was appointed on the spot, the Rev WC Eppstein.

At the end of the year the first AGM was held on 8th December, where the treasurers account showed a balance of £2 9s & 2d, with 55 members on the Association's roll. In the immediate years thereafter, dinners were held annually in London, Old Boys teams were fielded in soccer and cricket, and the Association became a valuable and integral part of the School's fabric.

✽ ✽ ✽

Private Richard John Green was the last OT to be killed. He joined the Royal Fusiliers as soon as he was 18 and saw service in Palestine, Egypt and France. He had returned from leave in England, on 16th October 1918 to rejoin his unit on the Western Front having volunteered for service with the 4th Royal Sussex Regiment. On 2nd November he was at a dressing station attending to the wounded when he was killed by a German bomb dropped in an air-raid over the British lines, this just 9 days before the Armistice.

In total 193 Old Boys had served in the Great War, 32 lost their lives. DSOs were won by Captain WG Bailey (with two bars), and Major DP Shaw who distinguishing himself in the initial attacks across Ancre. Shaw was also in command of the 6th Battalion of the Dorsets. Henry Shrimpton won the Military Cross as did Lieut. R Rhodes, Capt. Reginald Harris, and 2nd/ Lt Frank Mitchell. Captain EW Rose was awarded the MC after being killed in action. Captain R Lidington was mentioned in despatches as was Reginald Harrison.

More detail of OTs who fought in the Great War can be found in Volume 2, and both authors also made important contributions to the *Thame Remembers - the fallen,* project, which is available both on-line and as a book.

CHAPTER 18: A SECOND NEW BEGINNING – WALTER BYE 1920-1929

SHAW'S REPLACEMENT was Walter Roderick Griffith Bye (1889 – 1953). He was a young man to take on the headmastership of a grammar school as he was only aged 31 but his parents were both elementary school teachers and in one sense teaching was in his blood.

Bye's academic career was similar in many ways to his predecessor Shaw. Like Shaw he had an external London degree, though in mathematics rather than modern languages. Like Shaw he had taught in two schools for relatively short periods, in his case, King Edward VI Grammar School, Chelmsford for a year and Queen Elizabeth Grammar at Faversham for four terms. Like Shaw he seems to have decided that an Oxford degree was needed if he were to gain the headship he wanted. While it is unclear how Shaw supported himself and his family while studying for his degree, Bye chose to combine the role of undergraduate with that of teaching at Oxford Prep School (later re-named The Dragon School).

At this point their careers temporarily diverged. On the outbreak of war, Bye temporarily suspended his university studies and teaching career and enlisted initially in the University and Public Schools Royal Fusiliers before joining the 8th Battalion West Surrey Regiment, and then the Hampshire Regiment. At the end of the War he was temporary Captain and had been awarded both the DSO and MC.

In 1919, he returned to complete his degree, but rather than immediately resume teaching he studied for a year at the Oxford School of Education before returning to Oxford Prep for the summer term 1920. Thus, like Shaw before him, and indeed the School's first headmaster Edward Harris, he was the right man, at the right place, at the right time when Shaw resigned in 1920. He was, no doubt, the governors' obvious choice.

The nation needed reconstruction after the war and there was a longing to build a brave, new and peaceful world to replace the old order. Bye was said to be symbolic of the new spirit that was in the air. He threw himself into the task of making up the leeway lost because of the war and was determined to make the School one of the best of its type. At a dinner of Old Tamensians, he announced his aim was 'to send boys out into the world who would be first-class Britons – that stamp of boy which has 'Briton' written all over him – clean, manly, honourable boys.'

The Regulations of the Board of Education now stipulated that boys sent to grammar schools should remain for a minimum of four years and, hopefully, until they reached the age of 16. Forms at the School started with Form I, a preparatory class for eleven-year olds or younger while the core of the School was Forms II to V.

In 1917 the Secondary School Examinations Council had been set-up, and the following year the School Certificate and the Higher School Certificate were introduced but we now have no record of how many pupils took these exams in these early years.

All we know is that in the early 1920s, most boys left after four years, some but not all having taken the Oxford School Certificate while only a few remained in the Sixth Form to take the Higher School Certificate. Quickly though more boys sat the exams. While numbers varied year-to-year, 1926 seems typical when 16 boys passed the School Certificate, and four the Higher School Certificate,

One of the first things Bye did was to introduce the reading out of the names of the School's Fallen, done on Armistice Day, first at the School and then at a short service in St Mary's. He also recommended that the Cricket Pavilion, opened by the local MP Valentine Fleming who had been killed in the war, should also become a permanent memorial to the Fallen, many of whom had enjoyed many a summer's day on the cricket pitch, and who were now playing cricket on some new Elysian Field.

He established the Army Cadet Corps and 51 boys quickly joined up. Bye reassured parents that the Corps was 'purely educational and not a militarist movement.' They were drilled in square-bashing at lunchtime, and each cadet had a shortened Lee Enfield rifle. Shooting practice took place at Thame's rifle range, with the cadets marching through the town with their weapons carried on their shoulder. In time honoured tradition, the cadets' uniforms rarely fitted, and putting on the breeches and puttees was said to be always a struggle.

The Fallen were also commemorated by the 1920 presentation of a War Memorial Tablet by GE Shrimpton, Secretary of the Old Tamensians's Association to Mr Wykeham, the Chairman of the Governors. It was inscribed with the Arms of the School and the names of the Fallen, whilst a War Memorial Prize was created to be awarded to the pupil who exercised the best influence in or out of School. The Memorial was unveiled by General Sir Hew Fanshawe, educated at Winchester, a local notable who had been sacked as a Commander of V Corps by General Haig during the first days of the Battle of the Somme, though seemingly not because of military incompetence.

Bye also wanted to encourage extra-curricular activities. In the December 1921 issue of *The Tamensian* it noted:

Entertainments have been varied. Perhaps the most enjoy-
able of all was a visit paid to the Dragon School where a
special performance of Gilbert and Sullivan's Patience was
given for our benefit by the boys of the School. It is hoped
that we, too, someday will be able to produce Gilbert &
Sullivan opera with equal success. At any rate, we see what
can be done.

Indeed, the following year a Gilbert & Sullivan production was mounted at the School and this became an annual event for a number of years. (For further details of musical drama at this period and later, see Volume 2.)

Rowland Hill, a day-pupil who joined in 1924 described school life in the 1920s. Initially he cycled from Chinnor and recalled that the roads lacked tarmac and it was essential to carry a puncture outfit and tyre levers, as punctures were frequent.

Subsequently as Hill noted, the first-ever school bus was introduced: the Local Education Authority contracted House Brothers of Watlington to provide the service. This turned out to be a Renault ex-troop carrier with canvas sides and two benches for the boys to sit on. (House continued to provide the bus service to Chinnor and Watlington for many decades thereafter.)

Each classroom had a stars and stripes board: stars for outstanding work, stripes for particularly bad work, and dis-order stripes for unruly behaviour. Those who received two of the latter in a single week had to stand outside the head-master's office before morning assembly thereafter receiving two strokes of the cane.

Another strict school rule read, 'No day-boy is allowed to bring any articles whatsoever into the school premises for a boarder without special permission. A breach of this rule will render a boy liable to removal from the school.' The main object of the rule was, apparently, to prevent notes coming in from the Girls Grammar School. However the son of one of Thame's bank managers was caught breaking this rule, and to avoid being expelled had to do public penance in front of the whole school at morning assembly.

Hill also remembered that at weekends, selected boarders, (undoubtedly those with plenty of stars to their name) would take afternoon tea with Mrs Dyer. He described it as 'tea with half-an-hour of stilted conversation.'

On the subject of food, Bye introduced the ritual of boys now taking it in turns to serve food from the trolleys that were wheeled into the dining hall on rails rather like a tram system, and the collection of dirty plates and dishes afterwards.

Sports included both rugby and football, cross country runs, athletics and cricket.

The inter-war years were ones of economic uncertainty and Bye took seriously the matter of future employment. In 1923, he set up a school employment bureau as he recognised that the country was facing a serious decrease in the number of jobs.

A proportion of leavers found employment elsewhere by emigrating to the Empire, some under the Empire Settlement Scheme that had been set up in 1921. Old Tamensians in the 1920s might be found rubber planting in Malaya, sheep farming in New Zealand, banking in India, cotton-growing in the Sudan and administering East Africa. (There is more on this subject in Volume 2.) In part this enthusiasm might have come from the school visits to see the Empire Exhibition at Wembley in 1924 and '25. Back in School they were asked to write an essay about the greatness of the British Empire.

In 1929 after nine years in the job Bye resigned to take up a new appointment as Headmaster of Skinner's School, where he would stay until his retirement. As he was only forty it was likely that the Governor's would have expected him to stay as headmaster for longer but nonetheless they were generous in their praise, not least 'because he had relieved (them) of a great deal of responsibility' and they noted the influence he had on the 'general manners of the School.'

Under his leadership, sixth-form work began to assume the importance that it has since retained, and university scholarships became an actual possibility. School numbers had been 113 when he started but had fluctuated over the years once reaching 134 but then falling back to around 120.

There is a sense that parents tended to treat the School as one best suited for the younger boys and that having reached fifteen or sixteen a boy would be taken out and sent to another more academicly-orientated school.

If Bye's relatively early departure for another headship seems odd, it may be that he felt he had achieved what he set out to do, and as still a relatively young man he relished a new challenge elsewhere. Not that Skinners was a bigger school at the time. Indeed, in many respects it was similar to LWGS in terms of size and structure. However it had the backing of the Worshipful Company of Skinners, was located in Tunbridge Wells, and was likely to have been on a stronger financial footing.

Bye's list of achievements is certainly impressive. More buildings were added, and electric lighting came to the School, which was said to be a great improvement on the ugly gas brackets and the burning mantles that would sometimes fall on an unsuspecting pupil's head. Better classroom equipment was provided, along with a general improvement to facilities all round, including the purchase of a nearby house, Highfield, to improve accommodation for boarders. He had a swimming pool built, and he greatly expanded the library. He introduced the Cadet Corps, and encouraged the setting up of school clubs and societies such as the camera club, and the natural history society.

In his tenure he formed a Scout troop and reintroduced rugby after a lapse of nearly thirty years. He also established Founder's Day to celebrate the founding of the School. This took place in November to coincide with the commencement of teaching, and initially took place in the School but then moved to St Mary's, the parish church. He also introduced a new House system using the names Williams, Harris, Hampden and Wykeham.

The governors' view of Bye noted that he had taken particular care of looking after the boarders and had a particular affinity with the younger boys, no doubt stemming from his time at Oxford Prep. This favourable view was not shared by all. George Moss wrote:

> When Bye came in many changes were made – some better some worse. The food was much better and traditions tended to disappear. Pupil numbers increased and the staff were brought up to a reasonable number, some of whom for the first time were non-resident. One change was not appreciated: we were run as a preparatory school with every moment of the day organised. Efficiency yes, but happy atmosphere doubtful.

After he left Thame, Moss said that at his new school in Northampton, 'I felt like a caged bird freed from captivity as I had much more freedom and free time.' He continued to teach until he retired in 1958.

The food must have been really unpalatable in Moss's war years as the new food was said to both look and taste terrible: boiled fish, potatoes and greens, curry, plum duff, putty and varnish (steamed pudding with the minimum of treacle) were just a few of the dishes served.

Elsewhere in Thame, the National School was turned into Thame's Senior (i.e. secondary) School. The Royal British and Foreign School – that had started life in 1836 as a non-conformist institution now known as Park Street School and later renamed John Hampden - became Thame's only primary school. Both would forge a close relationship with LWGS in the future.

It was also during Bye's time that John Howard Brown wrote *A Short History of Thame School* which was published in 1927. He had a thousand copies printed - at his own expense - but according to Brown very few were sold. Howard Brown had hoped to publish a second edition in the 1940s extending the history to include Bye's headmastership. However, the paucity of sales of the first edition, exacerbated no doubt by the general difficulties experienced during WW2, meant that the additional chapters were only published in *The Tamensian* during the early years of the war.

Had Bye spent longer at the School he might have achieved more. Perhaps, as noted earlier, he felt that the potential for what he would like to have achieved was not present in post-war Thame and that there would be more scope for his ambitions in another school. Indeed, at one prize giving ceremony he remarked that Thame was a difficult place to reach because of the lack of public transport and poor roads.

During WW2 he re-enlisted; promoted to Lt Colonel, he commanded the 22nd Battalion Kent Home Guard, and was awarded an OBE.

He died in 1956 having retired from the headship of Skinners School in 1953, leaving £7,121 to his widow. He was still relatively young, aged only 64 when he died.

CHAPTER 19: DYER – THE FIRST TEN YEARS 1929-1939

BYE WAS REPLACED BY Captain Arthur Cyril Dyer (1888 – 1954), who became the first Cambridge graduate to be appointed Headmaster.

He was one of four long-serving heads in the 20th century, staying for almost twenty years. The others made an outstanding contribution to the School's history. Shaw, the first as already described, rescued the School from almost certain closure, and restored its reputation. Goodall, whose contribution is related in a later chapter, transformed a thriving small grammar school into a successful comprehensive, while Kenningham steered the School in its formative years as it became one of the country's biggest educational institutions. One short-serving head also made a difference: Nelson in the early 1960s deserves credit for laying the foundations for the modern school, and abolishing many archaic practices.

Dyer's legacy is more difficult to assess. The only certainty is that he was the least popular head of the 20th century both with the boys and the staff.

Dyer had been born and then educated at a country grammar school in Bridgenorth. His father was a Baptist Minister. He had served as a Lieutenant in the King's Own Shropshire Light Infantry and was mentioned in dispatches. Before the war he was a mathematics teacher at King Edward VI School, Lytham. This had been founded in 1908 so he would have been one of the first members of staff. After the war, he taught at Giggleswick and became commanding officer of the Giggleswick School contingent of the Junior Division of the Officer Training

Corps with the rank of Captain. He was still in the same role with the same rank in 1928 shortly before he became Headmaster of LWGS in 1929, but he was promoted to Major, when he took on the post of Commanding Officer, the 4th Oxfordshire Battalion, Home Guard, No.10 Platoon, based in Thame.

He arrived with his wife Marjorie who took over responsibilities for the Boarding House. She had six staff to look after including the matron, cook and other kitchen staff. They had two children aged 6 and 2, and because of Mrs Dyer's duties, they took on a nannie to look after them.

A former school archivist, Gerald Howat, wrote of Arthur Dyer that he was more academically inclined than Walter Bye and his main achievement in the school was to raise the academic standards and get more boys to stay into the Sixth Form.

> *He shouldered a heavy burden and shouldered it well. He had a thorough grip on the School and knew the boys. He carried an exceedingly heavy teaching programme.*

On the other hand, Howat acknowledged Dyer's unpopularity with the pupils.

> *He was a strict disciplinarian, intolerant with younger staff, and introduced petty rules. Many pupils in later life recorded their dislike of the man, showing how deeply this was rooted.*

✻ ✻ ✻

The school day

The school day had remained largely the same since the refounding of LWGS, and indeed would continue very much in the same way for the next forty years or so.

For day-boys, school began at 8.45 am, with an assembly in the what was called the Schoolroom - after assembly it was partitioned to accommodate Forms I and II. (Today it is the Sixth Form Common Room.)

Pupils had to bring their own copy of *Hymns Ancient and Modern* and stand between the desks. The masters then filed in, clad in their academic gowns, which they also wore in class - as most did until 1971.

Dyer would then enter after reviewing a small parade of pupils bringing excuse notes for recent absences. He would stand behind the master's desk, and would first give out the day's notices before reading a passage from the Bible. A hymn was sung, accompanied by Howard Brown at the piano, and sometimes with senior boys also playing an instrument such as a violin or flute.

Assembly ended at 9am and the pupils would disperse to their form rooms to start the day's work. There were four morning periods of forty minutes split by a mid-morning break. The end of each period was signalled by the ringing of the school bell by a rota of fourth formers.

Lunch was between 12.30 to 2pm; some day-boys would return home, if they stayed they had to pay for their meal. One Old Boy said it was 'good plain food using the produce of the school garden cultivated by Old Jim.'

Afternoon school consisted of three periods - again with a short break. On Thursday and Saturday there were five morning periods, with the afternoons given up to games. Matches were played against other schools but also there were House matches to be played.

One pupil remembered life at School as not being the best days of his life.

I have often wondered who first uttered that hoary old platitude about school days being the best days of your life. It certainly was not the case for me. On the contrary, I merely longed for the day of liberation. As a boarder, life was to say the last circumscribed and decidedly spartan. We were woken by the loud ringing of a handbell at 6.45am. We washed in cold water.

Being an exclusively male company it was also monastic. The only females we ever saw or had contact with were Dyer's wife, a pleasant and kindly lady but somewhat remote, being only seen on formal occasions, or if one had the misfortune to spend a few days in the sick-bay, which was in the Headmaster's house. There she would take a personal interest by popping in to see the patient from time to time. It was rather like being visited by a member of the Royal Family.

Matron was a formidable figure in stiff white colllar and blue uniform. It was beneficial to keep on her good side so I always returned from the holidays with a box of chocolates.

The girls from their grammar school were seen as strange creatures and much effort was made to ensure that strict segregation was the order of the day. However from time to time joint entertainments were held but masters and prefects kept a beady eye out for any sign of friendship.

On the plus-side, ours was not a class-ridden little world. Generally speaking we were an ordinary mix bunch without pretensions. The only social rule was not to sneak.

I regret to say that as they were not the best days of my life, I never returned. I do not believe in going back to places because they are never the same.

It is worth noting that a pupil's home life might be just as spartan particularly if they lived in one of the local villages with few amenities. Moreton was said to always smell because it had no main sewage system, and whatever soakaways were used were prone to discharging their contents into the village ditches. One pupil lived in a two bedroomed cottage in rural Bucks. It had no bath, no WC, no electric light, and no carpets.

✽ ✽ ✽

Dyer the man

Rowland Hill (who we met in the previous chapter) was still a pupil when Dyer arrived. He wrote, 'sorry to say I did not take to him from the start.' One new boy, a few years later, remembered that Major Dyer was 'stern and black-gowned,' who insisted boys sat still and that the slightest move to scratch an itch would provoke his wrath. 'He would remain aloof and unsmiling.'

Patrick Harrison provides a wonderfully vivid but highly critical view of Dyer:

> *We saw little of our Headmaster. He would materialise unexpectedly amongst us from time to time: motionless, enigmatic and censorious. He was a small, reserved man with a big nose in a face of coarse, pallid skin, with floppy, fairish hair, pale, expressionless eyes and a pale, tobacco-stained moustache above broken, tobacco-stained teeth all surrounded by an invisible cloud of sour, tobacco-stained breath. He had come from Giggleswick in 1929 and taught maths quite well to the upper forms. He should never have been a schoolmaster. To be a solicitor in a rather larger country town than Thame might have suited him. He had little understanding of the compulsive lunacy of boys.*

'Aaaah! All I ask is that yah be rea...sonable' he would plead, tapping the ends of his extended fingers together.

He distrusted enthusiasms of any kind, partly because he saw it as an undesirable diversion of energy from school-work, partly because he was made uneasy by any evidence of spontaneous pleasure. He caught one boy who was keen on carpentry making something when perhaps he should have been doing something else. His toolbox was promptly confiscated. 'Aaaah! It's schoolwork we need Boughton, not woodwork'. Later, my brother, who had given evidence of the musical ability that was to become the basis of his career, had his gramophone taken away. However, although repressive, our Headmaster probably stimulated ingenuity and subversive non-conformity. Had we been at a school where spare time was thoroughly organised, we would have been left to ourselves far less.

In this at least, perhaps the Dyer era was an improvement on Bye's over-organised days.

Another critic, William Arthur, a pupil who started shortly after Dyer joined, wrote in his memoirs that when he was interviewed by Dyer he felt some antagonism then and, having joined the School, found that he was a 'really tough character who I disliked intensely and most of the boys hated him. The other members of staff were generally very pleasant and good teachers.' Near the end of his time at School when head of house and captain of cricket, Arthur had another, remarkable, encounter with Dyer:

There was one incident which marred my year as skipper, and basically it was my own fault...After one particularly hard match, which we lost, I broke a school rule by drying my legs on a school towel having dirtied them by diving to save runs on the field. To Dyer this was a dastardly deed and as ill luck would have it as I did it, he appeared in the doorway. I was caught and undoubtedly in the wrong. Dyer was furious and in his most stentorian voice proclaimed in the presence of both teams, 'You will come to my office immediately and I will cane you.'

The opponents and my team were stunned and most sympathetic but there was no option. I had to visit the Head in his study where I was lectured for a couple of minutes and then ordered to bend over the table. I politely refused and said that I thought that the disgrace I had already suffered at his hands by my public humiliation was more than adequate punishment for what had been a wrong act on my part, and that I would, from that moment, relinquish the post of cricket captain. Dyer was completely taken aback by my polite revolt and sent me to sit outside the door. Whether this was to recover from the shock or to make a decision as to his next move I have no idea. Suffice to say that I was not caned and I was not allowed to resign as cricket captain.

In dealing out corporal punishment Dyer was acting no differently to most headmasters for this was a time when corporal punishment was the norm, but his over-reaction and public humiliation of a senior boy for a not-so-heinous crime is further evidence of the kind of character he normally presented to the outside world. There is no lack of other evidence but there is other compelling evidence that suggests that beneath this harsh exterior was a much more humane and sensitive person. PM (later Professor) Holt, in remembering his days said 'as a pupil I found Dyer unapproachable but when I came to know him better after I had left, he showed an unexpectedly human side which usually was all too well concealed.'

Another pupil who left in 1936, commented, 'On the whole I did not like school but twenty years later, when I joined the Old Tamensians's Association I acquired a high regard for its attributes, missed at the time.'

Fortunately, Howard Brown acted as a counter to Dyer and brought a quasi-pastoral quality to his relationships with pupils. He was said to have been the most popular of the masters, and a trip in the back of his Bullnose Morris was one of the better treats that pupils could enjoy.

Jumping forward to the start of the 2nd World War, Alan Mitchell wrote, 'The two Aris boys who were sent over from Germany to escape the Nazi terror arrived without a single word of English. The Head spoke to us and told us to help them to settle in with us and treat them with kindness, which we all did.'

Dyer made sure that the two boys were well looked after and covered the cost of their fees. He also arranged for the boys to phone their parents. They were able to make a connection but apparently the younger brother was so excited to speak he accidently hung up in his excitement. That was the last time they spoke with their parents, who both later died in the concentration camps. Most headmasters would have done the same in such circumstances, but Dyer's supportive attitude towards the refugees shows that he could occasionally reveal his inner humanity.

Long after he retired, there is the evidence from the man himself. He wrote a letter to his son, who was also just embarking on a teaching career:

> Then will come the settling in a new school. I don't think you will make all the mistakes I made, certainly not the one that was perhaps the worst – the too frequent inability to see the best in people, colleagues and pupils. Both are not always good but they were probably far better than I often thought they were. On the other hand, you will be wise enough not to be misled by the rogue.

Such self-awareness may have only come to Dyer later in life but there is evidence to suggest that he was at the time of his headship someone who was not at ease with himself, and prone to contradictory emotions. It has recently come to light via his family that during the war he had suffered from severe shell shock and that he struggled emotionally afterwards. Though his wife was said to have been an extremely kind and gentle woman who supported him greatly both emotionally and in his work, he may still have struggled to maintain emotional stability, adopting the character of stern disciplinarian as a strategy to maintain control.

One pupil later observed, 'I still have a vision of him striding down the long corridor with bowed head towards the sanctuary of his house which lay beyond the door at the far end. It never occurred to me at the time how relieved he must often have felt.'

* * *

Dyer the Head

Popularity does not necessarily go with effective leadership. As indicated by Howat earlier, Dyer's achievement in the decade before war broke out was sound if not spectacular but this was partly because, unlike Shaw, Dyer inherited from Bye a school that was in good shape and he was helped, as described below, by active and effective governors and by some good assistant teachers who provided the qualities that Dyer lacked.

In the 1930s the financial benefits that the School was receiving were considerable but they were coming not from the School's own income but what it received from the County Council. The endowment income was only about £130 a year while the maintenance grant from the local authority was £3,300 per annum. Nonetheless the School still retained some semblance of an independent status. For example, when the

County wanted to raise fees the Governors were able to force the County to back down, arguing that this would only lead to pupils being withdrawn. One of the Governors at the time was HAL Fisher, Warden of New College but who had been President of the Board of Education. He knew the importance of affordable education to a small town such as Thame.

Dyer made small changes to the School's routine, for example soccer had now been discontinued to concentrate only on rugby as more schools locally played with the oval ball, but the first half of the School's first full season at rugby was a disaster. Perhaps in part because they were playing teams of much experience like Old Wycombiensians, Saracens 'B', Henley Grammar, and Reading School.

There was a Natural History Society, a Cadet Force, a Scout Troop, and Camera Club. A branch of the National Savings Association was opened - though it was said that not all its members were 'particularly keen on saving.'

Sports Days included the steeplechase, 1 mile, half-mile, quarter-mile, 220 yards, 100 yards, high jump, long jump and cricket ball. All the boys paid a visit to the Oxfordshire Agricultural Show, held in a field behind the School. Early in the 1930s an entertainment was organised jointly with the Girls Grammar School and was performed in the cinema - it told the story of a Red Indian. This is the first mention that we have found of joint activities and these would continue in one form or another for forty years; perhaps the rule about not bringing in messages to the boarders had been relaxed.

Early into Dyer's tenure it was noted not for the first time that whilst the boarders were active in out-of-school activities, the day-boys gave slender support. 'Within school rugby, there appears to be a noticeable lack of public spirit among certain boys, particularly the day-boys. Their play is lackadaisical; inclusion in the team appears to be a matter of small importance compared with a visit to the cinema.' This led to day-boys living within a mile of the School being banned from cycling and they had to walk so as to improve their health.

In 1931 Dyer closed the Cadet Force, having decided that the Scout Troop was a more appropriate activity for the pupils as it offered more useful activities. In making this decision Dyer was reflecting the spirit of the age when demilitarisation, in the form of the Locarno disarmament conference, and 'appeasement' were already starting to appear, but he was also perhaps reacting to his own personal experience of the war.

Michael Fenwick described why he joined the Scouts:

> *Partly because of the uniform - the broad-rimmed hat, the scarf fastened with a leather woggle and the green ribbons decorating the tops of knee-high socks. I enjoyed the rope work, knotting and whipping and splicing, and tracking. And I have happy memories of summer camps by the River Cherwell and another by the River Teme in Worcestershire where we constructed an oven from mud and dried grass, and actually cooked something in it. We also had a kayak that we paddled on the River Thame.*

In 1933, Dyer had persuaded Dr WW Vaughan to distribute prizes at Speech Day. He had been headmaster at Rugby, and it is possible that his comment that boys should form their own opinions, not take what their parents or schoolmasters taught them as the truth, might have ruffled some feathers.

By 1934 the day-boys, following the criticism of their lack of interest in curricular activities two years earlier, were now more active in societies and sports. School outings included visits to Huntley & Palmer, Reading, William Birch Furniture Works in High Wycombe, Kodak, and Long Crendon Gravel Pits. The House points system was amended in an attempt to increase the competitiveness of the inter-house competition.

The 1st XV were able to watch the Varsity game at Twicken-ham, though they were still playing poorly as a team. One of the Governors, Mr Wood, drew up a long-term plan for the renovation and development of the School that was presented to the LEA.

By 1935 Dyer's efforts to encourage pupils to stay was paying off and the Sixth Form was slowly growing - though most pupils still left at fifteen or sixteen after taking the School Certificate.

The Sixth Form was divided into two divisions: one studying languages and history, the other mathematics and science, with a view to taking the Higher Certificate, although some left without taking the exam, often after only one year's study. At Speech Day, Dyer still made a plea for more pupils to stay on for longer and 'not to be in a hurry to leave.' He was much of the opinion that the sixth-form years provided the pinnacle of education and were the most valuable a boy could have.

To further encourage the take-up of further education, the John Hampden Leaving Scholarship had been established in 1931 to provide financial assistance to encourage pupils to at-tend university. A Past President of the OTA, RE Crawford, had been the driving force behind the project.

By 1936, the number of pupils had jumped to 144, which was a record. Founder's Day was celebrated on 29th November and drew a congregation of 80 parents and OTs - much larger than had been seen for many years. The cricket field was enlarged and an Elizabethan penny dug up during the excavations - much of the work was to remove a good deal of the bank on the north side to a line where we see it today. (Or at least the last surviving remnant as more recent building work has all but obliterated it.)

In the Library, students could read *Punch, Listener, Motor, Aero-plane, Motor Cycle, Wireless World, Meccano Magazine, Armchair*

Science, Popular Flying, and *Geographical Magazine.* Boys leaving the School were expected to observe the custom of donating a book to the library and, for the first time, fines for the late return of books were introduced.

There were now seven candidates for the Higher Certificate Examination and three went onto university - including Colin Cuthbert to Oxford (who later lost his life in North Africa in 1943.) This was testament to the improving academic performance. Swimming matches were held against Wycombe Grammar School, Southfield School Oxford and the City of Oxford High School. The 1st XV was hitting its stride for the first time since rugger was reintroduced and the average weight of the 1st XV was 10st 9lbs. The School now had seven full-time assistant masters - having grown from three over the last 15 years.

Norman Good came to the School in the late 1930s,

> *At the time there was one female teacher. Miss Devine (pronounced Diveen) and referred to by us, irreverently, as "Ma Divine". She was appointed to teach Junior Maths and was very much of the old school. Her Maths lessons will be remembered for their philosophical interludes - over our heads at the time but, in retrospect, probably as much value to us as mechanical removal of brackets and manipulation of complex fractions - but I still remember her dictum: 'First remove your brackets and then multiply and divide before you add and subtract'. Long may teachers of this ilk survive in the system!*

> *The main extra-curricular activities were playing marbles, a form of bowls on the parquet floors, and collecting cigarette cards to complete sets that were stuck into albums. Most of the boys collected eggs and butterflies, the lethal substance in the killing bottle was sodium cyanide.*

*There were distinct friendship groups at the School: those
who lived in Thame, the 'bus boys,' and the boarders of
course all who tended to stick together. I was one of the
different ones as I cycled in from a remote area.*

Nationally, the Government was looking at the provision of
education in the country. The Spens report of 1938 on secondary education recommended equality across all types of school
in the secondary system, with a tripartite arrangement of
grammar, modern and technical that would match the needs
and aspirations of pupils. One of its conclusions was that,

*In every phase of secondary teaching, the first aim should
be to educate the mind, and not merely to convey information. It is a fundamental fault, which pervades many parts
of the secondary teaching now given in England, that the
subject (literary, scientific or technical) is too often taught
in such a manner that it has little or no educational value.
The largest of the problems which concern the future of secondary education is how to secure, as far as possible, that in
all schools and in every branch of study the pupils shall be
not only instructed but educated.*

In the months before the outbreak of the Second World
War the School of course had no inkling what calamity was
about the befall the country. *The Tamensian* noted that a new
Boarders' Common Room had been opened with a ping-pong
table, and a miniature billiard table. A new library was opened
and the Master's Common Room had been refurbished. At
Speech Day, the boys and parents were urged by the eminent
scientist Sir Cyril Ashford to find careers that were:

*Congenial in preference to highly paid uncongenial ones,
so that there need be no deep contrast between the outlook
in hours of work and hours of leisure. The art of living*

together, so as to combine individual freedom with respect for the rights and happiness of others was a problem which older schools had been working on for centuries with a large degree of success.

Numbers in the School had reached a record 154, and in the summer of 1939 one pupil took the Higher Certificate and fifteen the School Certificate.

On the eve of the outbreak of war, therefore, Dyer could look back to a decade of steady improvements across many areas of school life but probably with mixed feelings. Despite his faults, it is clear that during the 1930s, he made valiant efforts to improve the School's academic credentials with some success. However he was limited by lack of money to invest in facilities, but also it is clear that many locally-living parents sent their sons to the School wishing them to receive a level of education that would see them prosper in the trades and lower reaches of the professions but not beyond. Perhaps only the boarders aspired to greater ambitions. Nationally, by the end of the 1930s, less than 2 per cent of the 18 year-old age group were going on to university. Unfortunately, his own behaviour likely put off some from staying longer and this led to some pupils leaving the School and completing their sixth-form education elsewhere.

CHAPTER 20: THE SCHOOL IN WW2 1939-1945

SHAW HAD FOURTEEN YEARS TO RESTORE the School's fortunes before war broke out. Dyer had ten to implement his academic aims. For both, the war years meant coping rather than advancing. In World War 2, evacuees began to quickly arrive: in September 1939 some 17 of the 33 new boys (of all years) were evacuees from London. All came from the middle-class suburbs including Eltham, Hampstead, Pinner, Wimbledon and Epsom; they were billeted in Thame and the surrounding villages, or were taken on as boarders. The School was given four boxes of first-aid kit and two stirrup pumps by the Education Committee.

The Aris boys, refugees from East Prussia were mentioned earlier. Gunter Aris, many years later wrote:

As new boys at School it was tradition that they be ragged during the first night in the dorm. Hans and I thought we were being attacked because we were Germans so we took our belts off and defended ourselves until the lookout boy shouted 'Cave' then our attackers dashed back into their beds and our ragging was ended.

Hans and I sat at the back of the class because we couldn't understand what was being said...Mr Drane our English teacher could speak some German so he gave us extra tuition at his home in Thame...the regimented routine was good for us because we soon learned the times for meals, the inspection of hands before entering the dining room and our allocated seat according to seniority. Similarly, we were joined by Zopf from Bremen who, if I remember correctly was the son of the commander of a German battleship. It was not long before his father's death was announced.

There were 163 on roll; of the 33 new admissions, only four were from Thame itself. Most of the local intake was from the surrounding villages: Aston Rowant, Chinnor, Great Milton, Horton-cum-Studley, Kingston Blount, Little Milton, Long Crendon, Princes Risborough, Stadhampton, Towersey, Watlington, and Wheatley.

In the 1939 Census, Dyer and his family are recorded along with four resident schoolmasters, seven resident domestic staff, and thirty-one boarders.

Rationing was quickly introduced but seemed to have little effect, other than Wednesday becoming meatless. (Perhaps because the quality of school meals could sink no further.)

Peter Franklin joined the School at this time:

I followed all the others when it was my first break out into a large field with freshly-dug slit trenches down each side of the gravel path to the flat area at the bottom.

I, with four others (David Davidson, Pat Davidson, Ronald Goodearl, and David Walsh), we all travelled on the train from Princes Risborough. This meant not getting to morning assembly in time, as the station was the other side of Thame but the headmaster was surprisingly understanding.

One year it snowed on and off for several days until one day the snow was very heavy with a strong wind. On getting to Thame station were told that the cutting along the track had filled in completely so we decided that the only way

home was walk the 7 miles along the track. On the way we
found the cap that David Walsh had lost out the window - I
wonder who threw it?

More air-raid precaution trenches were dug across the lower part of the cricket field, the swimming pool was declared a static water tank, and tape stuck across all windows to prevent flying glass.

In 1940 pupils had to undertake voluntary work including work on nearby farms; salvage activities were carried out by the Scouts. Masters joined Thame's Home Guard, while the Scout troop was asked to impersonate the enemy in an exercise to test the Home Guard's defences capability.

Sport was disrupted; only one 1st XV match was played due to lack of transport, a problem that did not affect cross-country runs that were routed as they had been for years (and as they were continue for decades) out on the Oxford Road, on to the Moreton Road past the brick works, down into Moreton village, past the pond, over Cuttle Brook, along the lane to the level crossing, through to the 'rec' and then down the hill to Cuttle Brook again, through the fields (now the Chiltern Vale Estate) and back to the School.

As with all bells in parish churches, the ringing of the turret bell ceased. Since the School had reopened under Plummer it had rung between lessons, before meals, and to announce prep.

One tragedy that occurred at this time was that the Right Honourable HAL Fisher, Warden of New College, and a Foundation Governor was knocked down by a lorry and killed on his way to preside at a Conscientious Objector's Tribunal. He had been an active governor as well as being important nationally in education reform and a distinguished historian.

A bomb went off at the Prebendal and several fragments

reached the School but only a few tiles were lost. Another bomb hit Bailey's shop on 107 High Street on the evening of 9th November 1940, and one memory of the day was clear:

> I remember that evening as I ended up in a ditch in More-ton. I was riding my bike along the lane, the air raid sirens were going. I thought I needed to get home quick but a bomber came over & a bomb landed right next to the lane in the field. The blast knocked me and my bike straight into the ditch, covering me in dirt. Unscathed, but for a few scratches I managed to get back home. A very frightening experience.

Boys were also used for potato lifting on neighbouring farms: 27 took part and in October and November providing over 1300 hours worth of work. Already by 1941, 11 OTs had given their lives, most while serving in the RAF; Dyers own son John had joined the RAF. Some 20 pupils were acting as messengers for the ARP and the Home Guard or taking turns with first-aid practice or fire-watching. Eleven pigs were fattened on school swill.

But the pupils were largely insulated from the devastation taking place elsewhere. A memory from Nonny Tiffany, an Old Girl from the Girl's Grammar School in Thame perfectly captures the mood:

> I was at the School from January 1940 until December 1942 as one of the younger full-time boarders, when Miss Hockley and Miss Messenger ran the school. It was right after the beginning of the war when people did not know what to expect. My home was in Stockport, just south of Manchester; my mother had recently died, and my father wanted me to be safe! He chose well.
>
> Hitler wanted Oxford to remain intact and sure enough

while I was there in Thame, I can remember only one stray bomb falling on the town! But as a result of this, all the boarders had to sleep downstairs in bunk-beds in the lovely front hall.

I was known at the time as "Nonn Adams", and I have many happy memories of my time at the School. There was very little to tell us that there was a war on, and that there was such a happening as Dunkirk or the Battle of Britain! We really were almost completely cushioned from the war. By the time my father and I moved down to Surrey in January 1943, I was completely blasé about it.

Exams were still sat: in the summer term of 1941, three boys had sat their Higher School Certificate, and 21 had sat the School Certificate.

Over the summer the boys did various holiday jobs, mostly involving work on farms. One boy laboured at Haddenham Aerodrome, another helped produce army camouflage netting, and another became a lorry driver's mate. Perhaps less essential to the war effort was the boy who worked in the foxhound kennels which mainly involved feeding and exercising them, the hounds still hunting four days a week.

Towards the end of 1941 *The Tamensian* was reporting with some optimism that the war 'seems to have receded. We have happily but one further casualty amongst Old Boys, and in Thame the siren has been scarcely heard...and rationing continues but is hardly more severe than in the first six months of the year.'

The Headmaster was given petrol coupons. War work by the boys continued: collecting salvage, potato and kale picking, gathering rose hips for the extraction of Vitamin C, and beet harvesting. A vegetable garden was dug. An Air Training Corps had been established in the town and older boys joined this, and a few senior boys also joined the Home Guard. One unit based in Thame was the 4th Battalion Oxfordshire Home Guard.

Many of the younger teachers were lost to war service and the staff shortages were seen as a considerable handicap. For example Mr Bevan, who joined the staff in 1935, was called-up to join the Royal Signals in the North Africa campaign, and RM Miller joined the RAF. Gradually more of the younger members left, and in their place came a succession of elderly and temporary replacements who had a tendency to hurl hard blackboard rubbers at badly behaving boys. Sixth formers were also drafted-in to take lessons.

One exception was the artist Peter Greenham who later became Keeper of the Royal Academy Schools. He had come to teach a bit of everything to lower forms. In an article written after his death:

> Lord Williams's School was then a tiny country grammar
> school, a robust community and brutal towards weak or
> incompetent masters, of whom there were a number among
> the motley collection of transients who flowed through
> the place at the time. Mr Greenham was a shy tall man.
> He might have seemed an obvious candidate for torment.
> Instead he proved to be quickly liked and respected not least
> for his ability to produce swift feathery portraits. These
> were much sought after by the boys who owned autograph
> books.
>
> He turned this skill to unusual account in the classroom.
> As lessons progressed he would begin with a few deft and
> enigmatic strokes on the blackboard to sketch those who
> misbehaved. Anyone wicked enough to have his instantly
> recognisable face completed could expect to receive appro-
> priate punishment to the delighted acclaim of the virtuous.

233

The optimism of 1941 also carried into 1942 when *The Tamensian* recorded 'events on all fronts seem to be taking a more favourable turn, and everyone is in consequence in much better spirits.' 169 OTs were or had served in the Forces; six were known to be PoWs and 17 had given their lives. By now the roll was 197 with 38 joining in September but only two had taken the Higher School Certificate while 17 had sat the School Certificate. The Air Training Corps take-up was still strong and this was leading to many boys joining the RAF after leaving School.

By 1943 the roll had dropped slightly to 186 pupils including around 40 evacuees. There were few bombs and those that were dropped were thought to be mistakes; the craters quickly attracted souvenir-hungry boys. The safest place in the building was judged to be the inside corridor between the dining hall and kitchen, and here pupils congregated if any sirens were sounded, and when practice drills were held.

Pupils became voracious egg collectors and butterfly catchers, and although the war was at its height, they still had an enjoyable day's outing in the summer, taking the train to Princes Risborough, playing games on the hills, stopping at a café on the way back, and ending with a party in the dormitory.

Beyond the School, the mood was perhaps more sombre. *The Tamensian* noted that in 1943 the town made no effort to celebrate the three hundredth anniversary of John Hampden's death; in fact it was said that the town clearly had no interest in the patriot, and had not even put up a plaque to show where he had died, whereas Aylesbury had mounted a proper celebration.

In terms of academic achievement, in 1943 E Matheison won an Open Scholarship to Downing College, Cambridge, and RO Shawe went to Bristol to study engineering; they were the only two boys to sit the Higher School Certificate. 17 had taken the

School Certificate.

Alan Mitchell wrote:

> *Blackout was done every day by four teams of four boys who had to cover the whole school. Dependent on the time of the year of course but in autumn the blackouts were put up at 5.45pm and then taken down at 8.15am. There was a team who were also responsible for locking and unlocking every door every day as well as making sure all the windows were shut before the blackout teams went round.*
>
> *No school photographs were taken. 'Away' fixtures were cancelled; there were a few home rugby matches against Royal Grammar School, High Wycombe, who travelled by train, and an Oxford school team who travelled by Oxford bus. There was an annual match against a scratch OTA side on Founder's Day.*

On a lighter note, the whole school was taken to the town's Grand Cinema to see Charlie Chaplin in *The Great Dictator*, probably because of the long homily delivered by Charlie Chaplin at the end.

One boy wrote a lengthy recollection of these mid-war years.

> *A small group of us managed to sneak in to see Coastal Command featuring Sunderland flying boats. A choir of about 40 of us "did" Hiawatha's Wedding at the cinema. Parents were invited. Nobody had a personal wireless set. One evening Mr. Dyer, the headmaster, brought his set into the classroom where we did prep. We listened with rapt attention to a Winston Churchill speech almost an hour long, perhaps at the time of the turning point victory at El Alamein. About half of the School was blacked-out; the rest was kept unlit.*

To help the war effort, a gang of about 20 was sent potato picking, which we called spud upping. In the field along the Oxford Road opposite Rycote Lane about where the by-pass roundabout is now. We picked up potatoes left on the surface by the spinner machine, into buckets and emptied them into carts. A pair of horses drew the spinner, one of which was wont to start the day with a virtuoso farting performance to the delight of his schoolboy audience. On a very foggy nil-visibility day, someone started throwing potatoes along the row, knowing that this was where most people would be working. This called for retaliation. Soon the fog was raining potatoes. Farmer Jack Castle arrived. He ran up and down the row hollering at the invisible spud launchers to get back to work and stop wasting food in wartime etc. He sustained a couple of hits and lots of near misses. Some day-boys, having bikes, went to Goods' farm at Aston Sandford.

One day Mr Howard Brown took a party to Princes Risborough by train. We climbed White Leaf Cross. On the hill an American built International T.D. 14 crawler tractor, which had done work on the family farm, was hauling timber. Before returning to the station, Mr. Howard Brown bought us each a soft drink at a small general store. While awaiting our return train, a goods train passed through, hauled by an American engine, which was later destined for the Continent after liberation. Europe was greatly indebted to American industrial production.

We were allowed an occasional short weekend home visit. I was returning to School, on Sunday evening, on the top of a no.84 bus from Aylesbury via Haddenham. On joining the A418 at Scotsgrove, the bus became incorporated into a column of tanks. We went down Scotsgrove Hill in the middle of road at 40mph, surrounded by tanks. Great fun. Unusual experiences were usual during the war.

During the 1940s most aircraft flew much lower than they do today. Of all the many planes that flew over, the North American Harvard Trainer was the noisiest. It made a loud droning noise that echoed back from buildings. Much worse than a present-day low flying helicopter. Speech and all other sound was drowned out. It was said to have been caused by the propeller design.

As more evacuees arrived in the area, pupil numbers swelled to 196 during 1944. Two extra forms were created to deal with this and the Sixth Form was larger than ever before, but this did not lead to a proportional increase in those taking exams as few were interested. A fifth House was formed for boarders only: School House, with the Headmaster as its housemaster. In the summer of 1944, five boys took the Higher Certificate, and 14 the School Certificate. Not sure which one Dad did

American supply trains ran along the railway line, pulling over two hundred truckloads of supplies for the invasion of Europe. An impressive sight to boys who stood there amazed, and counted them as they passed. There was much interest about the work that E.R. Watts & Sons, undertook on Southern Road. They manufactured aircraft bomb-aiming equipment but it was all hush-hush but that just peeked the boys' interest more.

School life continued to be curtailed through problems of transport and the 'black-out'. There was a shortage of rugby boots, and school dinners were now meatless for two days a week. As there were few general staff the boys helped out in the kitchen and the grounds.

Twenty-five new masters had come and gone since the war began, some like Peter Greenham with greater success and others with less. It was noted that the boys appeared noisier and disorderly. 'Whether this is a result of slackening of parental discipline, frequent changes of staff, or just the strain of war,' observed Dyer, 'let another decide.'

As the war began to clearly wind down, staff members started moving to other schools. When three leave at once it is not unfair to think that in part this was to escape the Dyer regime.

The official announcement for VE Day was heard by the boarders on Dyers' radio, on the evening of 7th May. The next day the Union Jack once again flew proudly from the School's flagstaff. However, within the School, there was no official celebration and the mood was sombre and more of thanks that it had all ended rather than jubilant celebration.

In Thame, an open air service was held during the day to celebrate VE Day, and members of the School attended. In the evening large crowds thronged the High Street but this was off-limits for boarders, although day-boys were seen enjoying themselves.

Local Old Boys who had been PoWs were welcomed home: the School had been sending them parcels of cigarettes from time to time.

Come the end of the war, it was announced that Hampden House was the grand winner of the aggregated points for the last 16 years of the House competition. After three years of no swimming due to water restrictions the swimming pool was refilled. School-outings now returned: to Beaconsfield, Tring and the Pitts Rivers Museum among others. There had been 324 siren alerts in Thame but no pupil had been injured, and the buildings were unharmed.

After VE Day, wooden screens, black paper and netting were taken down from the windows. School life quickly returned to normal although staff shortages were still an issue. However, it was still remembered that for those Old Boys serving in the Far East, the conflict had yet to draw to an end, and would not until the Japanese surrender in August.

When sports fixtures resumed, the 1st XV won all its matches in the winter term. This was something to celebrate but conversely at Founder's Day, the church was filled with sadness as, for the first time, the thirty-one names of those who had fallen in the war just finished, were read out.

A month later, as part of an attempt to encourage a sense of normality, a carol service was held for the first time in St Mary's church.

A little bit of fun did return on the last day of the winter term:

In those days the School Hymn was sung at the end of the last day of School before we were all sent home, only on this occasion as the science master (Old Ping) sat to play, which ever key he tried the sound was terrible, as if it had been tuned with a pair of pliers. Dyer told him to stop and the Hymn was sung without music. Dyer then threatened the whole of the school with not being allowed home in order to find the culprit. He had no success and eventually had to let us go. I knew who it was, as did some others, and indeed the boy had used pliers to retune the piano but Dyer never found out.

CHAPTER 21: 1947 AND ALL THAT – THE SCHOOL LOSES ITS INDEPENDENCE

IN THE 450-YEAR HISTORY OF THE SCHOOL, there have been three dramatic and life-changing events. The first: the collapse of the original foundation and the re-founding of the School has already been described. The third, the change from a small boys' grammar to a large coeducational comprehensive is the subject of a later chapter. Superficially of the three the second, the loss of independence, least affected the day-to-day life of the School but in the longer term its effects had an equally profound influence on the School's development. It is safe to say that had it retained its independence, its history during the following 60 years would have been quite different.

* * *

The national context

To fully understand the events of 1947, it is necessary first to look back at the broader context of educational developments in England during the second quarter of the 20th century.

In 1926, the Hadow Report published by the Board of Education proposed that education be split into two: primary and secondary. Within the secondary sector there would be the existing secondary schools, which would be upgraded to grammar schools, along with a new type of school called 'modern' that would cater for the less academically inclined. However, during the 1930s, little progress was made in creating a new form of secondary education, partly due to inertia on the part of successive governments, and the economic problems of the decade.

In 1938, the Spens Report proposed that not only should there be two types of secondary school, the grammar and modern but that technical high schools should also be part of the mix. The war did not entirely put this thinking on ice. A White Paper, *Educational Reconstruction*, recommended evolving the education system to provide successive stages of primary, secondary and further education. After the age of 11, pupils should be able to go to a diversified set of schools dependent on their needs. However, it proposed that this be done not by only setting competitive tests but based on their school record, parental wishes, and some form of intelligence testing. It also argued that the 'academic training' characterised by existing secondary schools was unsuitable for the majority of pupils. Once again it was proposed that there should be three types of schools: grammar, technical and modern.

However, while these debates had been going on, little thought had been given to independent (endowed) schools of which LWGS was one. They had been going quietly on their way, but increasingly the smaller ones were suffering from financial problems, as was the case in Thame for both the boys' and girls' Grammar Schools.

In 1944, the Butler Education Act legislated for full-time secondary education, free for all, so as to secure equality of opportunity in education for all children regardless of the means or class of their parents.

The 1944 Act introduced significant changes:

- County Councils were instructed to organise education into primary, secondary, and further stages.

- Free compulsory secondary education was made available for all children.

- Children between the ages of 5 and 11 were sent to primary schools.

- Children between 11 and 15 were to attend a secondary school suited to their abilities.

- Fees in grammar schools (providing secondary education for mostly middle class pupils of high academic ability) were abolished. (This of course being a significant change for LWGS.)

- Grammar schools were intended to teach an academic curriculum to the most intellectually able, 25 per cent of the school population, selected by the 11+ exam.

- Elementary schools (providing basic education for children aged 5 to 14 from poor families) were phased out.

- The compulsory school leaving age rose from 14 to 15.

- Local authorities were to provide school meals, free milk and regular medical inspections.

- The Ministry of Education was created to control and direct the implementation of educational policy.

The 11+ exam was introduced, taken in the last year of primary school, to test intelligence and abilities in English and arithmetic.

From this three groups of children were identified:

• Academically able pupils, who went to the grammar schools. These schools provided the main route to a university education.

• Practically able pupils, who went to vocationally-based technical schools. However very few of these were established.

• The remaining pupils (and mostly working class) were sent to a secondary modern school where they received a more basic education.

On a national level, the Butler Act remains even today, the most significant piece of legislation determining the country's education policy. The *Times* once wrote that RA Butler was 'the creator of the modern educational system.'

The effect on LWGS was stark: it would have to make a choice as to its future either to become wholly independent, or to become what was termed as Voluntary Controlled.

✳ ✳ ✳

Independence lost

It was clear that whilst LWGS was jealous of its independence, there were insufficient funds available to maintain this state and the school buildings were clearly inadequate for any sustainable future. The Governors and the School's Trustees saw that either the School must close or accept voluntary controlled status under the Local Education Authority. The first was unthinkable and the latter aroused suspicion among sceptics (particularly Dyer) that took the then Chairman of the Governor's, Lt. Colonel S.E. Ashton, considerable skill to overcome.

The likely immediate effects on the School were argued to be small: the abolition of the preparatory class as no pupils were taken into the School who were below eleven years old; all prospective pupils had to pass the LEA's 11+ exam, and the number of new pupils from outside Oxfordshire would decline as their parents now had to bear the cost of schooling.

If the immediate impact was small, the future was viewed with more pessimism: it was foreseen that there would be a general decline in numbers and that the boarding house would be abolished as the numbers from Oxfordshire families was likely to be small. It was felt that the School would lose its mix of pupils from different parts of the country and different backgrounds; there was even the fear that perhaps the Sixth Form would be closed. Generally, there was apprehension. 'Such dire results could have hardly been in the mind of those who framed the Act,' wrote Dyer.

A full inspection of the School by the Ministry of Education took place in 1946. (The last had been in 1934.) The Inspectors stayed for three days, joining assembly and meals as well as classes. It was reported that all three inspectors took a sympathetic attitude. They noted the significant contribution made to the quality of the School by the 'Out-County' pupils (the boarders), and the large proportion of such pupils in the Sixth Form. In the eight years since the last partial inspection, they noted that 22 had gone on to university. The concluding remarks of their report stated that the general life of the School was vigorous, that it had striven bravely to do the best for its pupils (and better than many comparable schools), and that it deserved commendation.

By early 1947 the School accepted that it could no longer remain independent. By an instrument of Government dated 14th March, it moved to voluntary controlled status under the Oxfordshire Education Committee. This meant the School would have all its costs met by the State, and would be controlled by the LEA. For the first time since 1575, the School had become as intended by Lord Williams: a school that offered free education.

It is apparent that the root of the School's loss of independence lies in its small endowment, as has always been the conventional wisdom, but not for the reasons normally given. Close examination of Williams's original endowment, as described in Chapter 3, reveals that, though not exceptionally generous, it was in 'the upper quarter of endowment income in this period.' From this we can conclude that financially LWS should have been in a strong position over the years.

It was not, therefore, Williams's parsimony that ultimately doomed his School's independence but the failure of succeeding heads and governors, especially New College and the Norreys and Wenman families, to add to those endowments. As is well known, Thame School was *alma mater* to many powerful, influential, and probably wealthy alumni in the 17th century. These could have been approached for additional endowments to cover the increasing cost of education, but the heads and governors failed to do what many other schools and university colleges did and continue to do: persuade wealthy alumni to support the institution that provided the education from which they benefited.

With the wisdom of hindsight, we can now see that fundamental reason for the School's loss of independence dates from well before Dyer's time.

The catchment area of the School was extended in order for sufficient numbers of pupils to enter each year and now reached Risinghurst, an outer suburb of Oxford in the west, and all areas in between; it also extended to Chinnor and the eastern county boarder, and southward down to Watlington. Those living locally in Thame who failed the 11+ went to the National School where they were taught English Reading, Composition, Geography, History, Mathematics, Science, Handwriting, Spelling, Gardening, Handiwork and Drawing.

At the same time, a grammar school for girls was established at Holton Park, near Wheatley, with the same catchment area.

With the start of the new academic year in September 1947 some thirty new boys entered the School in the First Form including 11 boarders, an encouraging start in this the first full year of the School's new status. This is one of the boy's memories of that first term:

All members of the Form have had quite a successful first term in work and games and we can provide some good scholars and sportsmen in the future. We are impressed by the School grounds, which we think are very well-kept, and the gymnasium. We have none of us such a good gym before and have enjoyed our work there and particularly the games conducted by our PT instructor.

Our favourite subject is Science – we like doing practical work in the Chemistry Lab – but some of us are linguists too and a few even enjoy Latin, though we have yet mastered the School Hymn. We are proud of the fact that one of our members sang two solos at the Carol Service (Finney 'who though his pace was slow surprised us with by the volume and purity of his voice.') and we are all agreed that the cases of stuffed birds in the Form Room look nice.

Alsworth and Morton seemed to have got off to a good start by achieving high alpha scores in their first term.

Thursday 18th Sept was a half holiday to visit Thame Show, and later in the term the School was closed to install a boiler.

A Taylor was the Head Prefect with P Mirams as School Prefect. P Mirams was also captaining the 1st XV and they had a mixed season, winning 4 and losing 4. One of the matches lost was 0-24 to the OTs. School and Harris did well in the House matches. And by the end of the Term, School was leading the House Challenge Shield. On 18th December the Carol Concert was held in the Parish Church. The weather was reasonable if showing both wind and sun rain and snow – though the first frost was on 23rd September. Fog was also frequent and snow fell on 18th November.

Yet, the accommodation at this time was wholly inadequate for the needs and size of the School. Indeed, the hope that new buildings would appear quickly was a decisive factor in the Governor's decision to seek voluntary controlled status. The deficiencies included the lack of an assembly hall and good science laboratories. The gym was too small; most classrooms were small and airless, and the boarding accommodation was spartan.

A second pupil at that time had a different set of memories:

> *I was in the first class admitted to Lord Williams's after passing the 11+. I was a boarder and had a county scholarship to cover the cost. All the boys older than us were fee-paying and looked at us as little better than yobs and swats. The School was incredibly old-fashioned in my time. We were forced to swim a width of the filthy old pool every morning, even if it meant breaking the ice with a pole.*

❋ ❋ ❋

The John Hampden War Memorial Fund

At an Extraordinary General Meeting of the Old Tamensians's Association in 1947 it was decided to amalgamate the First War Memorial Fund, seemingly in the gift of the Governors, with the newly launched War Memorial Scholarship Fund, which also absorbed the 1931 fund set up to provide scholarships to pupils going on to a university education.

The initial assets took in £255 9s 7d on deposit with the Post Office Savings Bank, and £33 at Lloyds Bank, but the response to the Appeal was sufficiently positive to allow the Trustees to think in terms of a Fund approaching £1,000.

It was decided that the capital and income of the Fund should be applied primarily to the provision of Scholarships and Exhibitions for the benefit of past and present pupils. The first Scholarship, of £25 per annum, was awarded in 1948, on the advice of Mr Dyer, to Peter Clarke, training as a Vet in Liverpool.

RE Crawford, of whom we have already heard in an earlier chapter, emerged as the first chairman of the fund, and a meeting held at the Spread Eagle in January 1948 was attended by GE Shrimpton, as well as Messrs Dyer, Castle, Purser and Syson.

The same meeting also discussed the proposed unveiling ceremony, due to take place on the 26th June after the OTs Cricket Match. A decision was taken to invite Mr Churchill to carry out the ceremony. Failing which, Lord Greene, the Master of the Rolls, might oblige. Failing him, perhaps Viscount Hampden, AP Herbert or Quinton Hogg.

Perhaps as the result of an oversight, the Articles did not provide for the provision of a memorial to commemorate those who had died in the war, and this was funded by the sale of residual assets in the 1914/18 Fund. The new tablet was designed and made by Maile & Co, of Euston Road, who had made the First World War memorial.

It was reported at the next meeting in May that all those actually approached had proved unable to accept the invitation. It was decided to approach Air Chief Marshall Sir Arthur Barratt, Inspector General of the RAF and, perhaps more realistically, Col GM Harper, an Old Boy. Time was of the essence.

In the end, the Memorial Tablet was unveiled after the cricket match with a ceremony that started on the steps of the pavilion and ended in the dining hall. The unveiling was conducted by Brigadier-General CAL Graham, DSO, who had served for many years in the Royal Artillery.

✳ ✳ ✳

Dyer retires

In 1948 Dyer retired at the age of 60 and, given his views about state education, was no doubt glad to do so. He went to live at The Red Cottage, Picket Twenty, Andover. In his last year only three boys took the Higher School Certificate, down from five the previous year, and sixteen sat the School Certificate with a 100 per cent success rate. It was recorded that the standard had not fallen below 85 per cent for many years. One of the last acts that he participated in was the unveiling of the War Memorial tablet in the dining hall in memory of those who had fallen in the 1939-45 war.

At his final Speech Day, Dyer noted that the School was in dire need of a hall equipped with stage and screen - though also noting that the highest priority was man-power and boy-power and that industry was enticing away potential teachers coming out of the Services with offers of remuneration far in excess of what the teaching profession could offer. He also noted that for the boys, too many still wished to leave school aged 16 or thereabouts even though they had better prospects if they stayed on.

The Tamensian was fulsome in its praise of Dyer's nineteen years' service, commenting that the School had flourished and academic attainments had been high.

In a lengthy piece in *The Tamensian*, William Guest (a long-serving master) went out of his way to be fair. He noted that Dyer clearly felt lonely at times in his position, and while he had made efforts to form relationships with the assistant masters these was not always close. Indeed, Guest said few would willingly seek him out to discuss anything to do with teaching.

And while outside the school day he showed a strong sense of humour, this was not evident during school hours. Clearly, he was not someone who was looking to introduce any new theories of education: he had 'no great faith in gramophones, cinema projectors, and BBC loudspeakers as aids to education.'

He stood for all the traditional values of hard work, serious play, punctuality and orderliness but his intensity was both a strength and a weakness. 'When he left the classroom,' Guest wrote, 'you could hear an audible sound of suppressed breath being released.' On the other hand, he wisely avoided interfering with the way the masters taught; conversely, he had a penchant for interfering when it came to games 'not always with the happiest of consequences.'

It was noted that Mrs Dyer had been a tower of strength in the boarding house and had shown unflagging thoughtfulness. She outlived her husband for many years and died in 1982, having moved to Australia where their son and his family had earlier emigrated. [He had two sons, John and Arthur, who he had sent to Bromsgrove School in Worcestershire. John joined the RAF during the war, then went up to St John's Oxford, returned to the RAF, and eventually became a Wing Commander. Arthur also went to Oxford but entered the teaching profession, and emigrated to Australia.]

The Governors presented him with a pair of Dutch paintings, an apposite choice for someone who liked things to be clear and detailed, lacking at least any superficial emotion.

Dyer did not live long to enjoy his retirement. Six years later he died over the Christmas holidays. He was 66. His relatively early death, as with Shaw and Bye, perhaps a result of the stresses of coping with wartime conditions and, in his case, the added tensions of dealing with the School's loss of independence. At a memorial service held in St Mary's, the vicar spoke of Dyer's high ideals and strong character, a man of sound scholarship and learning; a firm disciplinarian, he saw the path of duty and pursued it without regard for popularity or approval. While one might query Dyer's strength of character, the vicar's characterisation is otherwise a fair judgement.

CHAPTER 22: MULLENS - ENLIGHTENED CONSERVATISM? 1948-1957

IT WAS HOPED THAT A NEW ENLIGHTENED START would be made under the headship of Hugh Mullens. When he arrived, the School was still suffering from the staff shortages that Dyer had highlighted in his final public speech. Mullens had to rebuild the teaching staff but undoubtedly he was responsible for starting the transformation of the School to an entity closer to what it is today.

Mullens was a bachelor and arrived with his mother, his sister who looked after the domestic arrangement in the boarding school, his dog Towser, and his pipe. He was educated at Dean Close School, Cheltenham, a graduate of Keble College, Oxford in Mods and Classics, and he came to Thame having been Senior Classics Master at King William's College on the Isle of Man. During the war he had served with a commission rank in the Hampshire Regiment, and then later as an instructor at the Army School of Chemical Warfare.

His ambition was clear: like Dyer he wanted to build numbers staying on to the Sixth Form and significantly increase the number entering university. In his time, he saw the Sixth Form grow from a handful of pupils to close on twenty when he resigned – a number that today seems insignificant but then was a major achievement.

Since joining the School, he had been clear that a school should be judged by 'its Sixth Form and by its ability to keep up a steady stream to the universities'. In those early years, despite

Mullens' goal, too many boys still left after the Fifth Form, and some then left during the course of the Sixth Form having decided that in fact they were more suited to employment, and that a final exam would be of no benefit.

He realised the need to broaden the curriculum and improve the quality of the teaching facilities. Greek was added and he ensured that the new science labs - called the Boyle Laboratories - were planned, and eventually built even though this was after he left.

Attracting and retaining suitable staff is a continuous challenge for all head teachers. One of the critical problems in Mullens' early years was the difficulty in finding teachers with science degrees, a recurring problem as earlier chapters have indicated. When he first arrived, a pupil was studying chemistry in the Sixth Form by means of a correspondence course with Wolsey College, Oxford. Later Mullens was able to recruit part-time, two research students from the university.

He said that the root cause he and other heads faced was the comparatively low pay offered to teachers, and that science graduates in particular were being offered more lucrative careers in industry. 'The new Burnham Scale solves nothing. It was obviously inadequate and should never have been accepted by the professional associations and it is a grave injustice to the profession.'

In 1951, he wrote a letter to the *Times*:

> *Sir, The President of Corpus Christi suggests children's*
> *allowances as part solution of the present inadequate*
> *salary rates for teachers. It is, however, well-known in the*
> *profession that a batchelor as a rule gives better service*
> *to his school than a married man. The worth of a school*
> *master is measured by what he does for his boys over and*
> *above what he is paid to do: a married man because he has*

family responsibilities is often prevented from doing much more than he is paid to do. This is, of course, especially true in boarding schools, few of which have accommodation for married men.

Further it seems more equitable that there should be the same pay for the same work; and that difference in pay should correspond to difference in qualification and length of experience. It is for the State to give special privileges to the married man if it thinks fit by means of tax relief etc. It is not for the employer to dispense such privileges.

If Mullens struggled at times to attract staff he was successful in retaining them; within a few years he recruited science teachers such as Norman Lilley and Norman Good who then remained at the School for many years, and all of whom were married. It was a general characteristic of his era that staff turnover was low.

Peter More who had joined in 1951 as Head of Geography 'found the atmosphere rather quaint and archaic, with croquet for staff on the Headmaster's Lawn and my wife, Audrey who taught part-time, being admonished by a governor for appearing in Thame whilst shopping, wearing trousers.' Clearly there were many teachers who found the 'quaint and archaic' atmosphere congenial and shared Mullens' belief in the virtues of a small, traditionally run but forward-looking school. More looked back at this time as 'a very stable and peaceful period in the School's history, with the staff timetable virtually unchanged year-to-year for the simple reason that none of the staff left.'

Not that school punishments had diminished. Pupils were expelled - albeit very few - and Mullens could administer the cane, albeit now restricted to a maximum of six strokes on the backside. Prefects could administer the slipper. Mostly though it was the use of detentions, taken either during the Wednesday games period or Saturday afternoons.

As Brian Finney, a boarder, remembered:

> *I never warmed to Mr Mullens' delegation of almost all the domestic running of the boarding house to the prefects who were the primary disciplinary force and more feared than the masters. I remember all too well some of the slipper thrashings we received in our pyjamas. Many of the prefects were power-hungry and unsympathetic to the smaller boy's feelings of insecurity and loss of parental love. Fear was upper-most - there was a fear of bullying, the frequent slipperings, the alliances and betrayals among kids, the benevolent fascism of the entire regime.*

Cliff Nixey observed:

> *The pressure to behave and to perform was kept up in various ways: weekly performances were assessed in each classroom by the awarding of points - both good and bad. A bad behaviour point meant a visit to the Headmaster's study for a caning. They were guaranteed to leave blue weal marks.*

Bullying of weaker boys took place frequently and was usually ignored by the masters who thought it better to let boys sort out their own disputes and establish their own hierarchy.

Those arriving in the First Form had to put up with debagging and their trousers being hidden; beatings were common. These would carry on for few the years, particularly if the boy was not a sportsman as achievement at games was viewed as the pinnacle of success.

A system of 'fagging' also existed where new boys had to work for senior prefects and head-of-house. This involved a broad range of menial tasks particularly if both boy and prefect were boarders: shoe-cleaning, bed-making, clearing the prefect's room, shopping and being a general dogs-body.

Mullens oversaw academic improvements across the board. In 1951 when it could be said the School had settled down and staff numbers had risen, five boys took the newly introduced A-Levels and nineteen sat O-Levels. Two years later, the number passing O-Levels had risen to thirty, though A-Level candidates had only increased by one, but by 1956 the numbers taking A-Levels had doubled to twelve, and O-Level numbers had remained steady.

Mullens had done well at persuading boys to stay on into the Sixth Form. He was to leave the School having achieved the best O-Level results in the county, and with ten Old Boys up at Oxford - a record for the School.

But his achievements were not only confined to academic work. He fostered continuing progress in sport. In 1956 four boys represented Oxfordshire in the All-England finals, and the School participated in the first school's seven-a-side rugby tournament that had been organised for twenty teams across Berks, Hants and Oxon. They reached the final but lost 3-8 to Lord Wandsworth College.

Not that sporting conditions were ideal: the rugby field was rented from a farmer, and when it was not being used for games was grazed by his cattle. Before inter-school matches on Saturday afternoon, the boarders were sent out to clear the cow-pats.

All of Mullens' predecessors had tried, with varied degrees of success, to improve academic and sporting achievement, but he was the first to realise the importance of a broad range of extra-curricular activities and to foster them, thereby demonstrating that time spent on activities other than lessons and games in no way undermined academic standards.

He introduced the annual school play, performed at that time in an outdoor theatre, and appointed Gerard Gould, the inspirational Oxfordshire drama adviser, to be Head of English, thus ushering in a period of excellent drama both within and beyond the formal curriculum. The Combined Cadet Force was reintroduced, having been abolished in the early 1930s, and it quickly became a flourishing activity.

He realised the need to publicise the School and to show that it was not an 'ivory tower' isolated from the town and national events. In 1953 the School celebrated the Queen's Coronation by setting up floodlights so as to make it look attractive but unfortunately the inclement weather prevented people seeing the building all lit-up in the evening. (Rain had also marred the coronation itself.) The School had closed on the Friday afternoon and would not open again until the following Wednesday. To commemorate the Coronation, an oak seat was placed on the south-east corner of the cricket field, and the Chairman of the Governors Lt. Colonel Boyle planted a deodar cedar on the Headmaster's Lawn which, he said, might grow to 250 feet. (It was eventually chopped down in 2015 to improve the view.)

Despite Mullens' manifold successes, he was not entirely happy. He was uncomfortable with LEA control and in his Speech Day addresses often criticised their failings and the direction they were taking. Above all else, he wanted to keep the School as one that had fewer rather than more pupils.

His stance remained consistent over the years:

> *1953: I believe the School is doing its job. Our only fears are when we read in the Press, the ignorant theorising of politicians and others who, believing in equality of opportunity, will not believe that it exists until we have equality of results, which is not attainable nor even desirable. Remember that any grammar school is trying to give its boys as good an education as a public school. It is a commentary on the present system of state education that the public school is*

still immeasurably better than the state grammar school.

1954: The grammar school course demands work done by the head and not by the hands, and I deplore the latest proposal to create a new examination system in such subjects as 'plastering and puppetry' and to call it a General Certificate of Education.

Mullens' mother died in 1954. One pupil remembered how Mullens told them in an O-Level Scripture class of her impending death. Mullens was at pains to point out the importance of treating people with dignity at all times no matter how ill they might be.

In 1955, Mullens expressed frustration at the LEA's inability to execute promised plans particularly in the building of new accommodation. Plans had been proposed, then abandoned, and then replaced by new and different ideas. This was the case with the plan to build new science laboratories. Not a brick had been laid. This meant that most of the sixth-form pupils still took arts-based A-Levels and not science. Neither had new classrooms been built.

He also pointed out that the LEA was 'imposing a cut of 11 per cent on books and stationery - the lifeblood of grammar schools'.

Come 1956, he complained that in the last few years the grammar schools had been comparatively neglected in favour of the secondary moderns, and often had to teach with meagre resources.

He also criticised the idea - already under discussion within Government circles - of abolishing the three-tier system based on the 11+ exam and making secondary education comprehensive and non-selective which, it was claimed, would lead to greater efficiency and be more economical in operation. In part this was because it was acknowledged that too many secondary modern schools were not providing any meaningful education for their pupils.

In light of his views, there seems to have been little surprise when Mullens resigned in 1957 to take up the headmastership of the Royal Masonic School, Bushey. It was clear that he had loved the School but found being part of the state system not to his liking. Not least had been the failure of the LEA to provide - other than the new science labs, which were now being built - the accommodation that had been promised in 1947.

In his final speech he said,

> *'I cannot honestly say that I have ever felt at ease working under a local education authority. Previously I had always been in independent schools. Now that I have seen both I cannot believe that the local control in its present form is the best machinery for guiding and administering education in this country. I think that it is something that all friends of Lord Williams's must regret that it was necessary to accept controlled status in 1946. But that step has been taken and is unlikely to be reversed.*
>
> *Controlled status too often results in the essential differences between a grammar school and a secondary modern school being obliterated. In all essentials grammar schools are the same as public schools and in my opinion it should be the constant aim of everybody concerned to bring them up to the standards of the best public schools in the country.'*

In the final analysis, the impact of Mullens' relatively brief headmastership should not be underestimated. In a short time he started the transformation of the School into what became its modern entity, one that lasted until it became a comprehensive and in the immediate years beyond. He recruited some excellent teachers, four of whom who having arrived young would see out their careers at the School, making much impact, until they retired some thirty years later.

David Green in his book about life at Lord Williams's in the 1950s concluded that:

> *Most Old Tamensians look back at their 1950s schooldays with pride and affection...[even though] by modern standards a 1950s education would seem quite narrow - lots of language study, almost no creative work in the Arts, limited opportunities for scientific enquiry, no choice of sporting activities, narrow assessment methods, and almost no pastoral care or career advice.*

CHAPTER 23: JONATHAN NELSON 1957-1963

MULLENS WAS REPLACED BY JONATHAN NELSON, who had taken his degree at Christ's College Cambridge, and had been teaching history at Exeter School. In the war he had attained the rank of Major in the Royal Armoured Corps. He joined just as the new science laboratories finally opened, and arrived with his wife Phyliss, who ran then ran the boarding house.

It can be persuasively argued that there is no such thing as the ideal head. None are equally gifted in the many skills that are involved. The best head is the one whose strengths are a close match to the needs of a school at the time of his (or her) appointment; in the phrase used earlier 'The right man at the right moment'. (The idea that a woman might be the right head was generally inconceivable to the governors and, indeed, there has only been two woman at the head of the School since its foundation and only one through choice.)

Thame had its fair share of such 'ideal' heads: for example its first, Edward Harris who established its reputation, and Alfred Shaw who rescued it from near collapse. It also had its fair share of disasters: the pluralists of the 18th and early 19th century, and the sadistic Fookes. Most heads, however, fell somewhere between these two extremes. They added value to the School without fully meeting its needs. Both Mullens and his successor Jon Nelson fall into this middle category. Their broad aims were similar but they were very different in their approach.

Mullens' achievements have been described in the previous chapter but his frequent and public criticisms of the LEA did the School no favours. Nelson proved to be a safer pair of hands. He did not ruffle the feathers of the LEA, but he was not a man of great vision, more analytical and deliberate than a man with flair.

In his first public pronouncement of how he viewed the future, he envisaged the roll hovering around 180 pupils - what he called the normal figure to be expected in a single stream grammar school - with the five lower forms having a maximum of thirty pupils in each year, a fair number leaving at aged fifteen, with some thirty pupils across the Lower and Upper Sixth Forms. He did not foresee any expansion.

He noted that the School was more 'local' than it had been at previous times in its history: most of the day-boys came from Thame, Chinnor and its environs, along with fifteen from the Headington-Wheatley area; and fifty per cent of the boarders had parents who in fact lived in Oxfordshire.

Following a visitation by HM Inspectors led by Lady Helen Asquith in 1958, Nelson also announced that at long last the Ministry of Education had approved plans to spend £40,000 on buildings, scheduled to be opened in 1962: a new hall and gymnasium, a splendid new library, administrative space, a Masters' Common Room, and two new classrooms. Inexplicably, he envisaged even then that there would be no increase in school numbers but rather that the new buildings would mean that pupils and masters could enjoy more elbow room.

His only comment on the curriculum was that it would continue as present with perhaps an increasing emphasis on the sciences. There was no hint that he wanted to expand what was being offered at A-Level: Classics, Maths, English, French, Geography, History, Physics, Chemistry, and Biology. To deliver these subjects there were twelve members of staff.

In many respects Nelson's thinking was in line with the conventional wisdom about Britain in general and education in particular during the late 1950s and early 60s, the era of Macmillan's famous 1957 'never had it so good' speech. Macmillan advocated 'restraint and common sense - restraint in the demands we make and common sense on how we spend our income' and attacked the 'doctrinaire nightmare' of socialism, which along with its policies of nationalisation and central planning included comprehensive reorganisation.

On the other hand, the Crowther Report, which considered the provision of education for 15 to 18 year-olds, published in 1958, stated,

'The proportion of grammar school places to the total population varies so greatly from one part of England to another, and bears so varying a relation both to the social background and the distribution of ability in particular communities, that about the only thing one can safely say is that the grammar school will contain the ablest, and the modern school the least able, of the boys and girls in its catchment area. There is a considerable intermediate group of boys and girls whose abilities would in one place give them a grammar school education and in another a modern school one'.

Nelson's headship lasted for six years before he resigned to go to Hutton, a grammar school in the north of England, with over 500 pupils. As Headmaster, he witnessed stability, modest progress, and minimal innovation, although drama continued to reach new heights and Art at long last had a specialist teacher.

Possibly the most notable event of his time was the Quatercentenary of the School's foundation, held in 1959. Various events were held across the year including the third summer fête in as many years, and opened by the film star David Tomlinson.

Both his son attend the school with me

It was an essential source of income for the Quatercentenary Appeal, which in the end raised £2,500. What it was raising money for had gone through several proposals, the first of which was a commemorative arch, the second was a squash court but finally the School alighted on new hard courts for tennis, which were opened on Founder's Day.

[The squash court was revived a few years later, this time the Governors were prepared to fund the cost of materials but the cost of construction had to be found by the School. This was done by enlisting an army of staff, parents and pupils to self-build the courts.]

Nelson showed enthusiasm for drama but less so for music. The play in 1959 year was the UK première of *The Lion and the Unicorn*, which played to over a thousand people. This was followed in September by a tour of Germany with a production of *Twelfth Night*. (Volume 2 has more detail about the drama productions in this period.)

On Founder's Day, 1959, a special Act of Commemoration was held, and the Bishop of Lincoln preached the sermon. The new tennis courts were opened by the Countess of Macclesfield, and a special exhibition was held in the School of relics from the original foundation, many borrowed from New College. In the evening the Old Tamensians's held a dinner not only to celebrate the founding of the School but their own fiftieth anniversary. At the dinner, the artist and Old Tamensian Mr Walter Myall presented six portraits of some of the more famous old boys. (Some of these can still be seen in the Foundation Centre.)

The only disappointment was that the Governors had been unsuccessful in achieving a visit by royalty which would have been a high spot, and which many felt the School deserved.

Despite Nelson's prediction that there would be no increase in numbers, they did expand during his tenure until the roll reached 215. This was the result of the first wave of the post-war baby boomers entering the system.

It also should be noted that Nelson introduced modernising elements including a much widened house competition, the introduction of half-term holidays, significantly improved administration (reflecting his meticulous attention to detail), standardised period times, and elimination of some of the old bad disciplinary practices that were practised by prefects. He abolished his own use of the cane, seven o'clock swims for the boarders became a thing of the past, and he allowed second-year sixth formers to opt out of games.

There had been improvement in the numbers and quality of O-Level results, in part because he enhanced the structure of the teaching and allowed boys to drop their weakest subjects. But also because the threshold for passing the 11+ exam had been raised to dampen the number of pupils passing, as the number of grammar school places had yet to catch up with the baby-boomers now coming through the system.

In his final year, twenty-two pupils had taken and passed A-Levels and twenty-five the following year that he could claim to have nurtured, a steady increase over the years of his tenure as in his first year there had been only twelve entrants. Yet few LWGS pupils were going on to tertiary education; across his headmastership the numbers continuing to university remained in single figures each year.

Why few pupils went on to university is down to a number of reasons. The attitude of parents was always a factor: many still did not appreciate the value of a university education. To increase numbers, Nelson not only had to influence the pupils but also their parents, but he was a shy man and did not have a natural rapport with those he did not know well.

Neither should it be forgotten that until 1962, the State did not provide grants for students to cover fees. Before their introduction, students and their parents had to negotiate a jungle of grants and scholarships unless they came from wealthy backgrounds and could afford to pay out of their own pockets. This in itself was off-putting.

Nelson's tenure had been short, only six years. As was remarked when he left, 'the wind of change was not a hurricane but a steady trade wind.' However, unlike Mullens, he had an excellent relationship with the LEA and with Her Majesty's Inspectors and saw to the swift implementation of their recommendations. He had indeed been a safe pair of hands.

Peter More, who taught geography, later had this to say about Nelson, most critically that he had 'laid the foundations of the modern school.'

He had a dry wit and was convivial on social occasions. He was fair, just and widely respected for his integrity. He worked for the community, was a member of the Parochial Church Council and a Churchwarden. He introduced parents meetings and liaised with the staff of the primary schools. He became a Town Councillor and was judged an excellent committee man. In fact he laid the foundations of the modern school, with the welding of parents, pupils and former members into a team.

After the bachelor establishment of the previous nine years the boarding house echoed to the sound of what the then Chairman of Governors called "the boisterous Nelson children". Family solidarity was a key feature of the Nelsons. The Boarding House regime became less spartan with bedside lockers and colourful décor in the dormitories. Breakfast was made a quarter of an hour later and compulsory seven o'clock swims were discontinued! Phyl Nelson, his wife, was a great support and ran the domestic side with equal efficiency and care.

Nelson left at Christmas 1963, and as the new headmaster could not join until the summer of 1964, Peter More had to fill the breach, which meant that he, his wife and three children had to move out of their home in Thame to live full-time in the School.

CHAPTER 24: THE WENMAN, 1960S

BEFORE RECOUNTING WHAT PROVED to be the last age of the grammar school, it is worth digressing to provide a brief history of Thame's other secondary school, the Wenman, as in a few years time it would become part of the family. This account is based on the writings of its first and only headmaster, the late Geoffrey Chaplin, and the HMI Inspection report of 1963.

Across the 19th and first part of the 20th century, Thame's senior boys and girls who did not go to the grammar school, the towns private schools and later the girls' grammar, could attend either the British School or the National School until the school leaving-age. Both institutions also took in infants and juniors until 1929 when education for these two groups was consolidated into the British School, which was renamed the John Hampden School, and all senior aged children were then taught in the National School. In 1945, with the reorganisation of the school system, the National School became a secondary modern, with voluntary controlled status from 1949, and was renamed as the Thame Church of England (Voluntary) Secondary School. There were 160 seniors in 1950.

In 1955 the LEA started to discuss how best to provide education for the ever-increasing number of senior boys and girls in the Thame, Chinnor and Tetsworth area who had failed the 11+. Thame Secondary School was far too small to cater for the influx of additional pupils from outside of Thame, and in addition there was the expected growth of the pupil population as the birth rate increased.

* His daughter taught at Chinnor primary
and I had a crush on her.

Should the existing school be extended to cope with extra pupils or should a completely new school be built in the town, bearing in mind that Thame Secondary School at that time was well over 100 years old? And what of the senior children at Chinnor's all-age school which was now showing signs of bursting at the seams?

Following a meeting held early in 1955, the machinery was set in motion for building a new school, one that was large enough to cater for the needs of the seniors from Chinnor as well as those from Thame and Tetsworth. It was also suggested that a group of boys some 50 in number – who were taking a two-year secondary technical course at Rycotewood College - should be transferred to the new Thame Secondary School when it was built and the course extended to three years. (This plan was eventually abandoned because of the nation-wide discontinuance of technical courses beginning at the age of 13+ years, and only one set of boys taking part in the original technical course did, in fact, complete a full course in the new school.)

Approval for the proposed school was obtained from the Ministry of Education; the necessary money was guaranteed, farm land was purchased off the Towersey Road for buildings and playing fields, and plans drawn up. The school was to have normal classroom accommodation together with a large assembly hall, a science room and five craft rooms for art, housecraft, woodwork, metalwork and needlework – as well as cloakrooms, changing rooms, staff room and library. The all-important school uniform was to be a maroon blazer, worn with either a grey skirt or trousers.

A Governing Body was set-up consisting of twelve members: nine were representatives appointed by the Education Committee, one was nominated by Thame Urban District Council, another was the nominee of Bullingdon Rural District Council, and the twelfth was a co-opted member to represent parents.

By 1959 the builders were hard at work and the new school was ready for occupation by the promised date, Tuesday September 6th 1960. It had been built at a cost of £95,000.

The school opened with 202 boys and 129 girls on the registers. (The unusual gender disparity due to the extra boys from Rycotewood being part of the intake.) They were taught by a staff of 16. Some of the teachers had come from the old Thame Secondary School, some from Chinnor, and Rycotewood College, whilst others had been appointed from areas far away from Oxfordshire. Mr Chaplin had been headmaster of Thame Secondary School. Most of the teachers were full-time and out of the total number, around five were woman in the early years.

Geoffrey Arthur Chaplin was born in Headcorn, Kent, on 10th April 1917, the son of Arthur William Chaplin, a local grocer, and his teacher wife May. Arthur was something of a Winston Churchill look-a-like who 'may not run to large cigars but has the same flare for getting things done'.

Chaplin attended Judd School in Tonbridge from 1927 – 1935, being Head Boy in his final year. In 1937 he graduated BSc in Chemistry and Pure and Applied Maths from Goldsmith's College, London, and the following year gained a University Teaching Diploma.

He held several supply teaching posts in the south-east of England until he commenced military service in January 1940. He was perhaps fortunate that he was not required to go much further than Brighton in the course of his contribution to the war effort. Most of his service was with REME, working on the development of coastal radar equipment.

Other talents came to the fore including representing his Corps at sprinting and other sports. He made time in 1942 to marry Amy Ruth Kingsford, a young Kentish woman who had also studied at Goldsmith's College. They settled in Folkestone and were actively involved in the nearby Cheriton Baptist Church, particularly with the Youth Fellowship.

After the war, Chaplin took up a permanent post as science master at Dover RoadSchool in Folkestone, teaching science and mathematics from 1946 until 1952. He then moved, with Ruth and their two children Elizabeth and Tony, to a post as Senior Master at Arthur Mellows Village College in Glinton near Peterborough before taking up the headship in Thame.

There was also caretakers, cleaners, kitchen staff, and a school secretary to deal with the various needs of teachers and pupils.

The school leaving-age was fifteen and the school was divided into four years with approximately 80 pupils in each year. Each year was divided into two forms of roughly equal ability, and a third smaller form for those less able. There was no provision for those with special needs.

Pupil numbers would grow across the 1960s, as did the number of teaching staff, which reached 25 by the middle of the decade. In this respect both pupil and staff numbers were similar to the grammar school.

In the early 1960s opportunities existed for the transfer of pupils at the end of their fourth year to Northfield Secondary School in Littlemore, Oxford, in order to sit O-Levels - with the possibility thereafter of taking a sixth-form course at Littlemore Grammar School. In the three years since the school's start, twelve boys and fourteen girls had gone on to do at least another year. They reached Littlemore by taking the train from Thame. When the line closed in 1963, they were taken by coach.

The official opening did not take place until almost the end of the school year when, on Tuesday July 25th 1961, the School was honoured by a visit from Group Captain Leonard Cheshire,

VC, DSO, DFC who first opened the School officially and then presented the prizes at the first prize-giving ceremony. Earlier in the year the school Houses had been named after four distinguished, living Englishmen – Bannister, Cheshire, Hunt and Whittle – and so it was most appropriate that the opening ceremony should be carried out by one of these four in person. Also at the ceremony was the Vicar of Thame, The Rev. R H Faulkener, with the Rev. David Green representing the free churches of Thame. It would appear that either the Roman Catholic priest was not invited or he was unable to attend.

During the ceremony Geoffrey Chaplin made a speech and in conclusion, he remarked:

> *To all parents I would make this plea: do try to keep in close contact with the school...You must surely want to do the very best for your child; whether or not you always believe this, I can assure you that we, the teaching staff, have precisely the same desire, and the welfare of children is the concern of us all.*

He also made the point that the School was not there only to prepare its pupils for employment through their ability to spell, use tools and do arithmetic but the School should encourage pupils to acquire interests in the arts, music and drama, and they should have some knowledge of geography, current affairs and history.

The full curriculum covered English, Mathematics, History, Geography, Science (not divided into specific subjects), Religious Instruction, Music, Physical Education, Arts and Crafts, Woodwork, Metalwork and Technical Drawing. No foreign languages were taught, at least initially, nor was there provision for music or the learning of instruments. This was a disappointment for Mr Chaplin as he was someone who was much interested in music and, infact, had formed the Thame Choral Society in 1960. However there were insufficient funds to recruit a music teacher.

In the third year onwards two alternative courses were offered, differentiated by gender which was standard practice at the time: for boys a craft technical course, and a commercial course for girls where shorthand and touch-typing were taught.

The Library in 1963 had 2,300 books augmented once a term by books brought by the County Library's van. However this number was deemed insufficient for all subjects of the curriculum to be represented adequately. Pupils in the first three years spent one weekly period in the library when they were able to read a book of their choice.

During 1961 it was learned that approval had been given for the construction of a small swimming pool on the site, and work began on this project, the pool being finally in use by the summer of 1962 and opened by the Olympic runner Mary Rand. (Parents had been asked to contribute £25 per family towards the cost – or so it has been remembered by past pupils, although this seems a very high sum.) The sports facilities also included tennis and netball courts, two football and two hockey pitches, and a gym. However, HMI noted that the changing facilities were inadequate for the number of pupils. In the summer athletics took place, and cricket was played. The staff put together a cricket team - augmented with some pupils - who played local teams on a weekday evening.

Also in 1961 it was announced that the School was to have a new official name. In recognition of the services rendered in past years to education in the district by the Wenman family (formerly of Thame Park) it was decided that in future the School would no longer be called Thame Secondary School but instead would be called the Wenman County Secondary School.

During the next few years it became obvious that the existing buildings would soon be inadequate so further discussions took place regarding the kind of extensions which would be needed. The first of these extensions was a Youth Wing that could also be used by various youth clubs in the evening. This was built adjacent to the school and although the building was delayed for a time owing to unforeseen difficulties it finally opened at the beginning of 1967. One of the clubs that used it was the newly refounded Thame Youth Theatre on a Wednesday night. (There had been a youth theatre back in the 1950s.) Perhaps unsurprisingly, most of its members came from LWGS, the Wenman, and Holton Park GS.

The School also had seperate space for adult further education but which was also increasingly used by the School for teaching.

By this time work had already started on the major building programme to increase accommodation. Included in the extensions were two new science rooms, an art and pottery area, a needlework room and enlarged staff room and other administration offices. These, along with an extra classroom and a second hall, were ready for occupation by the end of 1968.

The day began with a simple act of worship and when the inspectors made their visit they were impressed by the 'serious and reverend bearing of the pupils on this occasion.' Then it was lessons. Lunch was cooked on the premises and was said to be 'palatable, reasonably planned and of good quality...with most of the diners appearing to enjoy their meals.'

The House system was said to be thriving and promoted healthy competition. Sixteen prefects including a head boy and head girl were chosen by the staff each year to undertake minor duties but they were said 'to exercise very little responsibility.'

The School produced a magazine called *Mosaic;* it organised trips overseas including Italy, Austria, Belgium and Luxembourg, and along with all the other secondary schools in the County, visits were made to the outward bound centres, Patterdale in the Lake District and Tregoyd in the Brecon Beacons. Many of the secondary modern schools would send pupils for four to six weeks, and in the 1960s these were often led by Fred Fox, a specialist outward bound teacher employed by the County, who became somewhat of a legend and is well-remembered by many Oxfordshire pupils.

Those who left school aged fifteen at the end of the fourth year would take a County Test of Achievement where pupils received a Pass or a Distinction in each subject. A Fail was left unnoted. This was not a recognised qualification but it did show potential employers the leaver's ability. It was a forerunner of what became the Oxford Certificate of Educational Achievement in the 1980s, and used by many other counties other than Oxfordshire to certificate the achievement of pupils of all abilities.

The majority of pupils would go straight into employment at the end of the fourth year. Most of the girls went into clerical work or the retail trade. Some went to work in factories, hairdressing or working for the GPO. Of the boys, a major proportion took up engineering or other apprenticeships, some went into factory work or farm labouring. Only a few entered the armed forces.

From 1966, pupils could stay on voluntarily for a fifth year and take the newly introduced Certificate of Secondary Education. These were graded 1-5, and a Grade 1 was the equivalent to an O-Level pass. There was no longer any need to switch to Northfield and now, if pupils wanted to try for A-Levels, they could join LWGS. However few did this.

It was also possible for pupils to be transferred directly to a grammar school at the end of the first year if it was clear that their failing of the 11+ was not a true reflection of their abilities but the uptake of this had been less than a handful.

There was still insufficient accommodation. Chinnor's population was growing fast and nearby Buckinghamshire pupils were beginning to press to cross the border for their education rather than travel to Aylesbury. So almost before the cement set in the first extension buildings, discussions were being held about a second building programme. However, by this time, plans for the implementation of comprehensive education were nearly complete, and so these discussions were put on hold. (And their short-sighted postponement ultimately led to the need to build a second lower school on the Oxford Road site.)

Inevitably pupil memories of the School's brief history are mixed. Some thought it was 'Brilliant. Changed my life' and remembered the teachers fondly. 'Touch typing got me lots of work over the years'. Others were happy to get out, 'You could leave school at Easter providing you were 15, I did and started work the following Monday.' 'Mr Dunsby gave me plenty of thrashings with his various sized bamboo canes.' 'I hated it at this place... although my fellow pupils were nice and some of the teachers were good.'

In the Inspection of 1963, it was noted that 'the staff work conscientiously and loyally; they are - apart from the senior handicraft master [Mr Davies] who is outstanding - a body of teachers of average ability.' It was also noted that the type of teaching offered too little opportunity for pupils themselves to exercise initiative and responsibility, and that the pattern of lessons varied very little.

However, apart from weaknesses in certain subjects due to staffing difficulties - something endemic to the whole educational system, i.e. shortage of qualified maths teachers, others temporary - the quality of teaching was reasonable for the majority of pupils of middling ability, but insufficiently challenging for the more able.

The HMI inspection noted that 'the School is kept in very good order. The pupils take care of it, and it is very well maintained by the caretaker, and his assistants.' They were at pains to point out that there was a pleasant atmosphere which they put down to Mr Chaplin's approach to running a school, and the respect and courtesy he showed to both colleagues and pupils.

In terms of running the School what occupied most of Chaplin's summer holiday was the preparation of the following year's timetable. Armed with a mass of coloured drawing pins, each colour representing a different member of staff, he would stand for hours in front of a large chart, rearranging the pins until satisfied that everyone was teaching who, where and when they should.

Overall, it seems that, in comparison with other secondary modern schools, the Wenman performed reasonably well during its short history. Although the summary below is from 1963, it is known that the school was able to make improvements. More staff were recruited including Bill Gilbert (mentioned elsewhere) as a part-time music teacher, and this gave impetus to the extra-curricula activities. Student teachers from Westminster College, who came to the school for a term, also made a difference.

> *Good honest work is being done at all levels, and in general the atmosphere is pleasant and co-operative. There is evidence, however, that more exacting demands might be made on the older boys and girls. Opportunities for showing initiative both in the process of learning and in the broader aspects of school life need to be increased. This is a challenge which, with the advantages of accommodation and staffing it now enjoys, the School should be well able to meet.*

CHAPTER 25. THE FINAL GRAMMAR SCHOOL YEARS 1963-1971

THE 1960S WERE AN ERA OF HOPE, innovation and experiment in all areas that broke the mould of British traditional culture and attitudes: the era of psychedelic experience, Carnaby Street fashion, Indian gurus, and a revolution in pop music led by the Beatles and Rolling Stones that penetrated areas of society never before reached. Contemporary photos show that even the headmaster wore his hair fashionably long at that time.

Increasing prosperity fostered social, economic and educational change. There were good ideas, and others that proved less so such as hideous city centre redevelopment and high rise blocks. Enthusiastic educationalists too were innovating with mixed success. In all, it was a time of hope, increasing wealth and a belief in progress.

Geoff Goodall inherited a situation full of promise, where the foundations had been laid for a modern school but still with some unfulfilled potential. When the School had been taken under voluntary control it was still another ten years or more before the LEA made any substantial investments to improve facilities. (Something that had frustrated Mullens and Governors alike.) It was under Nelson that the big investments arrived: first with the Boyle Labs, and then the new library, hall, gym and admin block in the early 1960s. (Although this building, it was discovered, was prone to serious leaks.)

Goodall stepped into something that had been already conceived not only in terms of facilities but key teaching staff who would make the School a leader in certain fields such as Gerard Gould with drama, or provided the backbone to the School's teaching success such as Norman Lilley, Norman Good and Peter More, all teachers who would spend most of their working lives at the School, and who had already introduced new ideas. *He was our Wedding photographer.

Other masters made an impact in their own way such as Mike Fethney. A pupil, D Tomlinson remembered:

> He was perhaps an unsung hero of my generation of LWGS's youth, but definitely a hero. I remember his Yorkshire accent and very down-to-earth Christianity – the sort I could have subscribed to if I had had an ounce of spirituality. Mike had also propped for the United Services, Portsmouth and beneath the unforced gentleness there was a no-messing firmness. Perhaps a 'school boy's story' but a local farmer discovered this to his cost when he fired some lead over Martin (alias Myrtle) Griffin's head; Martin was filching apples from the orchard behind Highfields, and the orchard belonged to the farmer. Unfortunately for the farmer, the entire scene was witnessed by Mike, who duly leapt over the Highfields fence into the adjacent field, raced over to said farmer, and flattened him with a single blow. The ensuing warning was gruff, and the dazed, supine farmer did not see fit to offer any opposition.
>
> Nor did Greenacres/Highfields residents ever have cause to fear repercussions from subsequent apple-filching. Nigel and I annually filled our games lockers to bursting with illicit fruit, and that we did so with impunity was down to Mike Fethney.

Goodall's arrival in Thame 1964 could hardly have been a better moment both for the School and for him. The School could benefit from a young and dynamic headmaster to accelerate its transformation into something that was thoroughly modern, reaching heights in music, drama, sport and academic achievement perhaps not seen before. But he was helped by the work done by Nelson, the public spending resources that were being pumped into education, the bulge in pupil numbers from the post-war baby boom, and the desire of the LEA that a greater percentage of 11+ takers would find a grammar school place. More pupils meant more money and more opportunities.

When Sir Edward Boyle, Minister of Education, had opened the School's new buildings in 1963, he made a speech where he promised that the Government would make increased resources available for the improvement of school education.

> *My department's plans assume that the local authorities*
> *will be spending at least £3,500 million of public money*
> *on school education not over the next ten years but over*
> *the next five. We are planning for an increase of school ex-*
> *penditure of over 13 per cent at a time when the total school*
> *population will rise by between 5 and 6 per cent. Thus my*
> *department are quite deliberately planning for improved*
> *standards in the schools - that is to say more teachers, better*
> *buildings and equipment, and wider opportunities for chil-*
> *dren of every level of ability.*

This increase in secondary-school-age pupils led to the introduction of two-form entry. Some fifty pupils entered the First Form in 1966. It was envisaged that total numbers from First to Sixth Form would ultimately increase to over 350, including increases in the boarding house numbers in order to preserve the traditional and essential character of the School.

* * *

Success

The last few years of the Grammar School's existence were arguably the most successful in its existence thus far. Though perhaps not producing as many figures of national importance as in the early 17th century, in almost every aspect of education it was a period of marked improvement, and excellence in several areas.

Most 20th century headmasters stated their aims on arriving in general terms, often at their first Speech Day. Their actual achievement sometimes fell short of these aims, albeit often for reasons beyond their control. Goodall, however stated his detailed aims in an interview. It is possible therefore to compare his aims and his achievement with some precision.

Goodall's seven stated aims were to: further strengthen the academic ability of the staff; improve teaching techniques; increase extra-curricular activities; expand foreign links; boost the quality of games teams; bring parents more into the frame, and strengthen the cultural side of the school. The following paragraphs illustrate the extent to which he succeeded during the final grammar school years. Interestingly, all these aims are about ways and means not outcomes. Implicit in them, however, is raising achievement, not just academically but across the board.

One of the striking features of the period between 1963 and 1970 was the growth in the proportion of leavers going on to a university education. As the number of leavers varied from year to year this trend is best shown by percentages rather than numbers: 36 per cent in Nelson's last year, falling the next year to 26 per cent in Goodall's first year but rising to 40 per cent over the next two years.

These years also coincided with the widening of opportunities for tertiary education: more places were made available and the grant system kicked in.

Thereafter the percentages grew and peaked in 1967 at 56 per cent before levelling off - despite the continued growth in the number taking A levels - until the end of the grammar school era.

Why more did not go to university is an interesting point. Some sixth-form leavers preferred the attractions of immediate employment and a salary. For example, the banks were frequent advertisers in the school magazine and indeed this was a popular career. Others decided to enter alternative forms of higher education such as art and teacher training colleges. This diversification was perhaps due to the varying academic abilities and aspirations of some of the boys who were successful in the 11+ selective examination, a point returned to at the end of this chapter. In the last year of the grammar school fifteen went on to university, three to Colleges of Education, two to Colleges of Technology, one to art school, one to agricultural college, and the rest into employment.

Some though, thought that there was too much emphasis put on going to Oxbridge and that was the only mark of success. Going to other universities was not celebrated in the same way, and so this in itself may have made some pupils wonder if there was much point in a university education at all.

Goodall's commitment to high academic aspirations and expectations certainly played a part in that steady growth of the proportion entering university but this can also be attributed to a number of other factors beyond those highlighted above. Clearly a new spirit had entered the School that encouraged tertiary education rather than going directly into employment or professional training. This sense of aspiration was not only directed at the pupils but also at the parents (most of whom were not degree-educated) in the hope that they too would accept the value of a tertiary education for their sons.

Secondly, increasing numbers of pupils enabled Goodall to enlarge teaching staff. In Nelson's final years they had numbered around thirteen. By the end of the decade this number had doubled meaning that more attention could be given to sixth form studies.

In part, the increase in numbers entering university was due to a nation-wide increase in student numbers as a result of government policy that saw twelve new universities being opened across the 1960s. Between 1960 and 1970, the number of students more than doubled: by 1970-71, there were 236,000 students studying at universities and 204,000 at polytechnics, and higher education participation rate had reached 8.4 per cent. (Compare this to 3 per cent who went to university in 1950 and 4 per cent in 1960.)

And as mentioned earlier, the introduction of student grants for both tuition fees and living costs meant that at least theoretically tertiary education was open to all who wanted it. In turn this led to the John Hampden War Memorial Fund, which was making some twenty awards annually to those going to or already at university, deciding that in future they would lay more emphasis on grants to pupils while they were still at School rather than for those in residence at university.

Finally, new methods of teaching were making education more enjoyable. Prior to Goodall, teaching had been very much based (as it was in most schools) on a teacher standing at the front of the class lecturing with pupils listening and taking notes. Very little work was done outside the classroom or done in a contextual manner. Masters paced, and pupils sat in orderly lines. Now there was an emphasis on activity, discovery and participation.

The character of the teaching staff was also changing as new, younger staff members were taken on. Hence Clive Hurst's somewhat *Goodbye Mr Chips* description of the five ages of a schoolmaster was rapidly becoming out-dated as a new breed entered the profession (of which two of his 'ages' are reproduced below):

> *Pity the poor teacher starting at a grammar school armed*
> *only with his twenty-odd meagre years of life and a scrap*
> *of paper to indicate his degree. Pity him as he struggles to*
> *adapt himself to a new set of companions with their anti-*
> *quated ideas, and trifling petty rules in the Common Room,*
> *with every day now lived to a strict and rigid schedule. And*
> *worse the hundreds of schoolboys: ignorant first-formers*
> *screaming as they hare down the corridors headlessly*
> *knocking him over and apologising with endless 'sorry sirs;*
> *hulking great fifth-formers who look down on the new man*
> *with threatening defiant sneers; aloof sixth-formers who*
> *tacitly ignore him.*

> *At fifty-five the master has reached the final leg of his car-*
> *eer. School is no longer the be-all and end-all of existence*
> *- the days aren't that long, the holidays are good, and the*
> *odd evening when marking cannot be avoided can be suit-*
> *ably eeked out with telly. The boys show respect for his age,*
> *and the new Headmaster is just losing his temporary zeal.*
> *There is time for fulltime hobbies if he can exert himself*
> *sufficiently, and the earlier money worries are no longer*
> *important.*

> *And so the teacher glides into retirement. With experience*
> *and the sagacity of old-age he refuses to consider what*
> *might have happened had he not fallen into the fatal teach-*
> *ing trap. Instead he counts his achievements as genuine; if*
> *not great ones.*

Slowly, very slowly, more women teachers were recruited, but by the end of the decade they still only numbered three.

Educational progress outside the classroom was more marked;

the highlights are described in greater detail in the Volume 2 chapters on drama, music and sport. What follows, therefore, is a brief summary. In some instances, as in drama, Goodall's arrival accelerated an already thriving activity. In others, notably music, he started almost from scratch.

In extracurricular activities little change occurred in the first three years of Goodall's tenure. In sport it is fair to say it was still business as usual. Rugby and cricket remained the two main team sports and it would be unfair to claim major improvements: both teams in the past had tended to win rather than lose against local opposition and, throughout the fifties to mid-sixties, players had been selected for county sides and had reached national standards. In athletics the School had representatives at county level while tennis and swimming were always poor cousins.

However, Dick Mainwaring who had joined at the same time as Goodall was able to build the 1st XV's overall standard. By the time he left in July 1969 they had lost only six games over five years. He also raised the level of gymnastics so that trophies and honours were won, and introduced basketball, hockey and golf. When the squash court was finally finished, he taught the boys how to excel at this.

In the arts, the standard of drama was as high as ever - in fact improving - but this was mainly due to the continued leadership and efforts of Gerard Gould. Goodall enthusiastically supported them and, as a modern linguist, was keen for the School to continue to demonstrate its dramatic excellence in continental Europe: two tours of Germany were conducted in these final grammar school years with the last one, when *Macbeth* was performed, generally thought to be the pinnacle of all Gould's achievements. Two UK premières were mounted: Noel Coward's *Post Mortem*, and the stage première of Giles Cooper's *Unman Wittering and Zigo*.

Gould wrote a seminal book for schools called *Dramatic Involvement*, and he recruited three outstanding English teachers who all became authors in their own right most notably with a series called *Explore and Express,* books taken up by hundreds of schools.

Performing arts also broadened with the introduction of dance led by the newly-recruited Jackie Kiers, an activity that was enthusiastically taken up by the boys. One of their early successes was to perform at Eton, a novel experience for everyone. They were given a rave review in the 1970 *Eton College Chronicle,* which noted the reactions of the boys watching, most of whom would have had little or no experience of dance. 'The group demonstrated that expressive movement was highly interesting and deceptively easy – it was difficult to believe that they had only been working together for a few months ... Many thanks to the students and their teacher for an entertaining and stimulating evening.'

It is said that the boys' main memory of the evening was the fact that they had shared cannabis with their sixth-form hosts while their teachers were enjoying dinner.

If there was one area where a major improvement was seen, it was music with the recruitment of Bill Gilbert as the full-time music teacher. (Well almost full-time. He also taught at the Wenman School and so his achievements are remarkable in that he could not devote himself fully to LWGS.) In earlier chapters it has been noted that music, while not necessarily entirely absent, was definitely a poor cousin. This was about to change.

Gilbert formed school orchestras and choirs, introduced the big combined-schools Easter Concert that mounted challenging choral works such as Brahms' *A German Requiem*, and Britten's cantata, *St Nicolas.* He brought in more part-time teachers so that it became the norm rather than the exception for a boy at LWGS to learn a musical instrument, and upped the standard of music education including the opportunity to sit Music O-Level that previously had not been made available on the curriculum. At least initially, sitting Music meant missing games on a Wednesday afternoon as there were insufficient periods to slot it in elsewhere.

Numerous visits to the Festival Hall, the Royal Albert Hall and other concert halls became the norm too, and it was common to have outside musicians perform concerts in the School.

If the LWGS had established itself as the leading Oxfordshire secondary school for drama, it was rapidly attempting to do the same with music. (It should though be noted that a number of teachers were also excellent musicians, and they too made a significant contribution to the School's success. The LEA too had invested in better music provision at the county level, and had set up a music school that was held on a Saturday morning, and which a number of pupils from LWGS attended.)

Operetta was reintroduced to become an iconic summer event when the new Head of Biology, Colin Brookes, produced *Iolanthe,* the first of a memorable series of sell-out performances.

The Combined Cadet Force had been in existence since Mullens's time and this thrived under both Nelson and Goodall. Camps were held in the wettest parts of the UK, cadets were sent on overseas trips, those in the RAF corps took to the air in gliders, and some were awarded Flying Scholarships and obtained their Private Pilot Licence. However in 1965, the concept of community service was broadened by the introduction of the non-military Pioneers as an alternative. One of their biggest successes was to move away from solely para-military activities to that of social service in which fifth and sixth formers made weekly visits to patients at Stone Mental Hospital. This became one of the great success stories of this era. At the same time the Duke of Edinburgh Awards were introduced.

The School also continued with the tradition of taking overseas trips but their breadth widened. This, though, was originally an initiative of the LEA who in turn had been directed by the Government to forge links with European schools. The pioneer school in Oxfordshire was Littlemore Grammar, and as their trips were deemed a success this was expanded across the county.

For LWGS this meant that for the first time, exchange links were formally established: with the Peter Dorfler Schule in Marktobedorf, and the College d'Enseignement Secondaire Michelet in Lisieux. *I went to both of these*

One memorable trip was in 1969 when an exchange was set-up with a school in Prague. LWGS hosted a party of Sixth Form boys who stayed with families in Thame and a group went to Czechoslovakia for two weeks. It was less than a year after the Russian invasion and the legacy of Dubeck and the 'Prague Spring' had not yet been totally eliminated. The Russians were somewhat trigger-happy as was found out in Mlada Boleslav when someone in the party unwisely took a photograph of a Red Army barracks and got everyone arrested. Fortunately after an hour of interrogation, the party was released.

Another break with tradition was the idea of pupil participation in the running of the School. In 1968, a School Council was formed that could vote and then propose changes to the way the School was run. Not always an effective nor necessarily a truly representative body, it was generally felt that at least it managed to raise a pupil-voice and it brought pupils and teachers together in discussion, which had to be a good thing.

In short, in these last few years, the breadth of extracurricular activity in the School was immense and it would surely be a dull boy who did not find something to interest them. But some did not and, as had always been the case, these were usually day-boys.

A typical summary of a boy's first taste of life at LWGS at this time was written some years afterwards:

> *It was literally a different world from what I had been used to. Our holidays were taken in England, none of my family had ever flown, we did not visit the theatre other than to see pantomines, on Sundays after church we went for an afternoon drive or visited an aunt. It was a happy but but far from exciting life but then my parents didn't have a lot of money to spend other than on the essentials.*
>
> *Suddenly a whole new vista of possibilities opened up. Even with sport: at primary school, the only sports we did were football and athletics and we rarely played any opposition. Now we travelled across the county to play other schools but more importantly there was a competitive spirit and a sense of belonging to something that was collectively ours. The School's history, the traditions, the winning spirit, all gave me a new sense of who I was. It would not be an exaggeration to say that I reinvented myself.*

✽ ✽ ✽

The School Calendar

Over the years a recurring calendar of events had been established, some dating back to the 19th century, and some already mentioned. For any pupil going through the School, this provided a sense of expectation, and perhaps excitement as well as a means of ticking off the days. (Looking back now, it is interesting, but perhaps not surprising, how little school life has changed little over the decades.)

Shortly after term started in mid-September, a half-day popped up to coincide with Thame Show. There was no expectation that any pupils actually had to go to the Show and few did.

The rugby season kicked-off with a game against the Headmaster's XV. Then it was time to start intense rehearsals for the School Play that would be performed mid October.

Founder's Day took place on the Saturday before the start of half-term, all pupils attended, the same hymns such as *For All The Saints* were sung year after year, and everyone was expected to watch the rugby game against the Old Tamensians in the afternoon.

The second-half of the Winter Term would see Speech Day when prizes were handed out and a guest speaker invited to make a speech that would inspire the boys to work hard, and aspire to greater things - although when the actor Robert Morley stood on stage, his message was that secondary school was a waste of time. A few weeks later, the term finished with the carol service in St Mary's Church, and with reports being taken home.

The major event in the Spring Term was the Combined Schools Music Concert that brought together well over a hundred pupils from LWGS, Holton Park Girls Grammar, the Wenman, and Wheatley Secondary Modern School.

During the Easter holidays, foreign trips were made.

Come the Summer Term, for some pupils the period was dominated by revision and public exams. Others could laze on the cricket pitch or run around the athletic track, a few would play tennis, or brave the swimming pool as the water was cold no matter the air temperature.

The final major event from the late sixties onwards was the

musical. Colin Brookes, the maestro who mounted them, said:

*The summer musicals meant so much to me. There were
trials, tribulations, heartaches and frustrations but I like
to feel that in the majority of cases the end justified the
means. I have always regarded the latter part of the summer term to be the happiest and most rewarding part of my
school year. It was always so heartening to see the response
not only of the cast but also of the audience. I consider it a
privilege for me to have been allowed to escape the confines
of the laboratory every year and enjoy a world of fantasy in
the company of so many terrific pupils and friends.*

Then it was time to pack-up for the summer. In those days
no Proms were held. Those who were leaving for ever hopefully dropped off their library books before fading away. Those
boys who would return gathered in the Hall, and sang the
School Hymn, and National Anthem. After a short speech by
the Headmaster reminding them to enjoy the holidays re-
sponsibly, the day-boys rushed for the school buses while the
boarders rushed for their trunks and hoped that parents or
relatives had arrived to pick them up.

David Price who left in 1970:

*It didn't strike me until a few years later. I realised that
there were many classmates who I had neither said goodbye
to or had ever seen again. And teachers too. After my last
exam I was so relieved it was all over and that I didn't have
to go into school again. And I didn't. Ever. In those days
the chances of remaining in contact were slim. Sometimes I
would see a few old classmates in Thame but only a handful
and of course our lives moved on. Most I never saw again,
and that was quite sad looking back now.*

A half-hour later, perhaps an hour, the School was empty save
for a handful of Boarding House Masters in their rooms, and

the odd boarder who was waiting to be taken to an airport to fly to Cyprus or Singapore or some other overseas military base.

There was someone else who remained behind. Reg Cadle walked through the hall with a broom. He led the caretaking staff and his summer weeks would be busy while pupil and teacher alike enjoyed themselves far away. He had much to do in the weeks ahead but now he worked his way through the buildings, turning off lights, closing doors, picking up battered text books, stained exercise books, discarded sheet music, and muddy clothes. Someone had forgotten their blazer. More had forgotten caps, scarfs and a vast array of games kit. Why do pupils lose only one shoe? Caps, Macs, ties, satchels, bags, brief cases and haversacks were gathered in a pile.

Rubbish was everywhere: potato crisp packets, essay papers, plastic cups, and Tizer bottles.

He had a lot to do: the floors needed re-waxing; the labs needed scrubbing. The lavatories, showers and changing rooms needed even more effort. Weeds were creosoted. Library shelves repaired. Furniture re-stuck or screwed, or dumped onto a heap that later would become a bonfire.

And then a few weeks later, it would all start over again. Not for Reg though. He died one lunch hour in the lobby cloakroom outside the lunch hall. Quick action had to be taken to conceal this from all the crowds of boys having lunch. *I remember that.*

* * *

Final words

Despite having all the advantages of a grammar school education, as Nelson had once observed, it did not suit all boys who had passed the 11+. Some did not sustain their 11+ promise either because they could not or would not. Others had parents who also did not see the advantages of a grammar school education let alone continuing into the Sixth Form. They had not made the decision to send their sons to grammar school, that was the State's, and as soon as they could at the end of the Fifth Form, they would pull their boys out of school - usually with little complaint from the boys themselves. These were the boys who, for whatever reason, had little appetite for what was on offer, were wasting their time at school and were feeling frustrated and unfulfilled. Over the late sixties, on average, 20 per cent to 25 per cent of the Fifth Form at LWGS would leave after O-Levels to enter some form of employment.

Demographically, they were mainly from working class families, and at least part of their parent's apathy was down to being unable to afford to keep their son in education for another two years. This was also an example of the bluntness of the 11+, and the need to fulfill quotas: across the country it had sent some boys to schools they did not wish to go and yet consigned others to a secondary modern education when in another year or so they might have bloomed and passed the exam.

Paul Gleeson, a student from that time:

> *There was a hidden barrier to coming - and staying - at the School including the cost of the uniform and all the different games kit. A couple of my friends at John Hampden who passed the 11 + didn't go because their parents felt they couldn't afford it.*

There were other costs too such as drawing and mathematical equipment; school trips; parents would have to pay for tickets to see plays and musicals. Inevitably this led to these pupils not participating in extra-curricula activities and hence from no fault of their own, were distanced from the main body of pupils.

Another pupils remembered:

My elder sister went to Holton Park. Her uniform was bought from Martin & Silver. I remember her telling me later how hand-me-downs were common within families but also between families. However there was no process at the schools like a second-hand rail to pass on uniform and games kit, which is more common today. Three years later when I got into Lord Williams's, she was still wearing the same uniform and continued to do so until the fifth form. Mum and Dad couldn't afford my uniform on Dad's wages so Mum went to work in the Co-op. It shows the expense. Dad had a mortgage on a newish semi-detached house and worked in Thame but Mum needed to work when there were two of us going to grammar school. We had a younger sister in John Hampden and so during the holidays we had to look after her.

The cost of uniforms and games kit was well over £150 at this time, when a manual worker's weekly wage was in the region of £25.

One pupil wrote about his own experience of trying to get in to the School:

There was no specific preparation for the 11+. I don't recall being told in advance that we would sit it but we did one day in January and the result came back that I was border-line. My parents and teachers were insistent that I resit it. My going to Lord Williams's was my Mum's dream. It was something she and Dad had talked about for as long as I could remember and we would sometimes drive past the school and talk about me going there.

So I did a re-sit. In fact eight of us re-sat the exam in early March so I'm unsure if anyone had actually passed first

*time round. Only in early May did I learn that once again
I was borderline. Looking back I was unsurprised. Now I
know I have a form of dyslexia called dysgraphia (not that
this was a known condition then), and had never been able
to spell as I can't naturally convert sounds into the written
word. All through my time at primary school, I had got
lowly marks in spelling, and my handwriting was terrible.
We had thirty in the class, and I would usually be something
like 15th for spelling and what was called 'reading recognition.' As the exam was mainly a combination of arithmetic,
reading comprehension, and spelling questions my ability
to pass was always going to be in doubt and so it proved.*

*Having scored border-line again, the next step was for my
primary school headmaster to argue for an interview at
Lord Williams's. This he did successfully and in early May,
only a week after I'd got the results, I was taken to the school
with an armful of special project and exercise books. I was
dressed in my best grey shorts, grey socks, black shoes, a
grey shirt, and my school blazer. A week later I heard I had
a place. We had thirty in our class and in the end, three
girls went to Holton Park and three boys to Lord Williams's.
What if I had gone to a secondary modern? Well the argument that I could have enjoyed more practical subjects
faltered as, because of my condition, I was useless at art,
technical drawing, or anything like woodwork. I really don't
know what would have become of me.*

Miss Clifford, one of the local primary school teachers, was to
write in her memoirs:

*Unfortunately those who did not succeed in passing were
too often regarded as 'failures' (by themselves and by parents) - this was a complete misconception because only a
certain number of places were available and often many
very able children could not obtain one of these. Also, these*

tests took little account of the meticulous slower-working child because they were timed - and those with imaginative flair and good ideas also often went unrecognised because of the nature of the questions.

Girls also suffered disproportionately as they tended to do better in the exam but of course an equal number of the sexes had to 'pass'. This led to poorer performing boys sometimes getting a grammar school place at the expense of a better performing girl.

Overall, it is clear that Goodall had largely achieved what he had set out to do. The circumstances of the time certainly helped, but favourable circumstances alone are insufficient to ensure success. Many examples abound in all schools that it is the driving force of the head that really makes the difference - for good or ill.

The School's achievement was recognised at national level. Its last year as a grammar happened to coincide with the centenary celebrations of state education and LWGS provided two features at an exhibition held in Central Hall, Westminster: one on music, and the second showcasing the teaching of drama.

The former consisted of a series of large photographs of pupils playing instruments, singing, rehearsing and performing; while drama was brought to life through a four-minute film playing on a continuous loop of Mr Gould and fifth formers discussing how at LWGS they approached a Shakespearean text. Apparently, Prime Minister Harold Wilson was impressed by the film since it was the only exhibit that showed a class in action.

It has been generally thought that the first female pupil had arrived in 1969: Carolyn Ward's parents had moved into the district but found that the local girls schools were unable to offer the right combination of A-Levels but LWGS could, so she joined the Sixth Form much to the excitement of many. However, very recently we discovered that Ann Matthews was in the sixth form in 1950-52 being taught science by Mr Bunney as her school did not provide science teaching (and specifically physics).

Further excitement could be found in Thame itself. Just one edition of the *Thame Gazette* reported that the youth of Thame were in turmoil - long hair and scarves round their heads leading to the Headmaster banning one fifth former from perfoming at the Thame Civic Carol Concert for looking scruffy. He did not want him representing the School in public. Cannabis was being smoked in Rycotewood College with the miscreants appearing before the local Bench. The older generation had enough to worry about too with fires at home and in pubs; fatal car crashes, and snow at Christmas.

Goodall had succeeded as a grammar school headmaster, but was about to face an altogether bigger challenge: comprehensive reorganisation.

His own thoughts about this style of education had changed since he first arrived. When he first came to the School he was not a fan - but then few of those teaching in grammar schools were. At his first Speech Day he had quoted from a letter to the *Times* from the Vice Chairman of the Headmasters Association which said that a grammar school education was not suitable for all:

> To claim that this regime is suitable for all children reveals either ignorance or hypocrisy. The secondary modern schools have shown brilliantly how many alternative roads to personal fulfilment are open to those pupils for whom Latin or theoretical Nuclear Physics is irrelevant.

Goodall went on to say that he did not believe that all children should be forced through an identical teaching regime. However he was all for the abolition of the 11+ and thought that pupils at grammar schools should be accepted on their academic records plus the headmaster's report.

Some final words on grammar schools, particularly as they are still an emotive topic. The argument for their retention is usually that they lead to better exam results, entry to university and, as a consequence, upward social mobility. Of course grammar schools gain better results overall because they select pupils who show the most promise, profit from selection bias, and then tutor them with academic-biased teaching geared to passing exams.

The social mobility argument fails too - other than for a narrow band of pupils - as once LWS turned comprehensive, a much broader demographic of pupils went on to university. The School in the 1960s was made up of three almost equally split groups of pupils: those from working class families, who lived in rented accommodation; a second group who's parents owned their homes and who's jobs were skilled workers, shop-owners, and clerical staff; and finally, not least because of the boarders, solid middle class families. As seen earlier, the working class group, almost to a boy, left at the end of their fifth year with little academic success to their name, and moved into the same sort of job they would have taken if they had been at a secondary modern. The middle class group usually continued on a rewarding path. It was that second group, whose working class parents did not have a tertiary education, who now had a university opportunity given to them, yet many still failed to take advantage of it.

CHAPTER 26: BULLYING

ANYONE WHO HAS WATCHED the Lindsay Anderson film if...
will not find this short chapter of any surprise. Anyone who
went to any school at this time, and who had their eyes open
would know that bullying was an issue. Not only at LWGS of
course but within the education system at large. Nor was it ignored at the School in the 1960s - unlike in the 1950s when it
was treated as being part of the growing-up process - as can be
read in Chapter 22.

Goodall:

> In all boarding schools you get bullying, and we had an in-
> stance with a boy in the Third Form who was being secretly
> bullied. He never complained or said who was doing it but it
> was mostly his class.

> So instead of getting in the Form and reading the riot act
> out, Gerard Gould changed the English syllabus to focus
> on some writing about bullying in schools. He took a radio
> play by Giles Cooper, Unman, Wittering and Zigo, about a
> teacher being bullied by the pupils. He had them all read it,
> they had to write essays about it, they discussed what it was
> like to be bullied, what it was like dealing with the bully.
> He had the class improvise scenes. The pupils knew nothing
> about why this had appeared on their syllabus yet after a
> month of this , the bullying just disappeared.

Some might believe that these things should be kept private,
that it hardly helps a school's reputation, and that it will gen-
erate bad feeling. Bullying is a problem that won't go away by

pretending it does not exist. Much of the time it is minor and transitory but it is undeniably true that it can also lead to serious consequences. Bullying will not disappear entirely but if we ignore it, then we side with the bullies.

In addition, we should not deceive ourselves: not everyone's school days were wonderful. Many harbour only fond memories, while some could not care one way or other – it was just a period in their life – but for a few it was more traumatic. One ex-pupil from this time, an Oxford graduate, resolutely refuses to come to any reunion event as he says his school days were the worst period of his life. For some it was.

* * *

My first memory of boarding school was the first night as soon as lights out, the tallest 2nd year leaned over the partition with words to the effect that we first years were 'plebs', if we were cheeky we would get beaten, and if we sneaked, we would get beaten badly. As my brother had been cheeky, the same was expected of me, unfortunately, I rose to the challenge and for the next 4 years the 'die' was set for me. The climax physically was Matron calling me in and asking how I had collected 40 bruises aged 12 years. I remember being tied up to hot radiators, head flushed in the toilet, spread eagled on a table and painted, locked in a wardrobe and basically becoming a punch bag. I had 40 bruises on the outside, but the bruises inside lasted longer.

* * *

My brother's bullying was worse than anything I can im-

agine: continuous and often violent bullying, not just cold showers and apple pie beds, but being locked in a laundry basket and skittered down the steps in the boarding house, hung upside down by his feet from the first floor dormitory window and being the target for group towel flicking. I didn't always realize how bad it was for him, but should have had the courage to stop my parents off-loading us after an out-Sunday: the first glimmer of the lights of the school after we had passed through Watlington and he would go silent, and my body would tense up.

We would be dropped off by parents not wanting to believe that they might be leaving their children in such a state. On out first morning my brother came down to breakfast with his tie just tied as one might a piece of string, because neither of us had worn ties before, and mine was a bit neater than his. The refectory went drop-dead silent and everyone watched him come in. My heart still quivers when I think about it.

My pleadings to the prefects and the house masters fell on deaf ears and I copped it for dobbing people in, and for trying to get others to protect him instead of sticking-up for him, and letting him fight his own battles. In the end I could do little, and he suffered incredibly, eventually leaving and undergoing many months of psychological rehabilitation before re-enrolling in the local secondary modern school from where he went on to study to be a teacher at Milton Keynes.

He was brilliantly creative, even wrote to and had tea with JRR Tolkein when he was 12. For some LWGS was great, but not for my brother. He could not understand why he was being punished when he had done nothing wrong. I have forgotten much of those who turned their backs on him when he called for help, and I cannot now find a way to for-

give, for each little act in its own way seems almost trivial now, but when put together they were a torrent that fell on his head.

* * *

I never had my head flushed down the toilet, and I seem to remember the bashings were more idle threats than actual events. I was certainly called a pleb, but this was rather standard boarding school vocabulary and many carried the title, handing it down to those in years below in due course. I certainly think that life as a boarder was fairly easy, and I wonder if in today's litigious society boarders would be given the liberty and freedom that we were then. Certainly we were allowed into Thame on a daily basis, and permission to travel further afield to Oxford was readily granted at weekends, a blind eye was turned to our hitching, (thus saving precious cash). Some may remember me because I was always playing with model aeroplanes. The staff were very understanding of this, and a few of us were even given a room to ourselves (when the smell of balsa wood glue, aircraft dope & model engine fuel became too evasive in the dormitory!)

* * *

Mine was the low level bullying. On my first day at school my cap was debobbled by a second-former. Nothing major but my mother was so proud of my new uniform and now it had been despoiled. I remember her being so upset when I showed her. Then across my first year if was this constant drip of verbal abuse by a fifth-former. It was a psychological form of torture and at the time was quite debilitating knowing that I had to face it every day and that many others were laughing at me. Why I had been singled out I don't know. He was a farmer's son, who left at that the end of that year, and later in life became a far-right fanatic.

Among the day boys though, verbal bullying was more common than physical bullying, and often it would take place on the school buses - as it was for me. Out of sight from the masters of course but I can't recall any prefects on that bus ever trying to stop it, and I always wondered thereafter what purpose prefects had at the school.

❋ ❋ ❋

Many people are surprised when I tell them about girl-on-girl bullying but when I was at the Wenman it was common. I was picked on and the girls had a nasty little trick. They would suddenly crowd around me so I couldn't escape, and then for a few brief seconds would pinch me hard and call me names before running off in all directions. To someone watching from a distance, it all seemed like innocent fun in the playground.

As stated in the introduction to this Volume, we have included this short chapter in the interests of honesty and transparency, not because LWS was in any way different in respect of bullying from any other school. As with all forms of abuse, those who suffered from it are loathe to speak or write about it until later in life, if at all. Our descriptions are therefore [mainly] drawn from those who were pupils in the post-WW2 period and we are grateful to them all for being willing to speak out on such a painful subject. This history needs to be on the record, but without evidence, history cannot be written.

What happened to these victims of bullying is inexcusable and it is true generally of the period they describe that those in authority tended to turn a blind eye to what they suspected was happening. Later generations of educationalists have done more to combat bullying. Neither this, nor any other of the descriptions, should be taken to imply any general criticism, or commendation, of the School or of boarding. They tell us nothing more than that bullying happened and that the School took measures to stop it. The extent of the bullying and the efforts that the School authorities made to curb it remain unknown.

This is perhaps the right time to also mention some other mercifully rare crises associated with the School. In the 1960s Goodall had to sack a hopeless French teacher at LWGS, whose drunken undergraduate son phoned one night to say he was coming over to kill the headmaster. Police protection was needed that night. Later another young PE teacher, who was very popular, was arrested at School, after a complaint of abuse by a young mother who used him as a baby-sitter for her toddler. He went to prison for 6 months.

Of parents one senior teacher was threatened in person by a vicious Brill parent, who was angry because the School had suspended his 14 year old daughter for repeated violence to other girls in the loos at break. One girl pupil from Long Crendon was murdered – as it later turned out by an abusive uncle. A very respectable sixth form girl was raped by a pupil on the Southern Road recreation field.

PART 3: THE COMPREHENSIVE ERA

CHAPTER 27: TURNING COMPREHENSIVE 1971-1980

IN 1971 THE LAST HEADMASTER of Lord Williams's Grammar School became the first principal of a comprehensive, now called Lord Williams's School but at least in the early years the ethos and the core values of the grammar school were carried forward. Whereas as the 19th century educational commissioners had eight years to re-found the School after it closed in 1872, the newly titled Principal and his staff had just 18 months, or in some respects, just eight weeks – the summer holidays: in the timescale of the School's four centuries of existence, just the blink of an eye, a seamless transition.

Seamless certainly but, unsurprisingly, not altogether smooth as explained in greater detail later in the chapter. The following story told by Goodall illustrates the bizarre, almost surreal two months before the School re-opened as a comprehensive.

In the depths of August, Goodall was accosted by a strange man with the words 'are you the headmaster?' On being assured that he was, the man continued 'I've got a school for you on the back of my lorry'. In reality the 'school' was one of the many Terrapins – temporary classrooms – that were to prove anything but temporary and a blight on the school landscape for years. Nevertheless, a Terrapin is better than nothing and for the first few weeks of the term, thanks to Indian summer, the School and pupils survived despite inadequate accommodation.

Despite the predictable difficulties, Lord Williams's School proved to be one of the most successful comprehensive reorganisations in the country. Bringing together two schools, with different histories, attitudes and pupils, is never easy. One of us experienced in the 1970s the all too frequent failures to adapt former schools to the new comprehensive model. But LWS met the challenges, not without difficulty on occasion, and demonstrated that, given the right circumstances, something approaching the comprehensive ideal could be achieved.

As described earlier, the idea of comprehensive education had been around for some time but it was not until the mid 1960s that it became government policy. At that time, in 1965 for example, there were 1,477 grammar schools in England & Wales. Circular 10/65 required all local education authorities to transform their secondary schools to comprehensives.

> *It is the Government's declared objective to end selection at eleven plus and to eliminate separatism in secondary education... The Secretary of State accordingly requests local education authorities, if they have not already done so, to prepare and submit to him plans for reorganising secondary education in their areas on comprehensive lines. There are a number of ways in which comprehensive education may be organised. While the essential needs of the children do not vary greatly from one area to another, the views of individual authorities, the distribution of population and the nature of existing schools will inevitably dictate different solutions in different areas. It is important that new schemes build on the foundation of present achievements and preserve what is best in existing schools.*

Some moved quickly to comply, others more sedately, and a few did nothing. Five years later in a new Conservative government, Margaret Thatcher, then Secretary of State for Education, ended the compulsion on local authorities to convert. However, many local authorities were so far down the path that it would have been prohibitively expensive to attempt to reverse the process, and more comprehensive schools were established under Thatcher than any other education secretary. Those LEAs, such has neighbouring Buckinghamshire, that had earlier dragged their feet, now made no pretence at taking any further action.

The people of Oxfordshire were perhaps slightly less conservative – and Conservative – than their Buckinghamshire neighbours. Nevertheless, such a radical upheaval was greeted in many quarters with reactions ranging from anxiety to outright opposition. On the national scale, 'going comprehensive' was unavoidably disruptive at first and unpopular with many parents and, as was already becoming apparent after five years, at least as often a failure as a success.

In contrast, for many education professionals, comprehensive reorganisation was seen as an opportunity, not only to bring together both boys and girls of all abilities but to introduce new and untested educational ideas such as 'mixed-ability' teaching. At the start, high-quality teachers were keen to be involved, and left-leaning middle-class parents chose to send their children to these new state schools in preference to independent schools. But the honeymoon period did not last long. Thanks in part to the appointment as head teachers of senior staff from independent schools with good track records but minimal experience of state education, many of the initially fashionable and superficially successful comprehensives were soon found wanting.

* * *

Plans for comprehensive reorganisation in Thame

Oxfordshire began to turn its secondary schools into comprehensives quite quickly. In the so-named Development Plan 1966, the Oxfordshire LEA proposed the creation of two junior comprehensive schools for the age range 11-14 at Wheatley

Secondary School and the Wenman School. At the same time, a single-site, mixed, senior comprehensive that merged Holton Park Girls Grammar with LWGS would be established at the Oxford Road site, which would take pupils from both of the junior schools. The existing Holton Park School premises would be taken out of use and sold to the Lady Spencer Churchill College of Education, which could be found close by.

At the time of the plan, it had been estimated that yearly entry into the senior school would rise to a maximum of 360 by 1980. Just two years later in 1968, it was realised that this figure was a serious under-estimate and that it was more likely to be in the region of 550 due to rising birth rates and expansion of housing in the Thame and Wheatley areas.

It was then thought that the more likely size of the Sixth Form would be around 500 including both girl and boy boarders, and that the total size of the senior school would be in the region of 1600 pupils.

In 1968 other issues were raised too, including the justified belief that junior schools separated from their senior school would not attract high-quality teachers, and that the daily transportation of large numbers of pupils from the Wheatley area would be expensive, likely costing around £14,000.

As a consequence, while retaining the junior schools, it was decided to abandon the 1966 plan and establish mixed senior schools at both Thame and Wheatley. Specifically for LWGS, it was also proposed that there be a closer association with Rycotewood College so as to increase the range of courses that could be offered to pupils in both establishments.

And finally, boarding. It was clear that boarding was an essential part of the School's make-up but it was also thought that perhaps a boarding facility could be established at Holton Park too, although the latter proposal was ultimately discarded.

By the end of the 1960s agreement had been reached and in March 1970 the Department of Education and Science approved the Oxfordshire plan to come into operation in September 1971. Perhaps remarkably, this only gave the schools eighteen months to prepare.

The proposal for Thame was very much centred on Lord Williams's. The Wenman School would be closed and its premises taken over by LWGS to form a two-site, co-educational comprehensive 11 to 18 with voluntary controlled status under the headship of Goodall. He would appoint a Director of Studies who would prepare proposals for a single unified curriculum and a single staff structure.

Mindful of how it might be received, the lengthy letter Goodall sent to all parents announcing the change did not actually use the word comprehensive nor mention that 'Grammar' would be dropped from the school name. Parents were assured that standards and values would not decline, that new buildings would be built, facilities significantly improved, that the new catchment area did not include slums. Last, but not least, it reminded parents that the LEA was both enlightened as it would leave many decisions in the hands of the School but at the same time they already had good experience of re-organising schools across the county.

❊ ❊ ❊

Implementation and impact

There followed a period of frantic preparation by Goodall, his Director of Studies, Dick Procktor, the School's first ever senior mistress, Betty Sadler, and a small army of secretaries needed to process all the paperwork involved. The most critical need was to appointment sufficient new teachers to cope with the expanded number of pupils as well as to replace the staff who resigned as they were unwilling to teach in a comprehensive school.

Peter More, a long standing, senior member of the Grammar School staff and Deputy Head realised the importance of both new appointments, Betty Sadler particularly.

> *She was an enormous help to me. She had experience of teaching girls; I hadn't, and a number of the ex-grammar school staff were in the same position. So Betty's role was crucial, not only as a figure of authority for the girls but as a mentor to the staff. She was an excellent teacher. Pastorally she was caring and understanding – but no pushover!*

Even more frantic and far from wholly successful was the provision of sufficient accommodation. Goodall, and More described the events during the first nine months of 1971.

> *(Goodall) A vast new building programme would be required. I decided that the newish Wenman buildings should house the Lower School, with pupils aged 11-14. Work started during early 1971 on the Upper School campus. During late August 1971, it became clear that by the start of term some eight classrooms would be unfinished. The Council's CEO promised some temporary classrooms as a stop-gap.*

That stop-gap was to prove larger and longer than anyone at that time imagined.

> *(More) At least 50 per cent of Upper School pupils were taught in temporary buildings called Elliotts and Terrapins. Often their heating was unreliable, the roofs leaked and pupils had to trudge through the mud to get to them.*

Young people are by nature conservative in the sense of being suspicious and often critical of any change. The advantages and disadvantages of the new regime were well summed up by one who experienced the School's dramatic metamorphosis.

I returned after the summer holidays facing two major changes. First, I was now in the Sixth Form, with fewer lessons to attend, and more free time. Second the School was now seemingly inundated with girls - those who had come into the School at the Fourth Form level from the Wenman and who intended taking O-Levels; some moving up from the Fifth Form at the Wenman into A-Levels, and a group of girls who had been persuaded to join by Geoff Goodall from a range of independent schools in Oxfordshire, Buckinghamshire and Berkshire. This was in contrast to the letter that had been sent to my parents that had said that the Sixth Form would remain single-sex boys.

In fact we had now had ten girls in our Lower Sixth year out of 44 pupils in total. Being mixed-sex created the sense that we were now in an adult and real world instead of the frankly cut-off, elitist and pampered world of my first five years at the School. It was also very interesting.

This notion of worldly chaos was further enhanced by the lack of facilities - the School was completely unprepared. Promised buildings had not materialised or were incomplete and instead we relied on the import of Portacabins to fill the gaps. The School seemed to wallow in a permanent mud-bath and it was quickly clear that those teaching staff who were shuttling back and forth between the two sites were feeling the strain. Did I care? Our lessons were largely unaffected as we were still using the same worn-out facilities, and activities like rugby, music and drama continued as normal. With the latter two the experience was better because we now had female talent on site rather than having to import it from Holton (as much as we loved the girls from there).

The School had never been particularly renowned for its pastoral care or for giving strong guidance about what to do in terms of education or career choice after leaving school. Unless you were Oxbridge material you had to work everything out yourself. With the strain on staff this became even more pronounced.

The School was noisy, chaotic and it was quickly apparent that some of the younger pupils who had come from the Wenman, were here under duress. We had no where to retreat to other than an overcrowded and frankly sweaty Sixth Form Common Room. Instead, I and others would walk into Thame and enjoy tea in the Malthouse or Bay Tree cafes. Or some took the extreme route and after registering would leave School entirely. The chaos of the School meant that keeping track of us was not the easiest task. This I did frequently. In truth, the sixth form largely retreated into its own insular world, dipping into the new School when it cared.

Bridget Thompson - one of several girls who had come from Headington School - was appointed as the first Head Girl. She remembers that initially the girls and female staff had to share a single set of loos, 'the loo situation points up how ready the School probably was for girls!' Another memory was meeting 'Tina, the goalie for the girl's football team. She was brilliant. She also smoked etc, something I had never come across in my age range.'

Two fifth formers were asked to write in *The Tamensian* about their perceptions of the change after one year had passed. They noted a wider range of activities, the introduction of new sports, and the fact that the girls had taken over the boys changing rooms. However one sixth former declared that the 'character of the School was dead'. He continued, 'one now looks back and remembers such events as Founder's Day and the Old Tamensians's Days as highlights – for they underlined the real character of the School. To carry on such traditions, in the half-hearted manner that we do today, is an insult.' Another noted that the girls were 'allowed to wear anything they like so long as it's not see-through.'

That was possibly wishful thinking on his part as the rules for girls were strict. They were instructed that jewelry was not allowed other than wristwatches, crucifixes and plain rings. Neither was make-up allowed. If blouses were nylon then white underwear had to be worn.

And not all traditions disappeared immediately. Ever since the death of George Plummer in 1891, his ghost would appear once a year in the boarding house, as it did still as Ken Hathaway wrote:

I can certainly confirm the Plummer tradition continued into the 70s before it was banned. I don't know the exact date of the 'event', but I'm sure it was always done in the autumn term. The key to a 'successful' night was secrecy, and our intake was certainly not forewarned of the coming events. This in spite of the fact that my older brother, Roy, had presumably been subjected to the same terror a few years previously (thanks for warning me)!

The first I knew of it was when I awoke to a ghostly figure standing over me holding a candle. I was wet through from what I took to be sweat, but I think we had been syringed with water (not blood-red thankfully) from the hatch to the loft. There may have been some background screaming too, but maybe my imagination added this later! Anyway, we were all well and truly terrified! Afterwards the lights came on and things were calmed down. I don't think anyone suffered any long term after-effects though.

I recall the whole thing was to do with the suspicion that George Plummer had murdered someone (his wife? the Matron? maybe a pupil?!) and hid the body in the loft above Dorm 1. Someone will no doubt know the full story. For some reason, it was always down to the firth-formers to commemorate the grisly deed, and although it was of course 'unofficial', I believe went on with the tacit agreement of the powers that be. That is, until it came to our turn in 1975. By then (and we might have been the first year) it was definitely 'outlawed', presumably as potentially too dangerous, and although there was some discussion in our year group about going ahead anyway, we were all terribly well behaved so let it pass. As far as I know, that was that.

It was hardly to be expected that everything would run smoothly from day one, nor that comprehensive education would immediately benefit all pupils. It had been promised that the transition to becoming a comprehensive would be smooth. After the first two or three years this largely turned out to be true, perhaps more quickly than might have been expected given such a short time had been allowed to plan and implement such a major upheaval.

None the less if university entrance is used as a yardstick there was no immediate change. Of the 27 boys that remained from the 1966 Grammar School entry, sixteen went to university after they sat A-Levels in 1973, two years after the reorganisation. This represented 30 percent of that original selected intake, indicating once again that the grammar school system did not inevitably lead to a university education - which of course was its purpose. This was also only a small percentage increase from Goodall's early years, although it also showed that the chaos and change had not been terminally disruptive to exam success.

But perhaps it also showed that grammar schools were not

succeeding in ensuring that most of those who had passed their 11+ were moving up to tertiary education despite the increased number of places that governments had created across the 1960s. In other words, a repeat of the same problem that Bye, Dyer, Mullens, and Nelson had encountered.

Of course, it could be rightly argued that at this time, a university education was not the be-all and end-all of those years spent in education. Just as important were the experiences that the pupils had that opened their eyes to a world broader than perhaps they would have experienced otherwise. To instil in them values that would stand them in good stead in their adult lives. As Goodall once wrote, a good education would lead to a 'growth in self-awareness and self-expression, the development of moral skills, widening of one's use of leisure and a sharpening of one's curiosity.' And, of course, some very bright pupils were still moving straight into employment.

The staff too had to adjust to the new regime. Examples abound from around the country of perfectly good grammar school teachers that were unwilling or unable to adapt their styles of teaching to suit the least academic as well as bright pupils. And vice-versa for former secondary modern teachers.

Peter More acknowledged that he had at first been opposed to comprehensive education but in time came to realise that the supposedly less-able pupils often achieved much more than was generally believed possible.

The rapid expansion in numbers created problems but also created opportunities such as providing a curriculum suitable for less academic pupils. For example the School was one of the first to offer a CSE in European Studies. In other schools this became a course of little value but thanks again to Peter More, LWS ensured it provided a valuable experience.

The large number of pupils and consequently staff not only allowed a considerable broadening of the curriculum, it also gave Goodall the opportunity to appoint some first-rate staff, no more so than the full-time Director of Music, Robin Nelson who, building on the foundations laid by Gilbert, raised the standard and breadth of music-making to heights that would have seemed impossible twenty years earlier. Within a few years, a musical *Star,* was broadcast on TV.

On the subject of staff, George Moss whose extensive memories of the School in the 1910-20s appeared earlier, died in 1973. He had been history master from 1913 to 1924, and because he had enjoyed his time teaching at LWGS so much he had become an Hon. Member of the Old Tamensians. Hugh Mullens who had been Head in the 1950s had retired from teaching, and was now living in Sheringham, Norfolk. He too had remained an enthusiastic supporter of the OTA.

Although the early 1970s were not an easy time for the School, it survived and soon thrived. In any case Thame itself was growing. Building of new housing estates had begun after the 2nd World War and in the 1970s the largest development, the Lea Park Estate, was started.

In terms of businesses and industry, the large Shell-BP depot had opened in 1958, and later a business and industrial zone opened up to provide diverse employment such as Angus Fire Armour, Hacker Radio, and King Harry Foods. However in 1971, the Census showed that almost half of the workforce worked outside of Thame: driving to Cowley for the motor works, working in High Wycombe across a range of occupations, and some commuted to London.

Eventually some excellent new buildings came on stream, including the Syson laboratory complex, the Music School, a computer room, a fine drama studio, and a lecture hall at Lower School East. A special needs centre was opened under the direction of Lally Lewis. However increasing pupil numbers eventually forced the School to open a second Lower

School campus of four forms of entry next to the Upper School site. This became known as Lower School West (LSW).

In 1975 LSW was officially opened by Joan Lester, Under Secretary of State for Education, on the Oxford Road site. A marquee was erected on the cricket pitch where the ceremony took place, and speeches made. Teachers were in a bouyant mood as despite the Labour government's need to cut public spending, teachers received pay increases averaging 27 per cent.

This changed a year later. 1976 was not the happiest year for Oxfordshire education: disputes within the County Council, controversy among parents and industrial action all caused concern. The most 'memorable' (if that is the right word) was the dispute with the National Union of Teachers when the Union ordered all their members in Oxon schools to down tools every Friday, and told all the Heads to close their schools on those days. As only 29 of the 137 LWS staff were in the NUT, Goodall refused, and took the NUT on. Thanks to the loyalty of the staff in Thame at least this particular strike collapsed.

The decision not to build a secondary school at Chinnor was leading to the School's roll growing, and Goodall commenting that with thirteen temporary buildings, the site was looking like a shanty town. Perhaps unsurprisingly vandalism was an issue.

By September 1977, the roll had broken through the 2,000 mark (including 80 boys in the Boarding House), entering a select group of just thirteen schools in England and Wales with over 2,000 pupils. From the outside this might have seen surprising as Thame itself was a small market town of 8,000 inhabitants but the School had a broad catchment area which included taking children from the neighbouring county of Buckinghamshire. This figure was a significant increase on the numbers predicted in 1968. Teaching those 2,000 pupils were 113 full-time staff and 11 part-time, about the same number of teachers as there had been pupils half a century earlier.

If success is measured purely by examination results, the School was now doing well. O- and A-Level results had improved substantially and in greater proportion to the rising numbers since the grammar school days, and a greater number of pupils were gaining admission to universities and other higher education institutions. Entry of pupils to Oxbridge had trebled because the School could now offer dedicated provision to aspiring entrants. The number of A-Level subjects offered was now 32 in all, more than double the number in 1971.

But this came at a cost both from local and national factors. Within the School, the Principal admitted that he no longer knew everyone's name. The schools were so large it was no longer possible for even each of the three schools to assemble everyone together unless it was outside. The sense of a tight school community had gone and, as was said at the time, 'an exclusive atmosphere of cloistered calm and study is impossible.' It was also said that the staff were near to exhaustion point from a heavy workload, massive expectations - and the fact that many had to shuttle back and forth across the town between the three school sites.

Beyond the School, the issues noted earlier continued. Disputes within the County Council about how best to develop education in the County had led to deep schisms. The Council too decided to cut the education budget by worsening the teacher-pupil ratio and this led to the first teacher strikes in the School's history with pupils being excluded from lessons on occasions.

During this period, a number of rather incredulous suggestions were made by the county councillors representing Thame and Chinnor, on the basis that pupil numbers were predicted to decline and hence the School would be too big and too costly for future needs, and that it should live within its means. These included closing the Sixth Form and making LWS a 11-16 school only with older pupils being educated elsewhere including Aylesbury and Oxford. Another was that some of the younger children too could also be educated outside the town. The idea then was to sell one of the School's sites for housing. Thirdly these councillors claimed that the School only had to live with the problems until the mid 1980s, when it was predicted that pupil numbers would decline again. (Clearly they had forgotten about the plans to expand significantly Thame's housing stock at the Lee Park Estate, and their plan to sell one site for housing.)

However, the national forecasts also showed (as turned out to be the case) that the average decline in a single school would only be approximately 100 pupils across the total roll (in other words LWS would go from around 2,000 pupils to 1,900) *and* that numbers would grow again in the 1990s.

In 1979, Goodall who had been Headmaster for fifteen years and had steered the School from a small grammar to this behemoth of an institution, resigned to take up a post in the independent sector. He was replaced by Peter Wells. In one sense this broke the final link to the grammar school past, even though there were still three staff members who had been teaching in the 1950s (Good, Lilley More) and another six from the 1960s, (Adams, Brookes Bradnack, Gilbert, Keirs, Burgess and Clarke). But whereas in those times they were nine out of twenty five staff, they were now nine out of one hundred. The School could now be said to be entering a new modern era.

❊ ❊ ❊

Reasons for success

On Goodall's leaving, the Chairman of the Governors, Sir William Hayter, said:

> *A man who has steered the School's transition from a two-form entry boy's grammar school into a 2000-pupil co-educational comprehensive can only be described as the school's second founder.*

He could well have added that, after eight years, LWS was an undoubted success, in strong contrast to the many comprehensives that failed or became no more than 'bog standard', and it is pertinent to consider why Thame succeeded when so many others did not.

Hayter himself can be credited as one of the major reasons for this success. A man of great wisdom and wide experience as former ambassador to the Soviet Union and Warden of New College, he provided constant support for the School in general and for Goodall in particular. The fortunes of the School had often mirrored (and still do) the quality of the governing body but they also mirror the state of education in the country at large. Not that this is surprising, and the late 1970s were an unstable period for education with changes of government, policy swings, all against the backdrop of an economy that was going into meltdown, and social unrest. There is a certain dependence on an environment that neither a headmaster nor governors can influence and hence credit should go to Goodall for ensuring the School remained a bastion of strength. He was the right man, in the right place, at the right time - twice.

In 1964, as already stated, he was the right man to fulfil the Grammar School's potential; from 1970 he was well qualified to plan and bring about the remarkable and successful transformation of the School. He understood the basic essentials of good education regardless of the type of school and he had the ability to make others share his philosophy and put it into practice. Through his earlier experience of independent school education, he was aware of and aspired to academic excellence within a broader liberal education. His knew how to deal with local authority educationalists, national policies, and teacher unions. He was able to learn from the successes and failures of other brand new Oxfordshire comprehensives, Banbury School especially. He was still relatively young and retained undiminished the energy and determination to make a success of what in most respects was a new school.

But circumstances helped him. If comprehensives were to succeed anywhere it would be at places such as Thame: a catchment area with a high proportion of relatively well-off parents, supportive of their children's education. Amongst other advantages of such a catchment area was the potential to create a large Sixth Form. Small sixth forms generated in less wealthy areas were the undoing of many a comprehensive. The limited curricular offer and, ironically, A-Level sets that were too small, adversely affected sixth-form students' education. The limited opportunities for sixth-form teaching also deterred the better qualified teachers from applying to join the staff. Thame's relative isolation was also a benefit. It had no serious comprehensive school competitors and therefore did not suffer from the, often negative, effects on schools of parental choice.

So Goodall was lucky, but there are many aphorisms that link luck and success. One of the most apposite is 'I'm a great believer in luck, and I find the harder I work, the more I have of it.' (Thomas Jefferson) or 'Luck is a dividend of sweat. The more you sweat, the luckier you get.' (Ray Kroc). Goodall and his staff certainly 'sweated' and it paid off.

CHAPTER 28: THREE PRINCIPALS IN TWENTY YEARS 1980-2000

HOWARD BROWN'S *Short History...* is not only short of words but stops short nearly 30 years before the time he published it. We took the decision to bring this history as close as possible to the time of writing.

A former Education Secretary once decreed that history stopped short thirty years before the present – thus presumably consigning all the university departments of contemporary history to academic limbo. But he did have a point. Writing recent and contemporary history poses particular challenges. As with using an old-fashioned camera, while distant objects/periods can be accurately defined, those close up in space or time lack focus and perspective. It is easy enough to chronicle events; much more difficult to assess their significance and long-term impact.

For instance, it is hard to judge whether the School's frequent changes of designation in the early 21st century after 400 years as a grammar school and 30 as a LEA maintained comprehensive, have made or will make a significant difference to its nature and effectiveness. In 1978 the *Times Educational Supplement* had written a full-page spread about LWS entitled 'The Comprehensive with the Public School Touch.' This touch remained with the School for the next fifteen years or so with the CCF, a Boarding House, a school magazine, and the Old Tamensians's Association but by the end of the 1990s only one of these would be left as a tradition.

Peter Wells succeeded Goodall but stayed in the post for only four years. After his resignation was accepted by the Governors, he went on to become a headteacher at Crown Woods in London. His short tenure at LWS coincided with the opening of a new Sixth Form Centre, and the Thame Leisure Centre - a sports and arts facility to be shared between School and community.

1982 was one of those years where a slight shift occurred in the nature of the School: Adrian Pritchard, the first married Head of Boarding House - other than the headmasters - arrived accompanied by wife Liz, a daughter Thomasin, two dogs and a cat. Robin Nelson who had done much to raise music to an extraordinary level left for Malborough College as Director of Music. Two teaching icons retired: Norman Lilley after many years as Head of Science and running the CCF (among many activities). He had joined the School in 1955. Peter More also took early retirement as the LEA were keen to reduce costs. He had joined in 1951, and finished as Head of Upper School. An OT wrote this about him, which we include as it accurately captures the workload and commitment of all the teachers from that era, men and women who really did dedicate their life to the School and its pupils.

There can be little doubt that Peter had an enormous effect on many pupils' lives over a long 32-year period at the School. He told me once that he nearly did not accept his appointment at LWGS after an interview with Mr Mullens, concerned that the School may be another 'public school' rendition of Caterham School in Surrey which he described as 'well-paid slave labour' and was his first post.

He was, too, one of the first teachers to be appointed after a year's teacher training in Oxford. His was not the glittering personality of a Gerard Gould or a Hugh Mullens, but like his close associate in Thame, Norman Lilley, he came across as a father-figure and a great organiser and facilitator –

a man who quietly instilled knowledge and confidence. He was well aware of the need for good preparation and flexible teaching strategies, and got boys interested and involved in all sorts of activities. In fact, his involvement in so many aspects of school life was legendary and one wonders whether his family saw much of him.

In his early years he was a teacher of geography, English and French; his extra-curricular activities included the CCF and particularly its new RAF Division. Peter did nothing by halves and made sure his c.20 cadets in the RAF cadre had every opportunity to experience the best: he arranged a visit to the Vickers Aircraft factory at Weybridge in 1960 to see the 'mock-up' of the VC 10 airliner; to Abingdon Airport for a flight in a Beverley aircraft and observation of control staff in action; a field day at Benson on the link trainer (flight simulator); regular 30-minute flights were also arranged for boys in the Chipmunk trainer aircraft at White Waltham, Berks and gliding courses at Oxford Airport (at Kidlington).

He revived the boarders' Stamp Club and Natural History Society in the early 1950s, and in 1959 he founded a flourishing Geographical Society with over 30 members showing films (e.g. The Lost World of the Kalahari and Daybreak in Udi – Nigerian village life resistant to change) and inviting speakers and slide presentations from ex-pupils (e.g. Geoff Cornish 1950-7, spoke on life in Salisbury and the native reserves in what was then S. Rhodesia).

Peter was heavily involved with school trips to Switzerland and Denmark and 6th Form Field Courses in Geography to Malham Tarn in Yorkshire and then Tyneside. He took a group to Russia in the early 70s. Later in his career he was Senior Master and took on the heavy load of school administration during and after the School's change from a gram-

mar to a comprehensive.

More himself had this to say:

> *These days people do not stay in the same job in the same place for thirty years and I have often been asked why I did. The reasons are complex. Perhaps there was an element of inertia and even laziness on my part. Certainly Thame is in a very pleasant part of the country, with easy access to the attractions of Oxford. There was without a doubt a particular sense of cooperation between staff, pupils and governors, which I thought would be difficult to find elsewhere. But chiefly, it was because of the excitement engendered by the radical changes and developments in the School, particularly from the mid sixties to the late-seventies.*

A year later another retirement was Norman Good's who had been a pupil at the School before the War, and then taught from the late 1950s. After his departure there were now only two teachers from the pre-comprehensive era on the staff and they left over the next two years.

The School continued to excel at sport: The 1st XV and the Colts toured Ireland – well Cork. A 1st VII were invited to play in the prestigious Rosslyn Park Tournament as well as in the Oxon 7s. The Netball VII were County Champions, and played in the All-England Finals.

Wells was succeeded by David Kenningham in 1985 after a gap when no head teacher was in place. Prior to coming to LWS Kenningham had been Headmaster of Cheney School, Oxford. A physicist, he'd previously taught at Malborough, RGS High Wycombe, Whitley Abbey School, Coventry, and in Massachusetts, USA. He served in REMR and had a spell in industry.

At Cheney he had made his mark as Headmaster and the school was highly popular but towards the end of his tenure, the LEA were looking at school provision in Oxford. Of the six upper schools it was clear that because of declining pupil numbers one would have to close. In the meantime - as another headmaster pointed out - all six heads would have to fight a bloody battle to ensure it was not their school that was axed. Perhaps unsurprisingly, Kenningham decided he did not want to be dragged down into this war of educational attrition and decided to move on. (That the war in Oxford then lasted for two decades possibly sums up the state of local education administration.)

He was a tall, imposing figure but most pupils would say he was firm but fair, with a wry sense of humour. He continued to teach physics as he thought he ought to keep in touch with the classroom and not be seen as someone who was remote. As one former pupil remarked, 'he was the nemesis of those who smoked on the estate...busted many of us with his stealth-like seeking powers but always very fair. He had a huge impact on me personally, in a positive way.'

Potentially the idea that would have most impact on LWS started to be formulated in 1984 when the County Council began discussions to move the whole school to one site on the Oxford Road. This time, they claimed, they were determined to make it happen.

One of the school's most influential figures in the modern era was Sir William Hayter. He retired as Chairman of the Governors and, typical of his generosity, he donated the funds contributed for a leaving present to found the Hayter Travel Award. He was someone who was known throughout the School as he ensured that he was not some aloof figure who would keep the school at arms length.

Hayter had become a Foundation Governor in 1957 and when he died in 1995, David Kenningham wrote, 'Sir William could have chosen to play a minimal part in this role. Instead he was active for 27 years, most of them as Chairman of Governors.'

He was someone who ensured he had a strong presence in the School rather than an anonymous or indeed invisible figure. Over the years, not all chairmen of the School's governing body have done this. It is less important for the students but can underpin the parents' perception of a strong team managing the School. If they see a strong team they are more likely to be supportive themselves of the School - a weak team and they tend to shrug their shoulders and are not persuaded to give much help.

He was replaced by Jane Bugg, the first women to head the governors and who proved to be equally adept.

We rarely mention the support staff in the School, so by way of some amends, in 1990 Rosemary Gill, who had been librarian in LWS and the Upper School for twenty years, retired. A difficult job indeed trying to maintain silence among an unruly group of pupils.

It was in 1990 that a combination of the school governors and the LEA decided to end some of the great traditions of Lord Williams's School.

In 1991 the Boarding House closed, ending a 400 year old tradition – Ellen Rudkin was the last Matron and Steve Warren the last Boarding House Master. (In the final year only 25 boarders were left.) No more getting-up at 7.15am for a cold shower. Putting aside frivolity, this fundamentally changed the School's nature. Since its inception and into the mid-20th century, it was the boarders who were at the core of the School. They were the pupils who provided much of the sporting talent and contributed greatly to extra-curricular activities. Many times in the seventy or so years between the School re-opening in 1879 and then coming under state control in 1947, headmasters had bemoaned the rather more lackadaisical attitude of the day-boys. (Although should we be surprised that they wanted to get home as quickly as possible after lessons finished?)

While the percentage of boarders decreased from 1947 it was a boarding house that invariably won the annual House Competition. Some might argue that this was because they had few alternative outlets for their energy and had to remain on the premises whether they liked it or not and while this is true the fact is their contribution was significant. In fact a deliberate decision had been taken across this period - so far as was possible – to recruit those with musical talent and sporting prowess.

Boarding also gave the School a very different character as numbers rose to over a hundred during the 1960s representing almost one third of the roll. However, in one fell stroke, when the School went comprehensive in 1971, the boarders constituted less than one ninth.

The decision to close the boarding house was hugely controversial but had the full support of the Principal. Already the two houses Greenacre and Highfield had closed at the end of July 1990.

As soon as the boarders vacated, plans were implemented to convert the boarding accommodation into the Foundation Centre for exclusive use of sixth formers. A fund-raising programme was put into operation, and an Elizabethan chest given to the School by New College, was sold at Sothebys to raise funds. A short-sighted move if there ever was one.

William Howe attended the School in the 1950s. Tragically he died from leukemia whilst still a pupil in the Sixth Form. In 1991, his father left in his Will a substantial bequest to the School to benefit students engaged in the study of music. These became known as the Willie Howe scholars. In addition, a further bequest was made to Headington Quarry Church – the parish where the Howe family lived. One result of this legacy is a beautiful stained glass window which features the essence of the seven Narnia stories (C.S. Lewis is buried in the church's graveyard) but also includes the crossed organ pipes from the School's coat of arms, im memory of Howe's time at the Grammar School.

In 1993, ACE Week became an important feature of the school: Active Curriculum Experience Week for the whole school where activities brough the curriculum to life in many different ways. Some were school-based, some were sent on work experience; some went camping; some attended lessons at Rycotewood College.

Another tradition came to an end in 1994 with the closure of the Combined Cadet Force. The Ministry of Defence regretted the School's decision but made it clear that for two years they had made attempts to keep it going despite increasing apathy from the School and governors. In their words, 'we received no response and were forced to conclude that there was little real interest in the School for a continued CCF presence.'

One issue that became an increasing problem for schools nationwide in the 1990s was the use of drugs. It was getting to a level where permanent exclusions were becoming commonplace. At Lord Williams's, Kenningham, was adamantly opposed to permanent exclusions. 'Pupils found in possession of cannabis are normally readmitted after three days and those found dealing after 10. The school offers a wide-ranging drugs education programme. When a group of Year 11 pupils was found with cannabis at Christmas, there were long talks involving their parents and governors, and the pupils were readmitted.'

The School was performing well when it came to exams and had an A-Level performance that was above many - but not all -of the other comprehensive schools in the county.

On a completely different note, in 1994 the 400th anniversary of the birth of John Hampden was marked by the planting of a tree in the grounds of the Upper School. The tree, a field maple, was planted by the Mayor of Thame, Councillor Mrs Jane Morbey, in the presence of the Principal, and the Earl of Buckinghamshire, Patron of the John Hampden Society.

In 1995 Lower School West on the Oxford Road site was closed and all Year 7-9 teaching was amalgamated on to the Towersey Road site. Of course the ultimate aim was to have a single-site school, something that had been discussed since 1984. However this seemed as far away as ever. (Just as the LEA had failed to resolve the number of upper schools in Oxford.)

The combined Lower School was opened with new facilities and upgrading of the existing classrooms. This was the realisation of a dream and planning process that had begun two years previously to overcome the difficulties of a split site. Of course some teaching staff still had to commute between Upper and Lower schools but at least the lower years were now all together. In turn, the buildings of Lower School West became part of the expanding Upper School as the Sixth Form now had over 400 students.

The younger students were excited:

> *The Lower School is great! One of our teachers said it was like the Tardis: old from the outside, and new and clean from the inside.*

> *The opening ceremony was brilliant but I kept getting pins and needles in my feet. We have been very privileged to have these wonderful facilities, and I hope they last forever.*

To make the opening *Pencils and Obelisks,* a sculpture commissioned from Old Tamensian, Peter Logan was unveiled.

Another welcomed opening was the school nursery - well a new nursery as one had opened in converted premises of Uplands in 1991. Not only did it provide childcare but it gave students at the school work-experience and became a much sought-after placement for NNEB students. This was now a purpose-built unit, and it also incorporated space for the Chinnor Autistic Unit.

Another tradition came to an end in 1996: *The Tamensian* ceased publication after 173 editions although various other school publications proliferated such as the Lower School's *Blue & Gold*. Some were short-lived but the *Sixth Form Yearbook*, published annually since the early 1990s, continues to thrive.

The closure of the magazine was in part due to financial constraints but also it was becoming increasingly difficult to put together an annual publication that in anyway could capture all that was going on at the School.

Perhaps unsurprisingly the School was still facing financial issues and sent out an appeal to parents, 'the School is currently facing continuing severe budget restraints...and we can no longer avoid turning to parents and friends for help.'

Founder's Day was yet another tradition that while not dropped, changed significantly. In 1982, it was reported that Founder's Day had a full programme including music, rugby, hockey and netball, tours of the school, a tea and AGM. The buffet lunch cost £1.75p and there was a bar selling wines and beer. That year, the rugby side was to be captained by Martin Fairn who also played for Coventry but on the day he had to play for Coventry and his replacement was Jon Cooke. Rebecca McConnell led the OT hockey side and they scored their first victory over the School. In the morning, a rugby tournament was organised for Years 8 and 9 before the service.

However by 1986, a joint committee of staff, OTs, the vicar and pupils was put together to review the Founder's Day format. The outcome was that in future, Founder's Day would no longer be organised solely by the School but be a joint effort between the school and the Old Tamensians' Assocation with the organising group headed by a member of staff. It was also agreed that attendance by pupils would be wholly voluntary.

In the 1990s, the School decided to experiment by making Founder's Day, a Founder's Week with a variety of sports and music events within the School as well as the church service. The format continued until the late 1990s when the School decided that because of changing lifestyles it would no longer support Founder's Day as part of the school calender. So the Old Tamensians's Association took over the organisation.

David Kenningham proved to be another long-serving Principal but in 1997 after twelve years he retired. His successor was Pat O'Shea, the second woman to head Lord Williams's School. She had come from being Warden of a community college in Cambridgeshire but had previously taught at Peers School in Oxford – and also worked with the Oxford University Department of Education.

In the final year of the millenium the Sixth Form students celebrated another good year, with the second best set of A-Level results ever. They achieved an overall pass rate of 94% with 20% at A Grade; and the School was ranked in the UK's Top 300. LWS supplied the Cricket captains for Oxfordshire at U13, U14, U15, U16 and U19. Luke Merry played for England U15 and took 1 for 29 against Scotland. Rachael Stoakes and Zoe Farrell were off to Australia to play for the England U16 touch rugby squad.

The School was also in the process of applying for Sports College status. The other option was Languages but despite the School's excellent record with its foreign exchange programmes it was decided that sports would be more inclusive for the students and community. That noted, the annual exchange with the Lycee Gambier in Lisiuex was in its 31st year and was now the longest-standing unbroken exchange in Oxfordshire. The link with Friedrich Ebert Gymnasium, Bonn was in its 18th year.

And the world did not come to an end at midnight.

CHAPTER 29: THE TWENTY FIRST CENTURY, AND SPORTING ACHIEVEMENTS

THESE FINAL CHAPTERS are not as detailed as the earlier chapters for two reasons: the first is that so much takes place at the School that it is impossible to cover it to the same detail; second, we have been unable to elicit an overview of what has happened at the School from anyone we have asked who was or is closely connected with the running of the School during this period.

The introduction of specialist schools was yet another government initiative whereby schools could specialise in certain subjects or areas in order to boost achievement levels. It was a policy that took sometime to get off the ground but accelerated from 1997 onwards.

At the end of 2000, the *Thame Gazette* reported:

> *Lord Williams's School has been designated a sports college by the Government – which could mean £200,000 a year more in its budget. It is now the seventh school in the county to achieve specialist status.*
>
> *The other schools which have specialist status are: King Alfred School in Wantage, which also has specialist sports status, Wheatley Park School at Holton (arts), St Birinus School in Didcot (technology), Peers School in Oxford (technology), Didcot Girls' School (language) and Banbury School in Banbury (technology).*

Lord Williams's deputy head teacher David Jones said: 'We are thrilled and delighted at achieving this status which operates from next September.' He said it did not mean major changes at the School – it remains a 2,000-pupil comprehensive taking all-comers. But the sports college status means extra Government money going to Lord Williams's. He said: 'We interpret sport in its widest sense, not just with traditional games. We will develop opportunities within PE with students being able to take GCSE in the subject. We will be able to extend dance into A-levels and there will be vocational training opportunities for people with special talents. We hope it will set up a more vibrant range of opportunities with something for everyone in the school.'

Mr Jones said the School selected to opt for sports-college status in May. He said there had been tremendous support from local industry, parish councils and individuals who helped raise the initial £50,000 needed to support the school's claim for sports college status.

Schools Standards Minister Estelle Morris said: 'As the recent secondary performance tables demonstrate, specialist schools are excelling academically. Three out of the top five in the list of 100 most improved schools are specialist schools. Crucially, specialist schools are also having a wider influence – raising standards in local schools and helping create opportunities right across the local community.'

Pat O'Shea's tenure was sadly an unhappy one for her personally. A brilliant teacher she resigned but fortunately she was not lost to the profession and ultimately became an Ofsted inspector.

Her replacement, Michael Spencer, had been the very successful head of the Warriner School, Bloxham but had taken early retirement to pursue his love of skiing and mountaineering.

Initially he was drafted in as acting head but fifty-five year old Spencer, then agreed to become the permament head in April 2001.

In 2003, nearby Rycotewood College closed. It had been founded in 1935 by Cecil Michaelis as a residential college offering training in gatemaking, wheelwrighting and later furniture and agricultural engineering. Some pupils had gone onto the College after leaving LWS but ties between the two institutions were not strong and some thought this was a missed opportunity. The College, the Oxford College of Further Education, and North Oxfordshire College in Banbury merged to form Oxford and Cherwell College. An idea was put forth that the building and assets could be amalgamated into the Upper School but the Council decided to sell the site to developers who turned the building into residential flats.

In 2004 the School and Thame were stunned by the sudden death of John Fulkes. Born in Thame, he had been a pupil in the 1960s, gone up to Oxford, became a member of staff in 1975, and the School's Head of Sixth Form since the mid-80s. He'd also been on the OTA Committee for nigh on 30 years, serving as President and Secretary during that time. His death left a void as he dedicated his life to the School, to Thame and the OTA. His dedication to cricket in particular at both school and county level had created one of the strongest youth teams in the UK - and that included the girls teams. Gerard Gould wrote:

> *Dear John – my farewell to you must be Horatio's to Hamlet: "Good night, sweet prince, And flights of angels sing thee to thy rest."*

A student wrote:

> *John was an inspirational English teacher and did much to encourage me to read as wide a variety of literature as possible; something I maintain to this day. He was also gen-*

erous by nature and, when he learnt that my parents had moved to Dorset, took it upon himself to chauffeur me home for the holidays without any thought of accepting the petrol money on offer. Last October I popped into the School to give my partner a quick overview of where my formative years were spent. This fortunately coincided with Founder's Day – I was delighted to meet John again after some 23 years and he seemed to be as full of good cheer and boundless energy as when I'd seen him last. His death must be a great loss to both Lord Williams's and the Old Tamensians.

Spencer remained in post until 2005.

Before he left he made the following comment:

The bid to become a specialist school was well under way when I arrived as head of Lord Williams's School in Oxfordshire in September 2000, and we became a sports college the following year. The specialism seemed to strike a particular chord with the local sports community and we wanted to build on that.

But when I looked at the School, I realised it had a wide range of strengths - not just sport. Although we were happy to be a sports college with all the advantages and developments that brought, I also wanted to make sure that this wasn't misunderstood by our local community.

The sports college bid was nicely varied. The three components we chose to focus on were dance, rugby and outdoor education - and we've recently relaunched the Duke of Edinburgh award scheme. Many of the children are participating in expeditions, so there's a big outlet for those who don't thrive in conventional sporting contexts but who do get fulfilled in other areas. But there was still a risk that people would think we were just a sports college, that pupils had to have sporting ability to thrive in the school.

Lord Williams's School, which is the only school serving Thame and the surrounding area, has a long tradition of artistic activity. The art department is strong, with some high-calibre work. In dance, drama and music we have high levels of performance and a wide range of involvement of children. All students study dance in Years 7 to 9. We also have A-Level groups in dance and theatre studies.

So when the Arts Council of England's Artsmark scheme (a national arts award for schools in England) came out, we decided to go for it. Our application involved a full audit of our arts provision. We had to describe our curriculum and extra-curricular provision, including performance data, participation rates, trends, staffing levels and expertise. There were supporting statements from people in the community with whom we have links in the arts. The application was followed by a site visit.

We won the Artsmark gold award a year ago. To some extent, it's an award that recognises what we already do - art education is important, and we have good people teaching it. But it's not just an accolade. It's also given us targets: to continue to ensure provision is wide and the extra-curricular diet is enriched; to provide access and high levels of participation. It's given us a real spur to maintain the quality of provision. It's important to give children confidence that their achievements across a wide range of activities are of interest and of value, and it is useful to encourage others.

In the last year of Spencer's tenure the Oftsed report on the School's performance showed it was ahead of the average in the county for GCSE performance but was slightly behind for A- and A/S-Level measures.

After Spencer's second retirement, there followed a short gap until the appointment of David Wybron as the new Head-teacher.

Wybron had joined the teaching staff in 1991 as Head of Humanities and a teacher of History. He progressed to become Deputy Headteacher before becoming Head.

When the Channel 4 TV programme *Dispatches - After School Arms Club,* was broadcast in 2006, the School became national media heroes. Students from the School's Amensty group were equipped with a letterhead, a mobile, and an e-mail address to find out how easy it was to broker arms and torture equipment all within the UK's legal guidelines. Anna Clayton went to the Westminster to present the School's findings:

> *I was shocked. A sting stick can only be used for torture*
> *and I was stunned when it was delivered to the School. The*
> *whole point of what we were doing was to make an impact*
> *on MPs to change the law and get the weapons we purchased*
> *put on arms lists and covered by EU treaties.*

Two years after Wybron's appointment - and for the first time in the School's history - a major catastrophe occured on the 30th June 2007 when a fire broke out at the drama studio of the Lower School campus. The emergency services received a 999 call at 9.42pm although it was believed the fire had started at 8.30pm.

Sixty-five fire-fighters from across the county were able to control the blaze and stop it from destroying a neighbouring building with fire-fighters from Thame, Wheatley, Watlington and Slade Park, as well as teams from Buckinghamshire Fire & Rescue coming from Aylesbury, Brill, Princes Risborough and Waddesdon attending the blaze.

The fire was the result of arson when a local man made a

botched attempt to burgle the School. He was later convicted. Subsequently the School set about raising £1m to build a new, state-of-the-art, drama and dance studio for both students and Thame Youth Theatre.

England Ladies hockey captain Kate Walsh opened the new all-weather pitch at the School in 2007 - and urged the students to follow in her footsteps by going on to represent their country.

Walsh had won bronze with England at the Commonwealth Games in Melbourne, and was impressed by the £650,000 facility which also catered for football, athletics and tennis. She told students at the official opening:

> I think it is a really great facility and you should be really proud that you have got it to play on. I wish I had this when I started playing because I started playing on grass. I hope it inspires you to keep practising and improving. Hopefully there is an Olympian or a world champion among you. It just takes practise - if I can do it so can you.

It may be recalled that the School had paid an annual sum for the upkeep of Lord Williams's tomb since its founding. Over the years it had made extraordinary payments for its repair and maintenance. In 2002 it was identified that some extensive conservation work was required to the alabaster figures but neither the church nor the School could fund this. So Graham Thomas, one of the authors, stepped in and funded the project through the Old Tamensians's Association.

Founder's Day was still an annual event. In 2007, the Head Boy and Head Girl described it thus:

> We had a great day and are really happy to have attended and been involved in Founder's Day. The weather was brilliant as we gathered at St. Mary's Church and were delivered an entertaining and poignant service by OT Rev.

Daplyn which was respectfully received and allowed us to have sincere remembrance of those passed. We were charmed with brilliant performances by Steph' Caulfield on flute and a song from Charlotte Smith, our lovely Wille Howe scholars. The congregation sang the hymn terrifically, well done to all those who sang in Latin (we were completely lost!).

Later at School as we drank tea and coffee, it was great to see Old Tamensians catching up with each other as well as engaging in friendly conversation with current students of the School. The visitors' genuine interest was apparent during the School tours especially as we showed off the brand new science block. The art installation was both thought-provoking and fitting to the occasion. Maybe it would have been nice for some paintings to be put on display in the buttery as well?

Joan and the team did a fantastic job providing us with a delicious roast, which we enjoyed with a glass of wine from a generous OT and great tunes struck up by the School's Jazz Band. Although upon hearing of the cooks' approaching retirement a collective heart sank and naturally Joan, Vera and Kath will be sorely missed. Fingers crossed they will return for next year's event.

Despite being very disappointed at not winning anything in the raffle(!), we admired the Committee President Aisling Begley's ticket-selling skills as well as, of course, her invaluable involvement in the event. We left with our bellies full and our hearts warmed by the overwhelming sense of community, pride and tradition. It was nice to meet some of the Old Tamensians as they shared their schoolboy stories with us and no doubt a great time was had by all. We certainly hope that we can enjoy such an event when we are older.

To finish this decade on another upbeat note, in 2009 the 450th anniversary of the School's founding was celebrated with a series of events across the whole year, and activities that involved students, teaching and support staff, and the Old Tamensians (who themselves were celebrating their one hundreth anniversary.)

Various exhibitions were amounted at both the Lower and Upper Schools, and at the recently opened Thame Museum in which both authors were involved; special cricket and rugby matches were held between the School and OTs. The BBC interviewed various people in several separate broadcasts across the year.

In July, an evening party was held in the school grounds with entertainment from students of all ages, a buffet meal, and finishing with a grand firework display. Later in September, a black-tie gala dinner was held for over a hundred Old Tamensians and teachers in the Hall at New College. Naturally, this included some who had celebrated the quatercentenary fifty years previously.

Finally a sell-out gala concert was held in November with music that reflected the many eras of the School since its foundation. Among the many pieces performed by over 100 current students and alumni was the world première of a Howard Goodall choral piece, *O Singe Unto New Songe.*

It was a thoroughly uplifting celebration of the School's history, and showed the importance of this historical legacy in making the School distinctive in the nation's education provision.

Inevitably there were some who felt that in the modern era, this history is less important if not irrelevant and old-fashioned, a distraction when teaching staff are under intense pressure to deliver the curriculum. There are many arguments as to why this is short-sighted but the most important is the ability to give students a sense of permanence. In an ever changing, topsy turvy, sometimes frightening world, the ability to demonstrate that some important institutions do survive despite whatever calamities befalls them, hopefully gives students a greater sense of security and confidence.

Our institutions are critical to the well-being of the country, something we sometimes only appreciate in times of crisis. England has a long history as a nation and there is national pride in many of its enduring institutions such as the Bank of England (1694), the Royal Society (1660), the House of Commons (1295), The Court of Chancery (1280) and the University of Oxford (1096). One of the institutions which we should also take pride in are schools, which precede all the above-mentioned institutions. As noted in the Prologue, the oldest extant grammar school is the King's School in Canterbury which was founded as a cathedral school in 597 AD. There are times when schools have faltered or failed and will continue to do so but the best survive and Lord Williams's School is one of the best.

CHAPTER 30: BECOMING AN ACADEMY, AND MODERN DAY PRESSURES

AS NOTED IN THE PREVIOUS CHAPTER, we acknowledge that we have only been able to skim over the surface of the most current history of the school. Hence without apology this is our view of the final decade in the School's history.

Government interference in education has been persistent since the Butler Act of 1944. We use the word interference deliberately as it is of course the ultimate responsibility of all governments to deliver education, yet it might be expected that this is done less on idealogical grounds and more grounded in wanting to improve education, with policies based on facts rather than fantasy. Not that all interference has been bad of course but there has been more than enough meddling and swings of direction that have stood in the way of good teaching.

But looking at this last decade in the School's history, what are the significant areas of government policy that have impinged directly on LWS and will do so in the immediate future? There have been three: decreasing expenditure on education in real terms that started during the period of austerity in 2010; changes in how examinations were assessed, and finally the policy decision to force schools (for that's what it was) into becoming academies.

The Institute of Fiscal Studies's papers on the subject show that historically the level of UK education spending rose significantly in real terms and particularly fast from the late

1990s through to the late 2000s, before falling in real terms from 2010 onwards. Most significantly, spending on sixth forms has seen a dramatic decrease of 20 per cent in real terms over the last decade. This coincided with the withdrawal of the specialist school funding as the new Tory/LibDem coalition decided to bring this programme to an end. Across the period 2017-2020 this led to funding per student at the School being cut by 8 per cent in real terms. On the other hand secondary pupil numbers have been rising since 2010 and currently number over 3 million. The Department for Education projects that they are expected to rise by 14.7% over the next 10 years.

Net: less money, more pupils.

A second reduction in funding came when the Tory government closed down the School Sports Partnership Scheme just as the London Olympics were taking place. The organisation, offered competitive sport to all state school children in the county until the Government stopped its annual £250,000 payment. Lord Williams's School was one of the lead partners helping less sports-orientated schools to undertake sport activities.

Under David Wybron, the School achieved an Outstanding Ofsted rating in 2011. Since then, the Governors once said, 'he continued to strive tirelessly for improvements and this resulted in consistently excellent GCSE results, including the School's best ever results in recent years. This was during the time when major changes were made to the GCSE and A-Level examinations.'

The reasoning behind the exam changes was the Government's claim that GCSE's were becoming too easy, and hence less meaningful. A radically new format was introduced - though those who took the equivalent O-Levels some decades previously would claim that it is a return to the format that they had to pass through:

- Most exams will be taken at the end of the two-year course rather than on completion of modules.
- There will be fewer 'bite-sized' questions and more essay-style questions.
- The content will be more challenging, with more substantial texts in English Literature and a number of new topics in Maths.
- Everyone will have to do at least two science GCSEs.
- Coursework and controlled assessment will disappear from most subjects, apart from practical ones such as art, dance and drama.

With A-Levels, the assessment was now also mainly by written exam, with other types of assessment used only where they were needed to test essential skills.

At the time of the change, the UK was experiencing full employment; GDP had been growing rapidly for the last few decades (other than the blip during the global financial crash of 2008, after which it recovered only for first the prospect of the Brexit effect to kick-in, and now COVID-19); inflation had been kept under control; the UK continued to contribute significantly to the world's bank of creativity; while in science a good indicator could be the number of Nobel Prizes won: the UK was the second highest recipient in the world and continued to win every year.

These are just a few key indicators; it does not appear that that there was anything fundamentally wrong with the way education was delivered in the UK. (But never let facts get in the way of ideology.)

In fact pupils not only felt their education was beneficial but enjoyed the whole LWS experience:

I was a student at Lord Williams's School from 2009 to 2016. I really loved the majority of my teachers, particularly the ones who really went above and beyond the usual requirements of teaching! They made the School a very welcoming place to be which helped to improve the sense of community. My experience with pastoral care at School was also very positive, and they were very supportive after my Dad passed away. The teachers were also incredibly inspiring and I am currently at university studying to become a teacher myself (a primary school teacher though!). One of my teachers even helped me write my personal statement for university, despite me having left School 2 years ago at that point!

This really demonstrates how lovely and supportive most of the staff are at Lord Williams's! The facilities at School were great, particularly at the Upper School. The science labs in particular were well equipped and were recently refurbished. Also, having access to the TLC at Upper School was great for PE lessons (and access to the vending machines!). I think pupil voices were listened to at School, but after researching and writing essays on this topic at university, I believe that this can always be improved upon!

Another student, Phoebe Groves, wrote:

Mr Rogerson was my tutor from Year 7 to Year 11 and he was one of the best people I have ever met. He was not only fully invested in all of the members of the tutor group and how well they were going to do, but he was passionate about his subject and made it so exciting. I remember at Lower School in geography we were learning about erosion and he made a line of tables with a load of cardboard boxes at the end and we slid along them then crushed the boxes at the end to show how a waterfall would erode the rocks as it fell.

*We also reenacted battles in history lessons and other inter-
active fun lessons. Also in terms of tutorials he organised
fun events for us like going paintballing and to Billy Elliot
in the theatre which was above and beyond for a teacher
(also I know teachers like Mr Cuell did this too).*

* * *

Becoming an academy

2012 saw the beginning of the next major change to the
School's status: it would no longer come under the control of
the Local Education Authority - as it had been since 1947 - but
instead would become an academy.

In Oxfordshire County Council's Strategy for Change Document, published in 2012, it had been stated:

*The drive to encourage Free Schools and to convert all
schools to Academy status instead of maintained Local
Authority status is strongly articulated nationally and endorsed locally through the March 2012 Cabinet report, with
targets to convert all secondary schools as soon as possible.*

Academies had been introduced in 2000 by the Labour Government under Tony Blair as a way of attempting to revitalise schools that were failing under Local Education Authority
control. They were allowed to become more autonomous in
their running, have their funding provided directly by the Department of Education, and would also have the opportunity
to raise further funds via, for example, being sponsored by
businesses or individuals.

In 2010, the Conservative/LibDem coalition took the decision
to widen the conversion of schools to academies to include
not just those who were failing; during the course of 2012-14,

many if not most state secondary schools converted to academy status.

David Wybron sent a letter to parents, which opened with the following paragraphs:

On 14th February the Cabinet at Oxfordshire County Council clearly stated its support for the conversion of schools to become academies and for the establishment of new forms of schools, including free schools, studio schools and university technical colleges. There will be strong political and philosophical views for and against becoming an Academy and the Governing Body has decided to consult with all stakeholders about whether the school should become an Academy or not. The consultation period is from Monday 26th March to Tuesday 8th May 2012. What follows is an indication of what a change in status would mean for the school:

•There would be no change to the core values and character of the school as a non-selective comprehensive school
•A broad and balanced curriculum would be maintained
•Our work through the Thame Partnership of Primary Schools would be unaffected.
•The pay and conditions of current staff would be protected.
•There would be little change to current arrangements for governance.
•There would be more control of financial resources.
•The School would not change its name.

For technical reasons, it may be prudent to convert to Foundation Status as part of Academy conversion, in order to safeguard the School's aspiration to become a single site school.

It could be argued that the consultation was a sham. No matter what the result, it was clear that Oxfordshire's LEA wished to bring to an end its responsibilities for schools. 'The direction of travel for the authority has been set and we cannot force the authority to have a relationship with us which it doesn't want to have,' was one response from the School.

And so the School became an academy. In one sense it had reverted to its pre-1947 status when it was an independent school - albeit with funding provided by the LEA but not control. By 2018, 95 per cent of secondary schools in Oxfordshire had converted, a figure higher than the national average.

It's worth summarising what had changed. Academies are schools managed by charities known as 'academy trusts' regulated by the government. In the past, LEAs oversaw the performance of schools in their area. They would intervene if any were under-performing and they provided a range of services: everything from payroll to psychologists to computer systems. This was usually done cost-effectively because of economies of scale. It also meant that the school's management had to worry less about the business side of running a school and focus on academic performance.

Now schools, governing bodies, and the academy trusts had to run everything and it quickly became clear that in some instances, the commercial skills to run a multi-million pound business (for that was what the trusts were) were lacking.

* * *

Financial pressures - again

In 2018, the School was once again facing severe financial pressures. Appeals were mounted in an attempt to raise money for critical items. One appeal went out to the Old Tamensians.

Our school budget is forecast to be cut by £500,000 by 2019.

Lord Williams's School alongside other schools is having to deal with a year-on-year reduction in funding. The School needs our help now!

Is it that bad?

• *Per pupil funding has not increased since 2012.*
• *Since 2009 we have had to deal with a 17 per cent reduction in our Sixth Form funding. That is approximately £250,000 (when government sources speak of "The Schools' Budget" this does not include Sixth Form funding).*
• *The money transferred from the Local Authority to this Academy, to run services hitherto run by the Local Authority, has been removed completely since September 2017.*
• *From April 2016 the School's National Insurance contributions increased by 33 per cent from 10.4 per cent to 13.8 per cent, adding approximately £150,000 to our staffing costs.*
• *Teachers' pension costs are expected to rise in 2019, potentially adding £135,000 to staffing costs.*
• *The ending of the pay cap for public sector workers is likely to make the funding situation worse by 2018/19. For example, a 1 per cent salary increase for staff in 2018/19 would add approximately £100,000 to our costs.*

In response, we are bridging the gap by looking at all areas of income and expenditure, including reducing staffing costs, renegotiating supply contracts, looking at efficiency savings, and significantly cutting back on capital investment projects in premises and ICT. As a result we have started to take steps to cut net costs, however any remaining shortfall is currently coming from school reserves, which are primarily held as a contingency for any major unforeseen events.

The School had an annual budget of £12m administered by the staff and the Governors. No longer could they call on the support services of the LEA. They needed to look after themselves.

Fortunately a wealthy OT was able to step-in and made a significant donation while other OTs made smaller donations. Not that this fully overcame the crisis but it relieved the pressure.

The School also set up a fund-raising and alumni development office. This has led to the preparation of a fifteen year capital plan with a Performing Arts Centre as its showcase project. (See Chapter 31 for details.)

On a day-to-day basis, life has continued as normal for the students, and the School continues to gain national recognition for the work it does. But what do some of the students think:

I attended LWS from Year 7 to Year 13 (2009 - 2016). I have mixed memories of my time there but most are positive. Of teachers, friends, and experiences. Two of my favourite memories are Year 11 and Year 13 leavers, having my shirt signed and dressing up as I did on my first day of primary school. Those events were always something we had to look forward to.

My most standout take away from LWS was the difference in support I received through my A-Levels. After failing AS Biology I remember my teacher, Dr Page, encouraging me to try again despite how bad I was at the subject. He showed that he really believed in me. Whilst another teacher told my parents not to allow me to apply for university as I wouldn't get through it, despite passing my exams. Luckily for me, my parents and other teachers had better faith in me as last year I graduated a Psychology degree with a 2:1 and this year I will graduate with a Masters degree in Early

Childhood Development from UCL.

There are also many more examples of the brilliant teachers at LWS including Ms Minnards who was so supportive throughout my time doing product design and Mrs Gibbins my other psychology teacher who was always a joy to be taught by, and Mr Pink and Mr Cassidy for trying their very best to help me through maths even when it really was not making sense. Also, other experiences like Marlow Camp, playing netball in Barbados. and going to Belgium with history I will never forget and were excellent memories provided by LWS.

In 2018 the School had once again been awarded the British Council's prestigious International School Award for working to bring the world into the classroom. This celebrates the work of schools that do exceptional work in international education such as the residential trips to Berlin, Munich and Paris, French (though now no longer with Lisieux), and German student exchanges in Bonn and annual sixth-form study-trips to The Gambia.

The School has a long-standing link with Brikama Upper Basic and Senior Secondary School in The Gambia that continues to grow in strength from year to year. The link has developed an appreciation of the wider world for students from both schools with the aims of forging well-rounded global citizens, gaining cultural understanding and developing skills they need for life and work. (More detail can be found in Volume 2.)

There is so much taking place across the School that making any attempt to cover it - as could be done when it was a grammar school - is impossible. Suffice to say that activities remain as diverse as ever, and academic standards remain laudably high.

The regular newsletter *Take Me Home,* sent to parents, is a window into current life at the School. Across 2019, we have picked out some of the activities that hopefully reflect the nature of today's School, or at least as it was before Covid-19 decimated the timetable.

The Christmas Carol Service is said to be as well-liked as ever. The newsletter mentions the 'Whole School Dance Production' *aLive With Style*, and the dance GCSE and A-Level classes and yet, as happened when dance was first introduced in the late 1960s, teachers were still sewing costumes in their spare evenings.

There was an annual drama production and a Lower School concert.

Other students were participating in an European Space Agency programme, while some from Year 10 attended a willow sculpture workshop.

On the sports front, by 2020 the School had an equestrian team. The U15 XV were crowned county champions and reached the last 16 of the National Schools Rugby Vase. Football was played successfully by both boys and girls. The U19 boys reached the Oxon League Cup Final. But sports were also for fun, as Sam Black remembered:

My favourite memory of Lord Williams was playing rugby for the school from year 7 to 13. The one event that stands out the most for me was when we entered a rugby 7s tournament when I was in year 12. We turned up as the obvious underdogs with our mix and match kits (some of us even wearing our school socks). Despite our appearance, we beat many 'better' schools such as Magdalen and went on to win the tournament. What really stood out for me with regard to sport at Lord Williams was how we were all playing simply for fun, there was never any pressure to do well and win anything. The relaxed nature however did not stop us from being one of the best rugby schools in the Oxfordshire/Bucks area.

Girls were playing rounders and doing well. Netball and hockey of course being their core sports.

And, as has been always the case, the School was strong locally in athletics with individuals going on to the All England games. Cricket was as strong as ever. And swimming teams did well in county events.

On a different note, the School now had over 200 Young Carers aged between 12-18 who care for close family members with an illness, mental health problems, or issues with alcohol or drugs. A co-ordinator was employed in the School, and much effort was made within both School and community to raise money to support them. The SEN provision under Lally Lewis was recognised as being particularly strong.

One important area of improvement is food. Sixth formers even have their own cafe in the Foundation Centre that sells decent cappuccino and appetising snacks. A sixteen-person catering team is on site and in one year students and staff managed to eat over 54,000 paninis, and drink 27,000 bottles of water.

The Lord Williams's Parents Association was established in the late 1960s, after a recent wobble, continues to go from strength to strength, and makes significant financial donations to the School through the many events it organises every year.

One area that has gained in importance over time is the amount of pastoral care that is offered to all students: this covers what subjects to study, career evenings, open evenings, university visits, talks by alumni, and work experience. The School Council, first established in the late 1960s, is still active, and senior students attend governor meetings.

Every year, over 100 students from other schools apply for a place in the Sixth Form, a testament to the School's external reputation. This is also reflected in the Ofsted parent survey: when asked 'would they recommend the School to another parent,' 93 per cent agreed.

The Sixth Form is now 500 students strong and over seventy per cent of those taking GSCE stay on, similar to the number staying on when LWS was a grammar school.

However, the School was not performing at the top of the league when compared to other Oxfordshire schools.

Taking just one typical but important measure, the percentage of pupils that attained a Grade 5 or above in GCSE Maths and English. For 2019 this was:

- Cherwell School (the top academy in the county): 64 per cent.

- Lord Williams: 49 per cent (with 16 Oxfordshire academy schools scoring a higher percentage.)

- England State Funded Average: 43 per cent.

In 2019, the percentage of pupils achieving AAB or higher in A-Levels was 11.4 per cent across 123 students. Looking at academy schools in Oxfordshire, sixteen achieved a higher percentage, and the average for state-funded secondary schools across England was 14.1 per cent. However, the School would argue that in part its performance is because it admits a broader range of academic abilities into the Sixth Form.

Other data points show the current nature of the School, and how much this has changed over the years. The School now has 136 teaching staff, 55 assistants and 84 support staff. The average salary for teachers is just over £39,000. In total, over £9million of the £12million annual budget is spent on staff costs. In 1970, the year before the School turned comprehensive, the average salary was around £1,900, there were 25 teachers at the grammar school, no assistants, and less than a dozen support staff.

And what of the School becoming a single-site on the Oxford Road?

By 2019 there had been much discussion, parent and staff consultations undertaken but no progress had been made at all. The town at this time had a population of 11,000 but the Town Plan envisaged that this would grow with the construction of around 775 new homes. If these plans were implemented around 150 extra secondary school places would be needed.

Increasingly it looked unlikely that the single-site proposal would move forward. Money was required to prepare a thorough feasibility study; the School did not have this money and the County Council had said they were not prepared to fund it. No study. No plan. No implementation.

In an early draft of this History, we wrote, 'And perhaps it is now time to draw a line under this and move onto other solutions rather than wasting time and energy on something that will never come to fruition.'

Prescient thoughts because at the begining of 2020, the Council said they would now not be prepared to provide a bridging loan to cover the cost of developing the Oxford Road site before the Towersey Road site was sold to developers. This was the final nail and it was decided that it was no longer possible to create a single-site school and, for the foreseeable future, the dual site will remain in place.

A few months before this decision, David Wybron had retired,

I find it hard to believe that I have been at the School for

28 years. I can honestly say that I have loved being a part of Lord Williams's School over this time. It has been a great privilege to be Headteacher over the last 14 years, to work and spend time with so many wonderful staff and students and to represent this splendid school in the community it serves.

His replacement was Jon Ryder, one of the two Deputy Head-teachers. He had taught at the School since 1991, grew up in London, supported Fulham FC, and studied Natural Sciences at Cambridge.

And then in March 2020, the School had to close for the second time in its history. This time because of COVID-19. GCSEs and A-Level exams were cancelled; students switched to e-learning at home.

Of course a School with such a long history can always find some direct connection to the past. The Statutes of 1575 had provisions covering what would happen in time of plague when towns and villages were 'depopulated by their own epi-demics and pestilential infections.' If this meant that studies had to be given-up or that the Master and Usher had to take whatever precautions were necessary for their own health, they would be paid in full even if they were absent.

However it was also noted that if the parents of the pupils wished to hire (at their own expense) other suitable premises in the country where teaching could carry on, then the Master and Usher would be expected to teach there.

David Kenningham died in April 2020. Although he had been ill for some time, he also had contracted COVID-19. Another death in 2020 was Phyliss Nelson aged 99, wife of Jonathan Nelson who had been headmaster from 1957 to 1963. Her hus-band had died in 2002.

The School reopened temporarily in September 2020. Jon

Ryder wrote a few weeks later that the students 'have been superb in adapting quickly to the new routines of life at Lord Williams's, with different timings, staggered lunchtimes, muster points, desk sanitising and face coverings.' There had been three unlinked positive tests since the start of term but the School was able to remain open.

The OTA also ensured that Founder's Day took place but this time it was a virtual event with a streamed act of commemoration. Over 1,000 people viewed the stream. Thereafter a series of Zoom meetings were held so that OTs could remain in contact with one another.

Come the end of 2020, Jon Ryder wrote to parents,

> Towards the end of November, things became particularly tricky with a number of staff required to 'shield', others poorly with Covid-19 and even more forced to isolate. We came close to having to close to at least one Year Group, but I have been so impressed with the Cover Supervisor Team who, in just one week, covered the majority of the 190 lessons where teachers were absent.

> It has been particularly tough for the students, whose learning experiences have been hampered by the reduction in practical and active learning opportunities due to the current limitations on movement and contact. In the light of these difficulties, I have been so pleased to see so much practical work going on in Art, Dance, Drama, Media, Music, PE, Science and Technology, where staff have developed safe routines and systems to allow students to participate in practical work whilst minimising the risk of transmission as far as possible.

Come the start of 2021, the School was closed again as part of a national lockdown programme. The way that the British government planned this was seen as not ideal by most teachers, students and parents alike, not just in Thame but nationally. In short it was a shambles.

Pupils went back to on-line home learning other than those who had special needs or whose parents were classified as critical workers. These could attend classes.

All schools were allowed to reopen on 8th March 2021, and students were asked to undergo lateral flow tests to detect the presence of Covid-19 or not. After Day 1, the School announced the following,

> We are pleased to report that the mass testing is running smoothly today. It is taking approximately 15 minutes for students to be registered and tested. Thank you so much to all the parents, carers and students who are engaging so positively with the testing operation. The testing team have said how brilliant the students are; calm, cooperative, patient and efficient.
>
> We conducted over 1000 tests yesterday, which is a huge achievement for the whole testing team.

The second shambles was how to hold public exams. These had been an unholy mess in the summer of 2020 when after the exams were cancelled, a poorly thought-through algorithm was used to award grades. This was met with derision by teachers, pupils, and parents alike. The Government backtracked and used teacher assessments to award grades.

Come September, the Prime Minister announced that in summer 2021 exams would definitely take place because of their critical importance and infallability when it came to grades. This message was repeated time and time again thereafter by Gavin Williamson, the Education minister.

Fast forward to early 2021 and in February, Ofqual published the plans for awarding grades to students who were due to take external examinations this summer. No formal exams would be sat and instead teacher assessments would once again be used.

The School wrote to parents,

> We will be working on our school processes over the next few weeks and will update you with all the information as soon as possible. We will obviously be doing all we can to ensure that students are awarded the grades that they deserve. We already have lots of assessment data from work that students have completed since they started their courses and I am sure that there will be further opportunities for students to demonstrate the quality of their learning once we have all returned to school.

There were exceptions with the performing arts such as dance, where some form of practical exam was deemed essential.

The School coped admirably but if truth beknown it was a government foul-up. The *Guardian* reported in August 2021 that the government's refusal to draw up contingency plans to protect schools and exams before a second lockdown was an "unforgivable" error that left teachers and parents in England to deal with chaos. They were reporting on an investigation into the government's handling of the pandemic by the Institute for Government. This castigated both ministers and the Department for Education for insisting schools in England would remain open and exams would go ahead this year, even as it became obvious a second wave of infections made a second lockdown inevitable. The report concluded that,

> 'What followed was easily the most disruptive period in children's education since at least the start of the second

world war ... When it came to education, U-turn was to follow U-turn. Well into March 2021, and indeed beyond, pupils taking GCSEs, A-Levels and BTecs remained unclear about precisely how they were to be assessed. At times it felt as though the school system was in chaos.'

When the 2021 A-Level results came out 44.8% of A-Level passes scored an A* or an A. (NB: A lot of media reports claimed it was 44.8 per cent of students but this is incorrect.) That's up from 36..5 per cent from last year and 25 per cent from the last time exams were sat - though given the system is different, comparison is difficult. But the underlying truth is that the government reforms to the exam system in the last decade made the pandemic exam problem more acute. Had more coursework/modular exams remained part of the system both this year and last there would have been more official moderated work for teachers to go on.

Of course school life has changed for many reasons not least with both the opportunities and challenges of the digital world. On the plus side it was IT that allowed lessons to be moved out of the classroom and into the home. Even in times of normality, homework and research is now done increasingly on-line by students. Beyond the ubiquitous school website, phone apps such as Edulink allow teachers, parents and students to be in constant contact and kept up-to-date.

On the downside, nationwide smartphones have led to bullying issues, sextexting, and problems such as inappropriate phone-camera use.

It seems that a small number of students have taken photographs of school staff without their consent and published them online. This serious infringement of privacy is being investigated and students who have taken photos of staff without consent and published them will face disciplinary sanctions. It would be very helpful if parents/carers could monitor students' phone use and ensure that any such images are deleted.

Not at LWS we hasten to add but the authors are aware of several instances where teaching staff have been sacked because of inappropriate content that has been discovered in their use of social media. It is, as they say, a sign of the times, and that issues with social media are not only student issues.

But as 2020 drew to a close let's end on a high.

Despite a second lockdown and Covid restrictions on singing, the spirit of Christmas resulted in a Herculean effort by staff and students to create this marvellous Christmas Carol Service in the very, very brief time between Lockdown 2 and the end of term.

The credit really goes to the students who were involved in making this. Their passion and desire to perform are special and they really are a joy to work with.

We are proud to share this with you to celebrate not only Christmas but the exceptional hard work and practice the students have done this year. Enjoy!

And a streamed video link could be clicked.

CHAPTER 31: POSTSCRIPT –
THE SCHOOL'S FUTURE?

IT IS NOW ALMOST ONE HUNDRED YEARS since the first history was published. Then it was a school with around 120 pupils on the roll, a mix of boarders and day-boys, most of whom left before the Sixth Form. For close on fifty years thereafter, LWS remained largely organised in much the same way, though growing both in size and scope until the introduction of comprehensive education transformed it from a school of some 270 pupils into something almost ten times that size, one of the largest schools in the country, and one of forty secondary schools Oxfordshire. It takes great pride in being a school for the community.

Today there is no longer the need to wait for another hundred years to update this history as technology allows for easy writing and publishing. But if we were to wait for another hundred years what would be found?

Without a doubt, the School will not have closed in a hundred years hence. Thame's population continues to grow and so there will always be a need for local education.

As noted in the previous chapter, currently Thame's population is in the region of 11,500 and the plan is to add at least 775 houses within the town's boundary, and more in the surrounding villages. South Oxfordshire District Council therefore suggested in its 2013 local plan that there would need to be extra primary school capacity provided either as a new school or as an extension to an existing one. An additional 120-160 secondary school places would be needed depending on the rate at which new dwellings are built and the type of housing stock e.g. family or single occupancy. Already the flaw is obvious: this expansion of secondary school places only reflects Thame's needs whereas LWS serves a significantly bigger area.

Since then South Oxfordshire District Council have published a strategic plan that goes through until the year 2034, which identifies a new housing requirement of at least 1500 new homes to be built in Thame, and over 700 in Chinnor.

This suggests that at some point, a new secondary school will be needed. This could be established in Chinnor as a lower school, along with new sixth-form provision in the Chalgrove and Watlington area in order to reduce the pressure on LWS.

But in those famous words 'who knows?' As can be seen from this History, strategic decisions about education provision change from one decade to the next, or indeed no decisions are made at all and a make-do strategy adopted.

Since the change in government policy where schools are no longer the direct responsibility of councils, this latest South Oxfordshire Plan now makes no mention of school provision. They must ensure that these houses are built but do not need to take responsibility for delivering education i.e. sufficient student places, which is the responsibility of Oxfordshire County Council (OCC).

In turn the latest OCC, 2018-2030 Plan for the county makes no provision for new secondary schools in the Thame catchment area, whereas it does for other parts of the county. Indeed at the moment, the strategy for the Thame area would appear to be based on reducing admissions from outside Oxfordshire. In other words no longer allow Buckinghamshire students to enter the School as a way of coping with increasing numbers. Excluding Buckinghamshire pupils regularly crops up as an option proposed by planners with little idea of geography and no sense of history. It can only be hoped that it will go the way of all the other attempts to ignore the realities of the School's natural catchment area.

The County Council is now working on a 2050 plan and currently this too makes little mention of education, reflecting the reduced role that local authorities have beyond ensuring that there are sufficient places available for students in its administrative area.

On the other hand, new technology (commonly called ed-tech) has the ability to ease the pressure on LWS. Rather than bussing in thousands of pupils perhaps small satellite schools will be created linked to a LWS main hub. Possibly older pupils will study from home – at least part time – as distance learning becomes more sophisticated.

Understandably and rightly so there is the argument that says that children should not spend their time in isolation and that coming together in social groups is an essential part of education, as is joining together in extra-curricular activities. But do they need to do that for every lesson?

Above all else, the overarching reason for change is to find a way to break the grip of underfunding. If one conclusion can be drawn from this account it is that the School for much of its history has suffered from chronic underfunding whether from its own income or when relying on government money. Sometimes the pressures have been less but they have never disappeared and once again at the conclusion of this chapter they are as bad as ever.

But look how successful the country is, some might argue, hence whatever the level of funding pumped into education, it still works. Our education system produces the goods. Putting aside the undoubtedly thorny issue of measuring success, the truth is that this is still a country which is dominated in both public and private sectors by people educated at independent schools who then go on to Oxbridge and the Russell Group universities. Perhaps all parents of state educated children should be made to visit a leading independent school to see the splendour of the facilities that these schools enjoy. It would be enough to make them weep. And there is a robust argument that it is still the independent sector that produces the superstars and the upper echelons of society - Prime Minister Theresa May - who went to Holton Park Girls Grammar - being the exception that proves the rule. Thame has never produced superstars: some very good people yes but otherwise it reflects its rural hinterland of comfortable, white, solid middle-class.

Perhaps the School will be able to raise the money to improve facilities through its own fund-raising efforts. Central to the School's vision is the realisation of long-held ambitions to improve facilities for teaching and learning at the Upper School site. This will provide exceptional state-of-the-art facilities, which will use modern technologies to provide teaching and learning spaces where students can thrive giving them the best opportunity to fulfil their dreams and ambitions.

The Capital Development Masterplan has 4 phases:

Phase 1
This will deliver a new Learning Resource Centre and English suite which has been commissioned and will be funded primarily through Section 106 funding and a six-figure philanthropic gift. The accommodation will benefit all Upper School students and will include a library and multi-functional teaching spaces supported by modern ICT equipment and fast internet connections.

Phase 2
This phase will provide a Performing Arts Centre which will include a 350-seat auditorium and a Music Centre.
Phase 3
This will bring significant improvements to sporting facilities

which will benefit not only the School, but also the local community.

Phase 4

The Capital Development Masterplan will conclude with a Design and Technology building to encourage the uptake of STEM subjects which are so important to employers and to apprenticeship programmes.

This programme will certainly please the current generation of parents. In a 2020 survey they voted for improved design and technology facilites when asked, 'Are there any facilities which you believe are more important to the school and the community at this time?' Number 2 on their list was better sports facilities. Most agreed too, that the school's facilities should be made available to the community. Their number one choice was no surprise as it is STEM subjects that are receiving most support from the Government as they are seen as the future for the UK's economy. This could mean that the planned Phase 2 is put back to later in the programme.

The School has always enjoyed a strong local reputation. Indeed it is the lifeblood and heart of the community; the biggest single organisation in Thame, the biggest employer, and the institution that very much defines the town. Its success also encourages families to move to the area, which in turn puts upward pressure on house prices. Higher house prices makes it more difficult to recruit teaching staff who are unable to afford to enter the local housing market.

After the 2nd World War, as life at the School expanded into more clubs, societies and extra-curricular activities, its reputation in the county flourished. Certainly, in the 1960s and into the 1970s, it enjoyed a national reputation in three areas, all at the same time: sport, drama, and music. It deserves in future to continue to be led by inspirational leaders, who will not accept the status quo, and given realistic funding to maintain its high reputation. Ofsted's judgements are not infallible, but to be rated by its inspectors as 'outstanding' is a powerful indication that Lord Williams's original vision for the School is still being realised, 450 years after teaching began.

As just written, Ofsted judgements are not infallible. In the light of the School's relatively modest position in the public examination league tables some might question whether such a designation is really justified. But to do so, at least on those grounds, would be a mistake engendered by the excessive importance given to high exam grades fostered by successive governments. The only real importance of exam results is to provide a key to open the door to the next stage of education or employment, though only a few very competitive universities and courses require the highest grades. Otherwise, exam results are no more than moderately reliable indicators of hard work and short-term recall of knowledge, most of which will be irrelevant to students' later education and career, and some of which will become outdated or even proved wrong within a few years.

It should be noted too that the marking of public exams in itself has been shown to be unreliable. Research by Ofqual showed that across all subjects some 25 per cent of grades were incorrect (and always too low.) Understandably the range varied according to the subject matter. Something like maths where an answer is usually right or wrong, about 96 per cent of the grades were correct. In history only 50 per cent.

Why are grades unreliable? Not because marking is erratic but because marking is imprecise. A written paper does not have an exact mark of 57 as different examiners can legitimately give the same script slightly different marks. For example the range of marks for that paper might be 56, 57 and 58. If these three marks lie within the same grade width, then all result in the same grade. But if the 6/7 grade boundary is 57, then marks of 56 and 57 are grade 6, but 58 is grade 7. One mark can, and does, make all the difference.

A 7 versus a 6 can then make a big difference when it comes to assessing a student's performance. A 7 is classed as a top grade, a 6 not so.

On top of that there are errors that come from poor marking, perhaps marking that is hurried, or the last paper marked after a long day. Again something that the authors have seen where results have been challenged with sometimes grades being upped by not just one but by two levels.

In short, the recent government's obsession with exams and the immutability of grades since coming into power in 2010 is just plain wrong.

Successive governments, while paying lip service to the concept of 'broad and balanced education' have made it ever harder for schools to achieve this. Truly outstanding schools have succeeded against the odds and LWS can reasonably be judged to be amongst them; increasingly so since the headmastership of Mullens. Such schools give due weight within the formal curriculum to subjects not currently deemed to be 'useful'; they provide an extensive and varied programme of extra, or co-curricular activities, within and well beyond the boundaries of the school, their mode of teaching and systems of pastoral care encourage students to think for themselves, to question, and to acquire key individual and positive social life skills and attitudes, none of which are tested by public examination. It is evident from the preceding chapters that over the last sixty years or more the School has achieved well in all these areas.

There is one more criterion by which to judge whether a school is outstanding, often overlooked but summed up, if rather inadequately and inaccurately, by the phrase 'the happiest days of your life'. School education is not just about preparing young people for the rest of their life; it is a part of their life, five to seven years at secondary school. There is a balance to be struck between living the moment and preparing for the future.

Geoff Goodall is on record as emphasising that experience of the school years should be as enriching and fulfilling as possible and since his era this has been manifestly so. Not of course for every pupil all the time, but true in general. For such as those young pupils, for example, who took part in the annual Lower School musicals, the older pupils touring Germany playing *Macbeth*, those gifted in athletics and sports representing their county or their country, volunteers helping to improve the educational provision of disadvantaged pupils in the Gambia, it is the experience at the time, not some possible future pay-off, that enriches their education. In these ways, it is surely fair to say that the School has been outstanding.

❊ ❊ ❊

As of 2021, the original school building from 1569 can be found on Church Road (or Row), now converted internally into offices.

The new school, built on the Oxford Road and opened in 1879, remains almost intact with little alteration externally except for an extension added in the 1970s. Internally, while the function of rooms may have changed, there is much that a pupil from the late 19th century would recognise.

The second historic building on the site is the cricket pavilion dating from 1909, and which came about after a massive fundraising effort. It was opened by the then MP for South Oxfordshire, Valentine Fleming (father of the James Bond author, Ian Fleming), who then served and was killed in the 1st World War. Winston Churchill wrote a moving eulogy in *The Times*. Fleming served in the Queens Own Oxfordshire Hussars; two

Old Tamensians were also members of the same Regiment and died in action: Hugh Kidman and William Roberts. As noted in Chapter 18, it had become part of the School's 'Living Memorial to the Fallen'.

In April 2021 it was demolished. (See Volume 2 for a more comprehensive history.)

Fortunately the boards in the Sixth Form Library are included in the Imperial War Museum's register of war memorials.

✻ ✻ ✻

One final note. In the future it should be remembered that a time capsule was buried under the new library on the Lower School site containing a school uniform, coins, photographs of the School and Thame, newspapers, and other items. If it has not been dug up already it should be uncovered and opened in 2100.

✻ ✻ ✻

BIBLIOGRAPHY, SOURCES, ADDITIONAL NOTES

GENERAL

1. Various volumes of accounts and ledgers relating to Lord Williams's School and Thame's almshouses are held in the archives at New College, Oxford and were examined *in-situ:*
NCA 789, 790: Thame Almshouses and School ledger and accounts 1618-1647, 1655-1814 (2 vols.)
NCA 3253: Thame Almshouses and School accounts 1575-1618 (1 vol.)
NCA 3254: Thame School accounts 1605-1660 (1 folder) 3254 Transcript

2. A Short History of Thame School. John Howard Brown. 1927

3. The Tamensian. 1900 – 1996. School magazine held in the School's archives. (NB: at the moment the archives are not able to accommodate visitors. It is hoped that at some stage they will be moved to bigger accommodation, though currently, after much discussion, no firms plans are in place.)

4. The History, Description, and Anquities of the Prebendal Church of the Blessed Virgin Mary of Thame, F. G. Lee, D.D., F.S.A., 1883.

5. The School's Statutes. 1575.

6. The History Of Thame and its Hamlets; Including the Abbey

of Thame, Prebend, and Free School. Harry Lupton. J.E. & F. Bradford. 1860.

7. Book of Thame. Gerald Clarke. Published by subscription. 1978.

8. Victoria County History, Oxfordshire. Various volumes.

9. John Williams, Baron Williams of Thame. Michael J Beech. 2009.

10. A History of Thame. John Howard Brown, William Guest. F. H. Castle, 1935

11. The Life and Times of Anthony Wood, Antiquary of Oxford, 1632–1695, Described by Himself. I. Oxford: Andrew Clark, ed. 1891. Clarendon Press.

12. The School's archives. (Catalogue information unavailable.)

13. Secondary Education in the Nineteenth Century. Richard Lawrence Archer. 1966. Frank Cass.

14. Making An Entrance. The Biography of Gerald Gould. Margaret Martin. 2010. D R Green.

15. A Twentieth Century Chronicle. Graham Thomas. 2009.

16. Reminiscences of Lord Williams's School. Collated by H.L. Nicolle. 1999.

17. *From Taunton to Butler: Lord Williams's School From 1866-1944*. Gerald Howat. 1995. Updated and expanded 1997.

Chapter 2

1. The main relevant primary sources for Thame during this period are the Chantry Certificates of 1548 and the main secondary source the editing of these by Rose Graham 1919 with a long and most interesting introduction.

Chapter 3

1. Henry VII: The Maligned Tudor King By Terry Breverton. Chapter 3.

2. Amanda Jones ' *Commotion Times': The English Risings of 1549*. Warwick PHD 2003

3. Lords lieutenant and high sheriffs of Oxfordshire. 1086-1868. Online

4. Thomas Cromwell. A Life. Diarmaid Macculloch, Penguin, 2018

Chapter 4

1. A. Monroe Stowe, English Grammar Schools in the Reign of Queen Elizabeth. Published 1908. On-line version published by Columbia University.

2. A History of the County of Oxford: Volume 1. Originally published by Victoria County History, London, 1939

3. Wages and the cost of living in Southern England (London) *1450-1700*. Author: Jan Luiten van Zanden.

4. Thame School and its Founder. Francis Steer. 1975. New College.

5. Oxford Dictionary of Art. Ian Chilvers. Third Edition. OUP. 2004

6. Some account of Lord Williams of Thame. Latin Translated by the Reverend John Young. Published C Ellis's Machine Offices, High Street, Thame. 1873

Chapter 5

1. Bodleian Library. Rycote Collection.

2. History of Parliament. On-Line

3. The National Archives {An index note to one record of this progress in the National Archives
http://discovery.nationalarchives.gov.uk/details/r/C2583381
Ref: T38/500]

4. Naunton, Robert; Caulfield, James (1814). Memoirs of Sir Robert Naunton, Knt., Author of "The Fragmenta Regalia"; With Some of His Posthumous Writings, With Manuscripts in his own Hand, Never Before Printed. [Compiled by James Caulfield]. London: G. Smeeton; J. Caulfield.}

5. John Nichols's The Progresses and Public Processions of Queen Elizabeth. Edited By Elizabeth Goldring, Jayne Elisabeth Archer, Oxford, 2014.
6. The Portable Queen. Mary Hill Cole.

Chapter 6

1. New College of Magic and Wizardry: A Second Note on the 1566/7 Visitation. Jan Machielsen. Cardiff University (formerly New College, Oxford)

2. English Grammar Schools in the Reign of Queen Elizabeth. Published 1908. A. Monroe Stowe, On-line version published by Columbia University.

3. History of the County of Oxford: Volume 1. Originally published by Victoria County History, London, 1939
Oxoniensia

Chapter 9

1. Thame Parish Registers. (Available on-line and at the Oxford History Centre.)

Chapter 10

1. Oakeshott, A.M.d'I. (1964) Grammar schools in Hanoverian England, Durham theses, Durham University. (Available at Durham E-Theses Online.)

Chapter 11

1. The History of the Royal Grammar School, High Wycombe 1562 to 1962. J Ashford and C M Haworth. Published by the Governors of RGS. 1962.

Chapter 13

1. A Victorian Lady Cycles The World: Recollections of an Octogenarian. Isabel G. Homewood.

Chapters 22 and 23

1. The Eleven-Plus Adventure. Portrait of a 1950s English grammar school education. David R Green. 2010.

Web-sites (at the time of printing)

www.oldtamensians.info
www.lordwilliams.oxon.sch.uk

www.flickr.com/photos/oldtamensians/albums

Contact

lwshistory@europemail.org

ABOUT THE AUTHOR

Graham Thomas & Derek Turner

Graham Thomas is an alumnus of the School. He has authored a number of books, including books on Japan and various aspects of Japanese history. He is a Fellow of the Royal Society of Arts.

Derek Turner is the School's archivist. He was a history teacher, HMI, Ofsted and ISI inspector, editor of Sussex Tapes (for sixth formers), and author of two books for secondary school pupils.

Printed in Great Britain
by Amazon

65576783R00236